ENT[illegible]S WHO BUILT INDIA

Celebrating
30 Years of Publishing
in India

ENTREPRENEURS WHO BUILT INDIA

LALA SHRI RAM

THE MAN WHO SAW TOMORROW

SONU BHASIN

HARPER
BUSINESS

An Imprint of HarperCollins *Publishers*

First published in India by Harper Business
An imprint of HarperCollins *Publishers* 2023
4th Floor, Tower A, Building No. 10, DLF Cyber City,
DLF Phase II, Gurugram, Haryana – 122002
www.harpercollins.co.in

2 4 6 8 10 9 7 5 3 1

P-ISBN: 978-93-5699-138-5
E-ISBN: 978-93-5699-137-8

Typeset in 11.5/15.5 Warnock Pro at
Manipal Technologies Limited, Manipal

Printed and bound at
Replika Press Pvt. Ltd.

FSC
www.fsc.org
MIX
Paper from
responsible sources
FSC® C016779

This book is produced from independently certified FSC® paper to ensure responsible forest management.

To the two men in my life—Juggi and Karan. You guys are my anchors in the choppy seas of life.

Contents

Prologue ix

1. The Legacy of Badri Das and Bishamber Das 1
2. Growing Up in Barhwali Haveli 11
3. Dealing with Failures 25
4. Setting Up DCM 40
5. Shri Ram Joins DCM 53
6. Early Successes at DCM 65
7. Public Service Goes Hand-in-Hand with Business 86
8. Shri Ram Takes Control of DCM 92
9. DCM Has a Second Mill 104
10. Shri Ram's First Overseas Trip 116
11. Diversifying into Sugar 127
12. A Wedding in the Family and a New Mill 139

13. Acquiring Bengal Potteries 153
14. A Strike in DCM Breaks Shri Ram's Heart 166
15. Jay Engineering and Usha Sewing Machines 177
16. DCM Turns Fifty 195
17. A New Sugar Mill and Foray into Chemicals 211
18. Shri Ram Takes a Sabbatical 226
19. A Plane Crash Devastates Shri Ram 245
20. The Setting Up of Lady Shri Ram College 260
21. Shri Ram Fights His Health, but Fails 267

Epilogue 275
Appendix 281
References 289
Index 299
Acknowledgements 307
About the Author 309

Prologue

DCM is a name that most Delhiites, even those who have little or no interest in business, would be familiar with. It is possible that even those who have heard of DCM may not know that it was north India's first textile factory, set up in the late 1880s, and was one of the earliest joint stock companies in the country. DCM stock was once considered a blue-chip stock. And DCM was a nursery for talent such as Shiv Nadar, founder of HCL Technologies, and Ashok Soota, founder of MindTree Limited. Both were management trainees in DCM in the mid-1960s.

Most people believe that DCM was founded by Lala Shri Ram. This is not quite true. It is a fact, however, that Lala Shri Ram took over a middlingly successful company and not only made the cloth mill amongst the best in India but also created a large business empire under the DCM Group.

DCM was founded by Shri Ram's uncle, Gopal Rai, along with a group of businessmen when Shri Ram himself was five years old. In today's context Gopal Rai would be seen as a start-up entrepreneur. He was a man who had an idea for setting up a cloth mill in Delhi. But Gopal Rai had no funds for the venture. So, he went looking for investors. He found a set of investors, 'sold' them the idea of being partners in the proposed cloth mill, set up a company and took it public. The board of directors comprised largely of the investors, and Gopal Rai, as the secretary of the company, was the de facto chief executive officer (CEO)/chief operating officer (COO), running the business and reporting to the board.

It was almost two decades after DCM was set up that Shri Ram joined the company. He joined without a role and without a salary. But in less than fifteen years, Shri Ram, by dint of his hard work, business acumen and management style, had become the biggest shareholder of the company and hence the 'owner' of the business. As its secretary, he also became the de facto CEO/COO of the company. From there he first expanded the cloth mill and then diversified into sugar, pottery, ceramics, precision engineering, vanaspati, chemicals, fertilizers and silk mills.

At the time of his death the DCM Group was the fourth-largest in the country and one of the most respected business houses. After his death in 1963, however, the group was unable to last long cohesively and splintered into three parts in 1989–90.

The story of Shri Ram and the DCM Group is not a lone example of a thriving business empire, set up in pre-independence India, growing in stature and size in the following years and then losing its way as it was hit either by family feuds or liberalization or both. The Indian industrial and corporate sector is scattered with people and businesses that had seen their glory in the days that some consider to be the most challenging in the lives of Indian businessmen—the years between 1947 and 1991.

India became independent in 1947 and the newfound freedom brought forth not only the aspirations and dreams of individuals but also collective dreams of social, political and economic freedom. However, the first prime minister envisaged a developmental model that had the state playing a dominant role as an entrepreneur as well as funder of private businesses. The economic freedom that entrepreneurs dreamt of in the new India quickly withered away as the British Raj was quickly replaced by the Licence Raj.

Due to the restrictions placed by the License Raj, which many say was a complex and opaque system, being an entrepreneur in India meant a big headache. Further, the entrepreneurial spirit was kept on a tight leash by the complex and authoritative system. Entrepreneurs were successful not so much because of what they did as because of who they knew. Such was the dependence on the benign hand of the government that businessmen, due to their association with the politician and bureaucrat, were also enveloped in a cloud of corruption in the minds of the general public.

However, people forget that there were many entrepreneurs, and indeed businesses, during those particularly challenging times that worked tirelessly to make the new India. Shri Ram was one of them. It was certainly not easy, but he persevered.

During British rule, Shri Ram, like any other entrepreneur of that time, faced problems around transport, logistics, communication and even skilled talent. Most transport of material and supplies was on slow-moving carts or using the few motor vehicles available. Getting in touch with mills and factories in remote locations was tough. Most machinery had to be imported, and then it was a challenge to find the workers to run the machinery. There were no MBA institutes to churn out batches of management students who could run businesses; most entrepreneurs relied on family members to run their businesses.

After India became independent some of these challenges remained while some new ones were added. These primarily revolved around the new 'system' of doing business. True, Shri Ram did learn how to 'manage' the system, but it still required entrepreneurial skills to set up new businesses and manage and grow the existing ones within the tight framework of the system. Manufacturing is never an easy business, and the License Raj made achieving economies of scale even more difficult with the restrictions on the numbers that could be produced. It is to the credit of Shri Ram that he not only went about his work diligently but also created products that became household names at the time. Unfortunately, most of these have either been diluted or almost forgotten.

However, what cannot and should not be forgotten is Shri Ram's contribution in being part of a group of entrepreneurs who worked to lay down the foundation of Indian economy and industry. If it were not for him and other stalwarts who worked against the odds and set up businesses, provided employment to many people and kept the Indian economy growing, India would not be where she is currently.

Thus, it is important to bring these entrepreneurs out of their obscurity and present them to the new generation as the entrepreneurs who built India.

This is the story of Shri Ram, the man behind the success of the DCM Group.

The story of Shri Ram is a story of a single man's determination to overcome many handicaps. Handicaps of physical frailty, childhood loneliness, early failures in business and not being considered good enough for anything by his own father. Overcoming all these, Shri Ram set up an industrial empire with a foresight and vision of business practices that others did not even have an inkling of at that time.

As I spent time with Shri Ram, vicariously of course, reading about him, talking to people who knew him and listening to people describe the man and the times he lived in, I started understanding and appreciating the man better.

Shri Ram came from a family of modest means—they were not poor, but neither were they rich.

I found it extraordinary that Shri Ram, who in his later years was the centre of Delhi's social life, spent a childhood that can best be described as somewhat lonely. The only child in a household of six adults—parents, uncles and aunts—Shri Ram had inherited a delicate constitution from his mother. Frail-looking and of slight build, Shri Ram could not play with the children of his age. He would yearn for peer company but the other boys, looking only at his physique, shunned his company. The same Shri Ram, once a successful businessman, was sought after by all, and people vied to be his friend. It is indeed true that success has many friends!

Success did not come easy to Shri Ram, however. He had a sharp mind as a child and was good with numbers but was at best an average scholar and a simple 'matric pass'. Unable to find a job after giving up his education, he started a small business with a friend, which folded within a couple of years. Another failure in business followed soon after, and Shri Ram thereafter had to work as a munim with a cloth dealer in Rawalpindi. He was brought into DCM, which was a moderately successful company at that time, by his father almost reluctantly. He joined as an employee with no role and no salary. These were circumstances that could have crushed any other man. But Shri Ram took all of this on the chin, put his head down and went to work.

During my research I was struck many times by the strength of Shri Ram's character. This was especially remarkable because he was bereft of his father's love and influence during his life. A person's life and values are typically formed by parental love and guidance. In the absence of both, Shri Ram had to craft his own set of values. He was married off to a young girl, belonging to a family that had fallen on hard times, as a teenager. It was evident during my research that Shri Ram and his wife were two individuals bound only by the fact that she had borne him three sons. Shri Ram, however, stood steadfastly by his wife and did not take on a mistress or marry again for companionship. Nor did he allow anyone to disrespect his wife.

His values at work were noteworthy as well. He was amongst the first industrialists of his time who understood the value of shareholder and stakeholder wealth creation. Whenever he raised capital for his businesses, he would keep aside a small percentage of shares to be bought by his workers and other employees—giving them an opportunity to create wealth for their own families. He was also amongst the first of his times to actively bring in talented professionals as and when he could. True, his sons did become part of the businesses by default, but Shri Ram did put non-family members at the helm of his businesses.

The success of his businesses led to Shri Ram being the centre of Delhi's social life. There was never a day that he ate alone in his big house; never a day when the house was not filled with guests—some of whom stayed on for months. The sense I got was that it was almost as if Shri Ram was proving a point to himself in his later years—making up for the mocking and ridicule he had received as a child from his peers. It was also a part of his need to create an ecosystem around him in which he was loved and admired.

The lack of his father's love—almost an abandonment—affected Shri Ram in many ways. He was unable to channel his emotions properly and therefore had a complex relationship with his sons. Shri Ram was extra strict with his sons, but he struggled with it. He wanted a loving, caring and less formal relationship with his sons but was unable to express himself. This did not make him a cold person but one who was unable to articulate his emotions to those who were closest to him. This somewhat strained relationship came neither in the way of the love between the father and sons nor the success of the business.

It is my belief that Shri Ram worked extra hard on an aspect of his personality—that of business strategy and execution—to compensate for his emotional personality. All his emotions and passion were put into the business. DCM was a companion, a child, a wife that was the recipient of unadulterated and unconditional love and passion from Shri Ram. And Shri Ram received love and adulation back from DCM and the employees of DCM.

It is unfortunate that the business empire fell apart after Shri Ram's death, albeit after almost three decades. With the foresight and vision available to him, Shri Ram could have planned his succession better. To give him credit, he did write a will and had decided on the division of assets. But, like any other industrialist of his times, he did not prepare his inheritors to work in the business cohesively, leading the large group to break off into smaller businesses.

The story of Shri Ram is instructive even for the entrepreneurs of today who often complain about the many constraints they face in setting up and then running their enterprises. As I travelled in time along with Shri Ram—the entrepreneur—it was evident that he looked at constraints not as roadblocks but as minor speed breakers. Modern-day entrepreneurs could also learn from Shri Ram the art of caring for their employees along with a strict focus on discipline. But mostly the entrepreneurs of today will find, as they read the life story of Shri Ram, that hard work, determination, grit and focus go hand in hand with the spirit of entrepreneurship.

As you read the story in the following pages, you will find that my role as the author is that of a narrator. I have taken creative licence when recounting the stories of various people and their conversations, including those of Shri Ram himself. Most dialogue is imagined, though the situations are real. Some of the names used in the story are fictitious. Many of the people in the story are no longer alive and thus, the narration is based on the memories of the people and/or the archives of the Shri Ram family. The creative licence has been used with the objective of bringing alive times gone by and the man who was Shri Ram.

Now presenting to you Shri Ram—one of the entrepreneurs who built India.

1

The Legacy of Badri Das and Bishamber Das

SHRI Ram was born into an Agarwal bania family from Jhajjar, a small town about forty kilometres west of Delhi. Badri Das, his great-grandfather, was a treasurer in the Karnal Commissariat of the British Army.

During the years that Badri Das worked at the Commissariat he made a name for himself by virtue of his ability to handle accounts. He was also known for his integrity and sharp mind. These qualities made him stand out in the eyes of his British bosses. He was often given cash rewards for his good work as well as recognition through other awards. Since the British trusted Badri, he was posted as a kotwal in the Ferozepur Cantonment, an important cantonment for the British. The post of kotwal was a prestigious one and equivalent to that of chief of police of the area.

Badri Das spent over fourteen years as the kotwal. It was common in those days for a family to be known by their profession. Thus, Badri Das's family became popularly known as the Kotwal family. Badri may have been a kotwal by profession, but he was a shrewd bania at heart. He invested the cash rewards he received in buying land. Such was the diligent work done by Kotwal Badri Das that his cash rewards enabled him to become the owner of 75 per cent of the Ferozepur Mandi. Along with his salary as a kotwal, he started getting a significant rental income from the shops in the mandi.

Happy with his work in Ferozepur, the British transferred Badri Das to Delhi in 1855. He was given the charge of the kotwali or the police station in the city's cantonment.

Badri Das, already proficient in buying real estate in Jhajjar, saw an opportunity to buy a large house for the family in Delhi. The old city of Delhi was a thriving area in the mid-nineteenth century. Within the walled city, Bazaar Sita Ram was a busy business district. Just off this bazaar was a cul-de-sac that was called Kucha Mai Das. Badri Das was drawn to this area for two reasons. One was a temple, and the other was an iron gate.

At the far end of Kucha Mai Das Lane was a temple that was popularly known as Chaurasey Ghantey ka Mandir, or the temple of eighty-four bells. The eighty-four bells were supposed to represent the eighty-four lakh cycles of birth that an individual has to go through to attain rebirth as a human being, as per Hinduism. It was an old temple and popular with the locals.

The temple, one of the reasons for Badri Das's decision, was at one end of the lane. The other reason was at the head of the lane. This was an iron gate that secured the entrance to the lane from the Bazaar Sita Ram side. At night this iron gate was closed and locked. Badri Das liked this additional security and decided to buy a house for the family in the lane.

It was a big house built in the haveli style. A haveli typically has a large courtyard in the middle of the house. Badri Das's house, too, had a courtyard and it had a large banyan tree in it. Thus, the house came to be known as Barhwali Haveli, the mansion of the banyan. As the Kotwal family grew, Badri Das bought all the neighbouring houses in the lane for his sons. With the passing of the years, the entire Kucha Mai Das came to be owned and occupied by descendants of Badri Das.

As he was the kotwal of the British Cantonment, the entire area knew of Badri Das's association with the British and the fact that the wealth of the Kotwal family came through their work for the British. It was this association with the British that brought them to the attention of the mutineers during the 1857 mutiny.

Once the mutiny started, the mutineers went after not only the British but also any locals who were seen as sympathizers of the British. The local bankers, moneylenders and policemen were also targeted as they were seen as collaborators of the British. It was thus natural for Badri Das, as a kotwal, to come under the scanner of the mutineers.

Since he was a member of the police force, Badri Das was well aware of the danger he was in. When it became clear that the mutineers were going to storm the city of Delhi, Badri Das decided to stay at home, hidden from the eyes of people.

Finally, the day came when the mutineers rode into the city. There was an air of danger and expectation all around. Badri

Das knew that he was a marked man. He decided to hunker down even more.

It was just before noon when Daya, the local sweeper woman, ran into Barhwali Haveli. She was out of breath and was sweating profusely.

'Where is Kotwal Sahab,' she asked in between breaths. 'I have some important news for him,' she continued huffing as she wiped her face with the edge of her pallu.

Badri Das first peeked out of the window to make sure that there were no men with Daya. Once he was sure that she was alone, he walked into the courtyard.

'What is it, Daya? Why are you so agitated?'

Daya folded her hands and bowed her head before she spoke.

'Kotwal Sahab, your family has always been good to me. I don't want any harm to come to you. Therefore, I have come to you,' she said.

'Thank you for that, but what has happened, Daya?' Badri asked gently.

'Kotwal Sahab, my brother works in the market. Some men were roaming in the market asking about you. They wanted to know where you stay and where they could find you,' Daya said.

Badri Das's antennae went up. His back straightened as he realized the impending danger.

'Do you know who these men are?' he asked urgently.

'Kotwal Sahab, the men are informants of the mutineers. Till now the people in the market have not told them where you are. But you are not safe. Please get out of this house and the city if possible. The mutineers, my brother tells me, are killing many local people also,' Daya said in a rush, wringing her hands and crying.

Badri Das knew then that the danger was real. He thanked Daya and rushed inside the house. He briefed his family about the situation and told them that he was going to be away for some time.

As a policeman, Badri Das was prepared to handle any adverse situation. Since the rumours of the mutiny had started, Badri Das had, in fact, started preparing for this eventuality. He went to his room and opened his almirah. He took out a tin box from the top shelf and unlocked it. The box contained a Pathani suit and a false beard. There was also some money kept in a pouch. Badri Das quickly changed into the Pathani suit and stuck on the unruly beard. He put the money pouch in the pocket of the kurta. He took off his shoes and wore open sandals instead. Then he looked in the mirror. He was sure no one would be able to say that the Muslim-looking man reflected in the mirror was Kotwal Badri Das.

He quickly bid goodbye to his family members, who wished him well. He instructed them to tell the mutineers if they did come to the haveli that Badri Das had been away for the past week, visiting relatives in Jhajjar.

Badri Das walked out of the haveli and, instead of going towards the Bazaar Sita Ram gate, walked towards the temple end. He knew there was a small opening in the cul-de-sac that would take him away from the bazaar. He walked unhurriedly, not wanting to draw any attention towards himself. Informants lurked everywhere.

He was able to flee the city without any problems. No one recognized him as the kotwal of Delhi. He did see some mutineers as he walked through the streets, but he did not slink away or try to hide. He nodded to the men, touched his forehead as a mark of respect and walked on.

On 1 January 1858, the city was transferred back to the civil authorities—the government of the North-Western Provinces. A month later, in February, the government carried out a reshuffle and the province of Punjab was carved out. A lieutenant governor was put in charge of the new province. Delhi became a part of this province. The city began to limp back to normalcy.

It was time for those who had fled to safety to return home. The British government was giving out rewards to people who had been loyal to them during the mutiny.

The British rewarded Badri Das handsomely for his loyalty. He was given a cash award of Rs 50,000, which was a significant amount of money in the mid-nineteenth century. He was also given a piece of land adjoining Ghaziabad. Further, the British gave Badri Das and his family a contract for the supply of fodder for the cavalry and the military dairy farm in Jullundur Cantonment.

However, Badri Das could not forget the terror in Kucha Mai Das during the mutiny. Thus, after the mutiny he chose to leave the walled city and spent the rest of this life in Ferozepur before his death in 1874.

Badri Das's four sons continued to stay in Kucha Mai Das in the large Barhwali Haveli. After Badri Das's death the eldest son, Raghunath Das, managed the estate left to the family. Raghunath Das had inherited the spirit of entrepreneurship from his father and thus was able to manage the estate well. The youngest son of Badri Das was quite the opposite of his eldest brother. The family and the larger community regarded Bishamber Das as the least distinguished of the four brothers. This image of Bishamber Das had taken root as he was an introvert and a shy man. He was not gregarious or social. Thus, when seen in contrast to Raghunath Das, it was assumed that Bishamber Das was not as accomplished as his eldest brother.

His elder brothers moved out of Barhwali Haveli one by one. Bishamber Das's reputation as a shy and somewhat unaccomplished man had led the family to leave the house to the youngest brother.

Bishamber Das, however, was accomplished in his own way. He had inherited the ability to understand and work with numbers from his father. He was able to maintain the accounts of the estate in a four-foot-long bahi (account book) and could recite the religious texts with great clarity. He also learnt to speak English and took the trouble to learn a smattering of science. More importantly, he put his three sons through ten years of schooling. This focus on education paid rich dividends later in life.

Bishamber Das had three sons, Gopal Rai, Girdhari Lal and Madan Mohan Lal. While Gopal Rai and Girdhari Lal were a couple of years apart, the youngest son, Madan Mohan Lal, was more than twenty-five years younger than his brothers. As a result, he was treated like a child by his elder brothers; to his parents he remained a baby. Madan Mohan grew up somewhat pampered by the family and got accustomed to having his needs met by other people.

Bishamber Das was hawk-eyed when it came to the education of his sons. It was remarkable that all three sons were 'matric pass'. Clearing the matriculation exam in the 1800s was almost equivalent to clearing the IIT entrance exam of today! Not many Indians studied up to this level and even fewer cleared it. This education laid the foundation for the eldest son, Gopal Das, to set up the framework for an industrial empire headed by his nephew Shri Ram in later years.

By the time Madan Mohan was a young teenager, both his elder brothers had been married for some time. Gopal Rai, at the age of fifteen, had got married to the sister of Benarsi Dass, a prominent jeweller of Delhi. Bishamber Das had got his second son, Girdhari Lal, married a couple of years after Gopal Rai's marriage. However, it was a matter of great concern in the family that between the two married brothers, there was no son. Gopal Rai had only one child, a daughter. Girdhari Lal and his wife remained childless. Theirs was a sombre and unhappy sonless family, as it was commonly believed that a son was needed not only to take the family legacy forward but also to attain nirvana.

Bishamber Das was particularly concerned about the lack of a grandson. A deeply religious man, he believed that his afterlife would be affected if he did not have a grandson. So he turned his attention to his youngest son, Madan Mohan. The hopes of Bishamber Das, and in fact of the entire family, rested on the young boy.

As soon as he turned fourteen, Madan Mohan was married off to Chando Devi, daughter of a trader in Delhi. In almost no time at all there was the announcement of 'good news' by the young couple. There was a sense of excitement and anticipation in the family. The young girl was pampered by her elder sisters-in-law and was not allowed to do any work in the house. These were the days before sex-determination tests were possible, but no one in the family wanted to take any chances. Her sisters-in-law put up pictures of Bhagwan Krishna in her room along with pictures of other male gods. She was told to look at the pictures every day. It was believed that if a pregnant woman looked at photos of boys she would deliver a male child. Since almost all Indian gods are depicted as dark-skinned, Chando Devi was fed with almonds and milk to ensure the child would have a fair complexion.

The entire family erupted in jubilation when Chando Devi gave birth to a baby boy on 27 April 1884. Some family members took up brass thalis—plates—and clanged them together. Others took heavy spoons and started hitting small brass katoris—bowls—to imitate the sounds of bells. These sounds were heard across the entire Kucha Mai Das. The residents in the community had known that Chando Devi was expecting and realized that there was 'good news' at the haveli. As they started thronging the gates of the haveli they saw the family members celebrating and knew immediately that a son had finally been born. Bishamber Das was both relieved and delighted at the birth of his grandson. He could finally die peacefully knowing that his next life was secure.

The neighbours, who poured into the haveli, were fed sweets while a feast was being prepared in the kitchen. No one was allowed to go without eating the rich food. In the following days Barhwali Haveli was decked with marigolds and roses, and anyone entering Kucha Mai Das was hit with the sweet and distinctive smell of the two flowers. The pujaris of the temple as well as other Brahmins trooped to the house and were served food by the family members. On the other hand, hijras came in groups to dance and sing at the birth of a son in the family. They too were fed and given money for their blessings. It was an atmosphere of joy. The family priest drew up the horoscope of the baby boy. The boy was also given a name—Shri Ram.

Bishamber Das would spend a large part of his day sitting in the front courtyard of the haveli with baby Shri Ram. He would hold the baby lovingly and would keep talking to him.

'Your name is Shri Ram, my child. You will be a good human being and you will do great work in your life,' he would whisper in the baby's ears. The baby, not understanding a word, would look up at his grandfather and coo delightedly.

Even though he did not know it, the words of the proud grandfather were prophetic.

2

Growing Up in Barhwali Haveli

SHRI Ram was born into a traditional Hindu family. It was the convention that the eldest male member of the family was the head of the household. He took all decisions on behalf of the entire family and also managed the funds of the family. Bishamber Das was the eldest member of the Kotwal family in the Barhwali Haveli, and the house ran under his writ. He passed away in 1889, when Shri Ram was five years old. It was then that Gopal Rai, as the eldest son, became the head of the family. The deference and respect that was given to Bishamber Das by Girdhari Lal and Madan Mohan Lal was transferred to Gopal Rai almost automatically.

Gopal Rai was the secretary of Delhi Cloth Mills, which he had set up in 1889 along with his associates. In a few years it had become a modest-sized factory producing cloth. Gopal

Rai, though the secretary of the company, was paid a small salary. The household income continued to be modest.

Gopal Rai managed the affairs of the family business and took it upon himself to be responsible for the welfare of his younger brothers and their families. The middle brother, Girdhari Lal, was a naib-tehsildar in Kangra. It was a government job in revenue administration, and it kept him away from Delhi for the better part of the year. His childless wife, though, continued to be part of the household at Kucha Mai Das.

Madan Mohan, the youngest brother, was looked after by his bhabhis and brother. The bhabhis, sonless themselves, treated him like a son of the house. Gopal Rai too looked upon Madan Mohan less like a sibling and more like a son or a nephew. He gave Madan Mohan the responsibility of looking after a few small matters of the family. Madan Mohan had inherited his father's reticence. He was not someone who built relationships, preferring to stay away from people. Further, as he had been pampered by the entire family since childhood, he had also developed a sense of privilege.

Shri Ram was part of this all-adult household. Gopal Rai's only child, a daughter, had been married off even before the birth of Shri Ram.

Shri Ram, as the only child in the extended family of three brothers, was showered with love and affection by all. His aunts, especially Girdhari Lal's wife, who was childless, showed special affection towards him. The ladies of the family would not allow young Shri Ram to set his feet on the ground. He was carried in the arms of the family members. Young Shri Ram did not complain at all about this affection but wondered at the lack of it from his own biological father.

Madan Mohan, Shri Ram's father, was himself a young boy of fifteen or sixteen at that time. Until Shri Ram was born, it was Madan Mohan who had been the baby of the family. His brothers and bhabhis had pampered him and had showered their affection on him. But once Shri Ram was born, Madan Mohan saw all the attention and affection of the family shift to his son.

In the eyes of the family, Madan Mohan had 'grown up', but Madan Mohan continued to see himself as the privileged child of the house. The young teenager could not see himself in the role of a father. Further, he resented his own son for taking the spotlight away from him. It is usual to see this kind of rivalry for attention amongst siblings; but here it was the father who saw his own son as a rival when it came to attention from the family. As a result, the affection and the love between a father and son, especially a firstborn, was missing between Madan Mohan and Shri Ram.

Madan Mohan abdicated his duties as a father and let the elders in the family take care of his son. The elders were happy to do so. As the eldest in the house, Gopal Rai had a special place in his heart for young Shri Ram. Gopal Rai saw Shri Ram as the one to take the legacy of the family forward. He also saw Shri Ram taking forward the legacy of the cloth mill that Gopal Rai had started with some of his associates.

As Shri Ram was brought up in a household of adults, there was no one he could play with. The young boy spent all his time with adults. He heard them talk about matters of business, matters of trade, matters of family and other matters that are normally discussed amongst the adults in a house. As a result, Shri Ram acquired a solemn outlook towards life very early on.

He was a serious child. He was also a child afflicted by health disorders. Right from his childhood he was affected by stomach ailments. This left him weak in body. He was a scrawny child with delicate health.

His aunts, who were overly protective of him, did not let him go out into the dirty streets or dusty open grounds to play with other kids. The adults in the house did not realize that in protecting the young boy, they were keeping him away from the simple childish pleasures of young life and, in fact, were stunting the growth of a child they loved with all their heart.

It was usual for Shri Ram to want to go out to play.

'I want to go outside in the galli and play gilli danda with the other boys,' said Shri Ram as he went up to his aunt.

His aunt was busy in the kitchen and ignored the boy's request.

Shri Ram pulled the pallu of her sari and stamped his feet. 'Why don't you listen to me? You are always working. I want to play. Can I go outside?' he said in an agitated voice as he looked up at his aunt.

Mrs Girdhari Lal turned and looked down at the young boy standing with his face raised in anticipation. Her heart melted. She gestured to the servant to take over from her in the kitchen. She patted Shri Ram affectionately on the head and pulled him gently to the front courtyard.

'Beta, you know you fall sick if you exert too much. So why do you want to go out and play in the mud and dirt?' she asked gently as she ran her fingers through Shri Ram's hair.

'But I want to play. You are always busy with work. Who do I play with? Tell me! Tell me!' Shri Ram asked petulantly.

'I know, I know, son. But come, let me tell you a story,' Mrs Girdhari Lal said kindly.

As Shri Ram sat on the ground looking up at his aunt, she started a story. Most of the stories she told him were tales from either the Ramayana or the Mahabharata. Even though Shri Ram had heard the stories before, he was happy to listen to them again.

Shri Ram did not realize it as a child, but he grew up in a house that was deeply religious. There was a puja in the house every day and a purohit would come to lead it. On auspicious days, lunch would be organized for the Brahmins. The women in the house would cook the food themselves.

Shri Ram would sit in a corner of the front courtyard of the haveli and watch the Brahmins troop in. The women of the house would welcome the Brahmins and wash their feet with water. After this the Brahmins would be led to the dining area. There they would sit on the floor, cross-legged, and wait for the thalis in front of them to be filled with hot, piping satvik food. The women of the house would serve the Brahmins themselves. Shri Ram watched his aunts, their heads covered with the pallus of their saris, gently cajole the Brahmins to eat more.

Shri Ram needed no cajoling to eat food. After the Brahmins had finished eating, it would be his turn. Like the Brahmins, he would sit cross-legged and ask his aunts to serve him. The women would look at each other with a smile and then look at Shri Ram with loving indulgence. They would serve him in the same manner as they did the Brahmins. Shri Ram would insist that his aunts keep their heads covered with their pallus while serving him. He wanted to feel as important as the Brahmins.

But even though Shri Ram would eat to his heart's content, he remained thin and of slight build.

As he grew up Shri Ram had to sport a braid in his hair. This was in keeping with the beliefs of the Hindu religion. It was believed that god would use the braid to pull them up into heaven on the day of reckoning. Even though Shri Ram was not entirely happy about this, his uncle Gopal Rai was insistent. Gopal Rai also made the young Shri Ram follow other religious practices.

The family believed in cow worship. On religious and other auspicious occasions, the family took pride in feeding cows. They also believed that seeing a cow upon waking up made their day go well. A family servant was therefore instructed to take a cow to the bedside of each member of the house so that the individual would see the holy animal upon opening their eyes. The servant also carried a box of aata-peda, dough in the shape of a small ball, with him. As the person waking up looked at the cow, the servant would hand over an aata-peda to them, which would then be fed to the cow. Shri Ram too followed this ritual and would stroke the head of the cow gently before feeding it.

Shri Ram's family was Vaishnava—they worshipped Bhagwan Vishnu and his incarnations. The first thing that Shri Ram did after waking up and feeding the cow was bow his head before an idol of Bhagwan Krishna—one of the incarnations of Vishnu. Once he started going to school, Shri Ram ensured that he visited the temple at the end of his lane—the Chaurasey Ghantey ka Mandir. This was a habit that he grew up with. Even in later years, as an adult, Shri Ram never left for work before going to a temple. In his childhood, it was the temple at the end of the lane and later, it was the Lakshmi Narayan Mandir on the eastern side of Chandni Chowk. Even in later years, Sundays were reserved for a visit to the Bhaironji ka Mandir on the Ridge and Tuesdays were reserved for the Hanuman Mandir in Connaught Place.

Shri Ram grew up remarkably unspoilt even though he was the only child in the household. The haveli, though large, could be gloomy at times. There were no joyous shrieks of children nor the pattering of feet in the house. Shri Ram grew up to be a lonely child. A child who wished for company of his own age but did not have it. He looked forward to going to school. He looked at school as a way of interacting with other children. He also believed that his aunts would have no control over whom he could play with at school.

But his loneliness was compounded when he went to school. His early education was at a municipal primary school in Bazaar Sita Ram. Later, when he was twelve years old, Shri Ram was sent to the Anglo Sanskrit High School in Charkhewalan.

Shri Ram was a scrawny child with a tiny physique. And he fell sick often. Thus, he could neither participate in the boisterous games that the other boys played nor in any group activities organized by the school. The other boys picked on him and made fun of his thinness. They also called him rude names whenever he fell sick. All his hopes of having a bunch of good friends in school were dashed.

Shri Ram yearned for social relationships but could not find them amongst the boys at school. He tried many times to be part of a larger group of boys who could be his friends. But children can be very cruel. The other boys saw a scrawny, dark kid who craved their friendship. As can be the case with boys, they felt a sense of power over the young kid. They felt powerful in denying Shri Ram their friendship. They refused to include him in their games as it was the easiest way to exclude Shri Ram legitimately due to his delicate health.

Shri Ram pined for company for both social as well as intellectual reasons. Most humans have a social need—a need to be accepted and be part of a 'group.' This need of Shri Ram went unmet in his childhood. The other need that Shri Ram had was to talk to his peers. At home, his aunts and uncle talked to him all the time, but they were adults. Shri Ram wanted to talk and laugh with other people his age.

'These boys don't want me to be their friend,' Shri Ram said petulantly one evening after a rather harrowing day at school, his voice filled with emotion. 'They don't invite me to their houses and when I invite them to come here they laugh and make fun of me.'

His aunt could only pat his head with affection. Shri Ram continued looking down at the ground as if holding back his emotions and then looked up at his aunt with a determined look.

'When I am older I will have many friends. You wait and see, Aunt, you just wait and see,' he said seriously. As his aunt smiled indulgently, Shri Ram got upset at not being taken seriously. 'I am telling you, Aunt, my house will be filled with my friends. People will want to be my friends. They will want to come to my house. Today these boys don't want me to be with them. You'll see, one day everyone will want me to be with them,' Shri Ram continued with a steely look.

Rather than wallow in self-pity, Shri Ram poured all his energies into hard work. He worked on his lessons. Though he was not a genius or a prodigy, he had a head for numbers. This was one ability that he had inherited from his forefathers. He focused on learning arithmetic and started enjoying dealing with numbers.

As he sat alone watching other boys play, he took to observing them—watching them interact with each other, seeing the way they carried themselves when they thought no one was looking, the way they talked to each other, their body language. Over time, even as a young boy, Shri Ram developed a keen sense of human character and behaviour. In later years he could judge a person almost instantaneously, and he was right most of the time. The childhood years spent not playing but observing others paid rich dividends in his adult life.

Shri Ram also got into the habit of not speaking much. He realized that whenever he spoke to any of the boys in school, they only made fun of him. So he developed the art of listening at a young age. He would sit quietly, observing his fellow students and listening to them. Not only did he develop the patience to listen, but he also became adept at understanding the nuances of voice tones and the body language of others. He realized that if he let people speak, they tended to reveal much more. He also observed that others liked to talk more and listen less; he did the opposite.

The only person he spoke with proactively was his uncle. Shri Ram spent a lot of time with Gopal Rai. Starved of a father's love, Shri Ram actively sought to spend more time with his uncle. For Gopal Rai too it was a joy to spend time with his nephew. Like any other Indian at that time, he too had desired a son. But he had been blessed with only a daughter. He saw Shri Ram as the son he never had and encouraged him to spend more time with him. He could have used his clout as the patriarch of the family and instructed Madan Mohan to take more interest in his own son's welfare; he did not and revelled in the companionship of the young boy.

It was usual to find Gopal Rai and Shri Ram sitting together in the open courtyard of the Barhwali Haveli in the evening.

Gopal Rai, after a day's work, would sit on a charpoy in the courtyard. As he unwound after a hard day, he would call out to Shri Ram. The young boy needed no second call as he came out running. It was almost as if he had been waiting for his uncle to come home. Gopal Rai would pat the charpoy, gesturing for Shri Ram to sit near him. The young boy, however, preferred to sit on the ground. Sitting cross-legged, he would look up at his uncle. His aunt, as she came out to give her husband a glass of shikanjavi, would look indulgently at the two male members of the house who were deep in conversation. She would serve her husband and go inside to get her sister-in-law to come and take a peek at the two from the edge of the door. The two women would look affectionately at the scene in the courtyard. One old man and one young child deep in conversation, obviously enjoying each other's company. They would look at the scene outside and then at each other and smile—content in the knowledge that the two men/boys were doing all right.

Shri Ram would bombard Gopal Rai with questions. 'Why do you work so much, Uncle?', 'Why do we feed so many Brahmins in our house?', 'What do you do at DCM?'—the questions flew out fast from his young mouth. Gopal Rai would look indulgently at his nephew as he sipped the shikanjavi.

'Hold your horses, young man. I will answer all your questions,' said Gopal Rai.

'But when will you answer them? Answer them now. Now. I can't wait,' said Shri Ram in a rush. He looked up to Gopal Rai as a father figure and wanted to spend as much time as he could with him.

Gopal Rai answered all the young boy's questions patiently. In fact, he enjoyed these conversations. They gave him a chance to almost believe that Shri Ram was his own son.

Shri Ram may not have been a brilliant scholar, but he had a sharp mind. He could process information fast and come to the nub of a problem immediately. He asked his uncle searching questions, especially about business numbers. Even at that young age he argued with Gopal Rai if he thought that there was something not quite right with the numbers being discussed. The conversations with his uncle helped Shri Ram shape his own thoughts about many matters; they also gave Gopal Rai an insight into the sharp mind of his nephew.

Some evenings, Gopal Rai would tell Shri Ram stories from the Ramayana and Mahabharata. He also encouraged the boy to read these books. As he grew older, Shri Ram discussed the Gita with Gopal Rai. As part of his spiritual development, he read the Upanishads. He learnt humility from religion as also the sense to distinguish right from wrong.

Gopal Rai was an idealist and a patriot. He lived in a time when the nationalist movement had picked up momentum. He was a deeply religious man and believed in doing the right thing. He was also a superstitious man. Shri Ram picked up all these qualities from his uncle as they spent an increasing amount of time together. The feeling of patriotism was ignited in Shri Ram during his childhood as he heard stories about the glory of India and her people. Gopal Rai also talked about how industry could help India get on the path of development. Gopal Rai told Shri Ram with great pride that DCM was the first mill of its kind in the entire northern part of India.

Spending time with his uncle influenced Shri Ram's character. The household was neither rich nor poor. But Gopal Rai was careful when it came to spending money, and Shri Ram picked up this habit. To save paper, he would tear small pieces from a notebook to write on rather than use the entire page. This austerity percolated into other matters as well. He did not see the need to spend money on new clothes. He only allowed his aunts to buy him new clothes when the older ones had either grown tight or had torn. He also grew up to be deeply religious and somewhat superstitious.

Shri Ram also had a keen sense of curiosity. As a child when he went to the Ridge in Delhi, he would look at the chimneys in the distance. And then he would look up at the elder accompanying him and ask, 'Why is the smoke of that chimney different in colour from the smoke of the other chimneys?' It is not known if he got the answer!

Shri Ram's curiosity also led him to examine the earthen oil lamps that were lit in their house in the evenings. These and similar lamps were used by not only the Kotwal family but also by other Indians in general. But young Shri Ram felt that the lamps did not give off enough light and believed that it was the design of the lamp that was faulty. He spoke to his aunts about it, but they just waved him off. Undeterred, Shri Ram took a lamp and examined it minutely under the streetlight—which itself was a large earthen lamp. He believed he had the solution and then spent the next few weeks baking lamps of his own design in the large ovens of the family kitchen. His aunts tut-tutted affectionately and let him carry on with his experiments. He may not have achieved a breakthrough in the design department but his attitude towards a problem, and towards life in general, was applauded by all.

In 1896, when Shri Ram was twelve years old, his uncle Girdhari Lal was struck by a disease. Though the family got the best medical help, Girdhari Lal did not survive.

His widow was distraught. 'I have lost my husband and I do not even have a child. Why should I live anymore?' she cried aloud. The family members tried to comfort her, but she was inconsolable. She would not eat anything and even refused to take a sip of water. It may be useful to note that in India, in the late nineteenth century, widows were not treated well. Even though the Hindu Widows' Remarriage Act had been passed in 1856, this social reform took time to be accepted universally in India.

Girdhari Lal's widow was not treated badly by the other members of the family, but she, it seemed to all, had lost her will to live. Gopal Rai decided to take matters into his own hands. On the last day of the mourning for Girdhari Lal, Gopal Rai ordered young Shri Ram to sit in the lap of his widowed aunt. This was in the presence of the larger community that had gathered for the prayer service performed by the priest for the departed soul. By ordering Shri Ram to sit in his aunt's lap Gopal Rai conveyed to the community and to the family that the boy was to be adopted by the widow. Gopal Rai had seen the genuine affection that the lady had for his nephew, and he believed that this would give the widow a reason to live. But Shri Ram was old enough to understand who his real parents were. He continued to address Chando Devi as Ma and his aunt as Tai (elder aunt).

Madan Mohan, since the birth of Shri Ram, had shown scant interest in the young child. Now that the boy had been adopted by his sister-in-law, Madan Mohan believed that Shri Ram was no longer his responsibility. Though Shri Ram was the centre of affection for the rest of the family, the young boy grew up yearning for the love of his father. The affection given by the others was a poor substitute for a father's love. In fact, there were even times when Madan Mohan treated his son harshly.

By the time Girdhari Lal passed away Shri Ram had started going to the Anglo Sanskrit High School in Charkhewalan. The students there learnt their lessons in both Sanskrit and English. Modern science was also taught in the school.

Shri Ram completed his middle school examination and then went on to prepare for his matriculation. The headmaster, Bhola Nath, took him under his wing. Bhola Nath recognized the spark of intelligence in the otherwise quiet boy who kept to himself. Under the tutelage of Bhola Nath, Shri Ram learnt better English and commercial arithmetic. Bhola Nath actively encouraged Shri Ram to read English books and to speak in English.

Shri Ram, though still young, intuitively understood the value of the language and added it to his area of focus. In spite of his scrawny and slight build, he had a deep and resonant voice. People were often surprised when Shri Ram started speaking. They expected a squeaky voice to go along with the slight physique; the deep voice that spoke excellent English startled them.

He cleared his matriculation in 1900 at the age of sixteen. Matriculation was a high point in any student's life in those times. Passing the matriculation exam enabled a student to go on to study further. But more importantly, being 'matric pass' helped a person gain a higher status in society. It was a qualification that guaranteed the entry of the individual into the ranks of the 'educated'.

Shri Ram did gain the badge of being 'matric pass'. It was another matter that he cleared his exams in the third division. In later years, when he was a successful industrialist, he actually wore his third division as a badge of honour. 'I haven't done badly for a third division matric pass now, have I?' he would ask people with a twinkle in his eyes.

3

Dealing with Failures

ONCE Shri Ram was 'matric pass' the family started preparing for is wedding. In India it was customary then for boys to get married at a young age. A marriage was seen not only as a union of two individuals but also of two families. Some families promised their sons or daughters in marriage almost as soon as they were born.

Gopal Rai had found a match for Shri Ram when the boy was only nine years old. He had decided that his nephew would marry Phoolan Devi, the daughter of Bhagwan Dass, a filigree merchant in Chandni Chowk. Bhagwan Dass had his shop in Dariba Kalan, the hub of jewels and ornaments in old Delhi. The two families had exchanged gifts in a small ceremony at that time.

Now that Shri Ram was sixteen and had cleared his matriculation exams, the Kotwal family took stock of the situation. They found that Phoolan Devi's father had died in the intervening years, and the family had fallen on hard times. Many family members, relatives and others from the community suggested to Gopal Rai that he break off the betrothal and seek an alliance with a wealthy family.

'Shri Ram is the only son of the three brothers, and we are sure that he will command a heavy dowry,' said some. 'You are making a mistake, Gopal Rai. You can easily find a better match for your nephew,' said others. But Gopal Rai had given his word to the family, and he was unwilling to break it. He was heartened by the fact that even at the young age of sixteen, Shri Ram himself was unwilling to break the word given by his uncle.

Shri Ram was thus married to Phoolan Devi in the summer of 1900. It was a joyous occasion for the family, and they pulled out all the stops to ensure that the wedding was a grand one. The entire Kucha Mai Das was decked with flowers, and earthen oil lamps were lit in every house in the lane. The entire street was sprinkled with rose water and the heady, sweet smell travelled across the iron gate into the main Bazaar Sita Ram. Ordinary shoppers in the main bazaar could not help but peek into the gaily lit and bedecked side lane that was Kucha Mai Das to discover the reason for the fragrance that was wafting into the main street.

The sixteen-year-old bridegroom went to Dariba Kalan with his baraat and came back with his twelve-year-old bride, Phoolan Devi. Shri Ram's father, Madan Mohan, had not been happy when his son had refused to break his engagement. Madan Mohan, like many others, believed that the family had given up a chance to form an alliance with a better family. The ladies in the house, too, had wanted a daughter-in-law from a wealthier family. They also felt cheated as they did not get the expensive gifts they had desired. They made their displeasure felt by taunting the young bride. Resenting Phoolan Devi's comparative poverty, the women of the household used harsh language when talking to the new bride. They were even more upset when it was discovered that Phoolan Devi suffered from epilepsy. However, all their harsh language and taunts came to an abrupt halt once Shri Ram gave them a piece of his mind.

'I decided to marry her, and I am perfectly happy with her as my life partner,' shouted Shri Ram in anger one day. He was very upset at the treatment meted out to his wife. He had seen her crying in a corner once too often and had asked her what the matter was. The frightened young girl had not wanted to say anything as she was scared that the elder women would get angrier. But she had also been brought up, like all other girls of that age, to obey her husband. Thus, she told him about the mistreatment. It was then that Shri Ram made it clear to all the men and women of the household that he was very pleased with his wife.

Phoolan Devi was not an educated girl. She also had frequent epileptic fits. Shri Ram tried to get her treated but her condition did not improve. In those times most people did not realize that epilepsy was a disease; it was commonly believed that the patient's body was possessed by a chudail or a witch. In a sense, both husband and wife suffered from ill health.

Shri Ram, as the years went by, found that he had little in common with his wife. But he was a man of principle. And he had a deep ambition to do something more with his life. So, he focused his energies on academics and later on business. Phoolan Devi remained in the background, a shadowy figure in Shri Ram's life, the mother of his three sons who were born later.

Shri Ram, despite his third class in matriculation, wanted to continue his studies. He wanted a university degree. His uncle allowed him to join Hindu College, where he pursued his course of choice. However, it appeared that fate, and his father, had different plans for him.

Gopal Rai developed a chronic disease that sapped his energy. He could not manage the work at Delhi Cloth Mills alone and started taking Madan Mohan to assist him at the mill. As the weeks passed, Gopal Rai became more infirm and passed on the job of managing the family and all its affairs to his younger brother.

Once Madan Mohan became the de facto head of the family, he also started managing the finances of the household and business. His disinterest in Shri Ram had grown even more after the birth of his second son, Shankar Lall, soon after Shri Ram's marriage.

It was nearing Shri Ram's twentieth birthday. His life was spent between the haveli and college. Phoolan Devi remained in the background. She had borne a child that had not survived. Her health continued to be delicate.

Shri Ram, too, had always been frail and fragile. But now he had an acute attack of anaemia. He went to a local hakim who put him through a forty-day course of powdered steel mixed with some Yunani medicine. This harsh medicine brought on a fistula, which required surgery. Shri Ram's problems did not end there. The surgery resulted in severe sinusitis. This time Shri Ram turned to Ayurveda. The vaid put him on a diet of chana (gram) and asli ghee for seven days. The Ayurvedic cure worked. Not only did the sinusitis disappear, but a host of other smaller ailments also went away. Shri Ram enjoyed good health for the next twenty years.

Shri Ram's good health did not prepare him for what was to come next, though.

One evening, when Shri Ram entered Barhwali Haveli, he saw Madan Mohan sitting in the courtyard. It seemed that the father was waiting for his son to return. Madan Mohan gestured for Shri Ram to come to him.

'Shri Ram, you know that the family finances are not good. Your uncle cannot work at DCM as he used to. As you can see, money is a problem,' Madan Mohan told his son.

Shri Ram listened distractedly, not knowing where this was leading. Half his mind was on what his father was saying while the other half was on the lessons he had to finish before the next day's class.

'I want you to start managing your life on your own. I can't look after you.' Shri Ram was jolted out of his reverie as he heard these words.

'What are you saying, Father?' he asked in astonishment.

'I am saying that you need to start taking responsibility for yourself and your wife,' said Madan Mohan.

Shri Ram was flustered. But he knew, now that Madan Mohan had told him to be responsible for himself, there was no other choice. Gopal Rai was infirm and would not interfere in the matter; the women of the household, much as they loved Shri Ram, had no voice in any decision.

Shri Ram knew then that he could not continue his studies. It broke his heart to give up college, as he believed strongly that a good education was a gateway to a better life. He decided to look for a job so he could start earning money. He was thankful that Madan Mohan had allowed his wife and him to continue living with the joint family. He was relieved that he did not have to pay any rent and did not have to worry about food.

Finding a job was not easy. Madan Mohan was working at DCM and was doing most of the work of the secretary. But he did not want his son to work at DCM. Madan Mohan, the youngest of the household, was being recognized, maybe for the first time in his life, as an individual in his own right. His brother was infirm and was not present at the workplace. As the de facto secretary, Madan Mohan was enjoying the authority that came with the role. He thought that having his son at work would stymie his style and maybe dissipate his authority as well. He told Shri Ram clearly that there was no job available for him at DCM.

Shri Ram, though disappointed, was not surprised. He had stopped expecting any affection from his father a long time ago. The relationship he had with Madan Mohan was a functional one. He also knew that his father was emotionally closer to his second son, Shri Ram's younger brother, Shankar. Lall. Undeterred, Shri Ram took stock of the situation.

Setting up a business was not an option as the family did not have any surplus money. Madan Mohan, who controlled the family's finances, did not want to invest any money in a new business. Shri Ram had no work experience either. Nevertheless, he looked around for possible avenues of employment. His lack of work experience proved to be an obstacle in every job he applied for.

After being rejected by many potential employers Shri Ram finally found a job in a cloth shop. Mohan Brothers was a large textile shop in Chandni Chowk. The job was nothing great. Shri Ram had to open bales of cloth, measure them, cut lengths as required by customers and then roll up the bales again. This he had to do as many times as a sale was made. Shri Ram knew that one of the reasons he had got the job was because the shop owner bought a large amount of cloth from Delhi Cloth Mills and knew that Shri Ram was part of the same family. However, Shri Ram did not allow this to come between him and the job he was fortunate to have.

Shri Ram was also thankful for the Rs 25 he earned every month. As he was living in a joint family set-up, his living expenses were mostly taken care of by the household. He was thus able to save some amount each month from the salary he earned. Though he was thankful for the job he had, he was not very happy working at the cloth shop. He wished to start his own business, but he did not want to ask the family, which meant his biological father, for the money. He was aware of the feelings, or the lack of them, that his father had towards him.

Slowly but surely his savings grew. Meanwhile, he had been speaking to his friend Jagan Nath Ganju about his desire to do something on his own. Jagan, too, wanted to start an enterprise of his own. The two friends talked about the various possibilities, especially of the funding that would be required to launch the enterprise.

They focused on the idea of dealing in stationery but rejected the thought of getting into manufacturing. Shri Ram was aware of the importance that families were giving to education. Jagan and he talked about all the stationery items they could sell to students. They also thought of targeting various commercial ventures—shops, offices, trading units—all of which used paper and pens and other items of stationery.

The idea of selling stationery was good and appealed to them. But they had no money to even rent a shop. Shri Ram and Jagan would spend many evenings talking about various options.

'But Shri Ram, we definitely need a shop,' said Jagan as the two friends sat on a bench in a park in old Delhi.

'Why do we need a shop, Jagan?' asked Shri Ram evenly. He had been thinking about their lack of finances, and an idea had germinated in his mind. But he wanted to lead Jagan gently into it.

Jagan was eating a roasted bhutta, or corn on the cob. The park had a bhutta-walla who was very popular. Bhuttas, roasted on hot coals and then slathered with lemon, salt and red chilli powder, were everyone's favourite. Shri Ram could not have the bhutta with the red chilli as it upset his stomach. So, he had to be content with a bhutta with only lemon and salt.

Jagan took a bite of the bhutta. As he smacked his lips feeling the red chilli powder hit his senses, he looked at Shri Ram and answered the question he had been asked.

'Shri Ram, we need a shop so that customers can come and buy our products,' he said in a patient tone, as if explaining something simple to a child.

'Jagan, our business is to get customers and the stationery items together, is it not?' Shri Ram asked.

'Yes it is. You know it is. What kind of a question is that?' Jagan asked with a bit of irritation.

'Yes, yes, I know, but I was just checking. So, if we have to get customers and stationery items together, maybe we can take the items to the customers instead of asking the customers to come to the items, eh? How about it?' Shri Ram asked Jagan with a glint in his eyes.

'What do you mean, Shri Ram? How can we take the items to the customers?' Jagan asked, focusing on the last bit of chilli-slathered bhutta.

'I've thought about it. How about we use the bicycles we already have and go to customers to sell our products?' asked Shri Ram. 'We will be able to show the customers our products and we can sell them there and then. We won't need a shop, nor will we have to pay rent and other charges.'

Jagan had a little bit of bhutta still left, but now his attention was completely on Shri Ram. He looked at his friend with awe.

'What a wonderful idea, Shri Ram!' he exclaimed, throwing away the last bit of uneaten bhutta in his excitement. 'We have two bicycles, and we can meet twice the number of customers. Let's do this.' Excited, he stood up and dusted himself off as if ready to go to work immediately.

Shri Ram quit his job with Mohan Brothers and got down to work with Jagan on their stationery business.

The two young men were full of enthusiasm but lacked the experience of running a business of any kind. Unfortunately for them, enthusiasm could not compensate for the lack of experience. It did not get them far, as the market was full of experienced tradesmen in the business of stationery. The art of dealmaking, sourcing the right products at the right prices and selling to customers are key skills required in any business. Shri Ram and Jagan Nath lacked these skills, and their business floundered. Both men were loath to give up, as this would have meant admitting failure. So, they persevered. After a couple of years, however, when the writing was clear to them, they decided to shut shop. The first enterprise of Shri Ram's life was a dismal failure.

'So, we lost everything, Shri Ram,' said Jagan Nath forlornly. The two friends were back on the bench in the park. It was not bhutta season. They had a paper cone filled with shelled peanuts. Jagan took a small handful of peanuts as he continued speaking. 'At the end of all this time what have we gained? Nothing!'

'Nonsense!' exclaimed Shri Ram, almost jumping up from the bench. 'We may not have gained any money from our enterprise, but we have gained immense experience, haven't we?'

And then he answered the question himself. 'Of course we have. I know now what not to do in business and who not to trust,' he said softly to himself.

Having tasted blood by running his own venture, even if it had ultimately failed, Shri Ram did not want to look for a job to earn his living. He also did not want to ask his father for help as he knew that it would be futile.

Shri Ram, instead, turned to his brother-in-law, Sher Singh, who was married to his elder cousin Kalawati. Gopal Rai's only child Kalawati was many years older than Shri Ram and was fond of her young cousin. She had been married even before Shri Ram was born and saw her cousin as a child. In Shri Ram's time of need, she requested her husband to help him.

Sher Singh's father had been chief minister to the maharaja of Alwar. Even after he had retired, Sher Singh's father had maintained good relations with the durbar of the maharaja. Sher Singh had got permission to start a cotton ginning factory in Alwar, and he spoke to Shri Ram about the possibility of his working there.

Shri Ram jumped into the venture with great enthusiasm.

Yet again, enthusiasm proved to be a poor cousin of experience. Alwar was in a desert area and cotton was not grown for many miles around it. Obviously, a cotton ginning factory required cotton, but this had to be sourced from Delhi and the Punjab area. Further, these areas already had many cotton ginning factories. In fact, there were more cotton ginning factories than required, and almost all of them ran at half capacity. The cotton ginning factory set up at Alwar soldiered on bravely for some time but could not sustain itself for long.

Shri Ram's second venture thus also ended in failure. The factory had to be shut down. Though upset and disappointed, Shri Ram focused on what he had learnt during his time at the ginning factory. He had learnt how the cotton market operated; he had learnt how to run a mill; he had learnt the importance of workers in a mill. Overall, he mused to himself, the score was even.

Meanwhile, there had been both good news and bad news on the family front. The good news was that Phoolan Devi had borne him a son—Murli Dhar. This good news came one year after the sad demise of Gopal Rai. After having been ill for many years, Gopal Rai had finally breathed his last in 1906. Following his death, Shri Ram and Phoolan Devi had moved to Alwar, and it was in 1907 that Murli Dhar was born.

Shri Ram did not want to go back to Delhi after the ginning factory in Alwar was shut down. He was sure that his father would not let him hear the end of it. He was apprehensive of the taunts and the snide remarks that would not only come his way but also be directed at his wife. He was also sure that his father, who was now the secretary of Delhi Cloth Mills, would not help him find employment in the mill. Further, after two failures, no one from the family would be ready to help him start yet another business venture.

The two failures in business had not been able to dim the flame of ambition that still burnt bright in Shri Ram. In fact, whenever he was in a reflective mood, he went over his experiences and what they had taught him. After spending time running the cotton ginning factory, Shri Ram had learnt the importance of workers in any mill. He also realized that most mill owners saw their workers as a necessary evil—they could not do without them but also did not treat them well. Shri Ram was clear in his mind that whenever, if ever, he got a chance to be a mill owner, he would treat his workers very differently. He saw the workers as fundamental, and not incidental, to the success of any manufacturing business.

Even though it had been a very different business, the time spent dealing with customers and suppliers in the stationery business had given Shri Ram an insight into human behaviour when it came to matters of commerce. The role played by agents in selling products on the one hand and the role of suppliers on the other had been studied, retrospectively, in great detail by him. Once again, he was sure that if he ever got the chance to run a business, he would focus on these two sets of associates.

At this time, though, Shri Ram was practical enough not to seek another business opportunity. He decided to take a job with Rai Bahadur Boota Singh & Sons of Rawalpindi. Boota Singh was one of the largest customers of Delhi Cloth Mills. He was a contractor who bought large quantities of yarn from DCM and sold it to weavers and small weaving units who, in turn, produced cloth. Over the years, Boota Singh's business had grown within northern Punjab and had expanded to Kabul and Kashmir. He needed a munshi—someone who could manage accounts and part of the operations. Shri Ram started work as Boota Singh's munshi. His responsibilities covered handling orders, managing purchases, negotiating prices with all parties and arranging transport and logistics for the goods.

Shri Ram enjoyed his work, as he could read numbers better than anyone in the office. He needed only a couple of minutes to go over a ledger to spot any discrepancies. Further, dealing with the suppliers and logistics associates gave him insights into these aspects of a business.

While Shri Ram was working as a munshi, Boota Singh managed to secure an order for the supply of tents for the Coronation Durbar, which was to be held in Delhi in 1911. The Durbar is said to have been the largest extravaganza of the British Raj in India. It was held to coronate King George V as the Emperor of India. It is reported that over forty thousand tents were erected in the encampment of the Durbar. More than 2,50,000 people attended. It was at this Durbar that Delhi was proclaimed the new capital of India.

Boota Singh was ecstatic with the order for the tents for the Durbar, which was still more than three years away. Work in the office increased manifold to prepare for the procurement of tents and other material. Shri Ram, by now, had the pulse of the accounts along with some of the operations, and he worked hard, with diligence and honesty. Boota Singh had already been impressed by his work, but he now came to depend completely on Shri Ram, especially for financial and logistical work.

It was during a casual chat with his trusted employee that Boota Singh found out that Shri Ram was in fact the son of DCM's secretary, Madan Mohan. He was surprised that, instead of working at DCM, Shri Ram was working as a munshi.

'You should work with your father, Shri Ram,' said Boota Singh in his baritone voice, twirling his lush moustache absentmindedly. 'I can't understand why he is not taking advantage of your abilities—after all, the work you are doing for me is similar to the work that the secretary of DCM does.'

Shri Ram hemmed and hawed as he tried to explain his complex relationship with his father and the failure of his two business ventures. But Boota Singh was in no mood to listen to the somewhat rambling excuses being made by Shri Ram.

He cut Shri Ram short and gestured for him to keep quiet. 'You are a very capable young man, Shri Ram. So what if your earlier ventures were not successful? Look at me,' said Boota Singh, pointing at himself. 'You think this is my first business? No, not at all.' He wagged his finger at Shri Ram. 'I, too, have tasted failure. But it made me even more determined to succeed. And look at me now!' Boota Singh spread his arms out expansively.

'I too want to succeed, Boota Singh ji. I know I can. It is just that . . . ' Shri Ram tapered off hesitatingly.

'Nonsense,' said Boota Singh brusquely. 'I know you can succeed. Your father is an idiot if he is not using your ability. I am going to write to him and tell him exactly that.' He patted the young employee on the back.

Boota Singh wrote a letter to Madan Mohan in which he chided him for not recognizing the talents of his son. Shri Ram was sceptical about the efficacy of the letter but he was still disappointed when his father ignored Boota Singh's gentle admonishments. However, Boota Singh was not a man to give up easily. He wrote again and yet again, each time chiding Madan Mohan and extolling Shri Ram's virtues.

Madan Mohan remained unimpressed but could not overlook the many letters from one of his biggest customers. He decided to give his son a chance mainly to get Boota Singh off his back. Madan Mohan called Shri Ram to Delhi and gave him a job in the accounts department. However, he told Shri Ram that there would be no salary paid to him.

Shri Ram was happy to be back in Delhi and to be living with the larger family once again and thus did not spend too much time agonizing over the lack of a salary. His son Murli Dhar was two years old, and Shri Ram thought that the large haveli would be a good place for the young boy. Shri Ram also saw that his younger brother Shankar Lall was just six years older than Murli Dhar. Remembering his own lonely childhood, Shri Ram was happy that Shankar Lall and Murli Dhar would keep each other company. Phoolan Devi had no voice in any decision but she, too, was happy to be back in the more familiar surroundings.

Shri Ram entered DCM in March 1909, and, though he did not know it at that time, the destiny of both the man and the organization changed thereafter. Even though he was not the one who founded DCM, in later years Shri Ram's name came to be synonymous with it. People believed that it was Shri Ram who had set up the mill!

4

Setting Up DCM

DELHI Cloth and General Mills Company Limited or DCM, as it came to be known popularly, was the fulfilment of Gopal Rai's dream. He was able to manifest his dream with the help of four other people: Ram Kishan Dass, Sri Krishn Dass, Banwari Lall and Benarsi Dass. These four people, brought together by Gopal Rai, launched a cloth mill in Delhi in 1889 that was the largest and most modern in north India at the time. This cloth mill would later be the stepping stone for Shri Ram, helping him gain his own eminence in the business world.

Gopal Rai had started his career without any fanfare. Before he took on the responsibility of the Kotwal household following the death of his father, he had started working with Ram Kishan Dass at Messrs Chunnamal Salig Ram. A naturally curious man, Gopal Rai had been following the cotton industry and the cloth mills that had started burgeoning in India, especially after 1854.

It was in 1854 that three cloth mills were launched in Bombay. The first was by a British national named James Landon. The other two were set up by two Parsis—Cowasji Davar and Maneckji Petit. Davar's mill was set up in Tardeo, Bombay. Maneckji Petit was a prosperous merchant and set up Oriental Spinning and Weaving Mills, which was twice as large as the mills set up by Davar and Landon. In 1861, another mill came up in Ahmedabad. It was set up by Ranchhod Lal Chotalal, who had put together a group of businessmen to finance him.

In the 1860s, the Indian textile industry got a shot in the arm due to the American Civil War. Cotton supply from America to England was choked due to the war. India became the focus of attention both for raw cotton as well as the woven fabric. The boom continued even after the American Civil War ended. Between 1869 and 1882, more cloth mills were set up in India. Such was the interest in cloth mills that eighteen new mills were set up in one year alone—between 1873 and 1874. North India, however, did not see this textile boom as almost all the new mills were set up in other parts of the country, in cities such as Nagpur, Nadiad, Khandesh, Surat, Solapur, Madras, Calcutta and Halar. While the new mills used modern machinery to spin cloth, north Indian weavers still used the old looms in their huts.

Gopal Rai had been following the boom of the textile industry in India and was aware that north India was not a part of this textile economy. He also knew that Delhi was surrounded by thousands of square kilometres of land that could be used to grow cotton. Gopal Rai was a nationalist and understood the role played by industry in improving the lives of the people in the community. Even though the Mutiny had been crushed by the British, the desire for independence burnt bright in him. Independent India, Gopal Rai believed, would benefit from new and modern industry. The northern part of India, specifically, needed more industry according to him.

But Gopal Rai was not a trained engineer. He was not a rich man and did not have the funds required to set up a cotton mill. All he had was a dream.

He spoke to his employer, Ram Kishan Dass, about his dream. The astute businessman understood the potential of a cotton mill but was apprehensive about investing all the money required.

'Your idea is a good one, Gopal Rai, but it will be a risky business, no?' asked Ram Kishan Dass.

'No business venture is without any risk, Lala ji,' answered Gopal Rai in his measured voice. 'But look around,' he said passionately, waving his hands around, turning his head from left to right. 'Do you see even a single modern cloth mill in north India? I am certain that it will be a great venture.'

'All that is fine, Gopal Rai, but it is still a big financial commitment. You've just told me roughly how much a mill would cost. I don't want to put in all the money myself,' the businessman responded.

Gopal Rai was disappointed but also saw merit in his employer's argument.

'Lala ji, what if I find other investors? Will you at least commit to being an investor then?' asked Gopal Rai after a minute's thought.

'Of course, if you find other investors, you can be sure of my money,' confirmed Ram Kishan Dass.

Gopal Rai saw a dim light at the end of the dark tunnel after this conversation with his employer. He had a confirmed investor. He decided to find other investors and sell his dream to them.

One of the first businessmen he spoke with was Sri Krishn Dass, who belonged to the same biradari or caste subgroup as Gopal Rai. Sri Krishn Dass was a trader of jaggery and was known as Gurwala. At that time members of the same biradari typically helped each other out in times of need. However, Sri Krishn Dass was also a successful businessman, and he saw merit in the business proposition.

'You say that Lala Ram Kishan has already agreed to be part of this venture?' asked Sri Krishn Dass as he sat back and took a long, deep pull of his hookah. He looked at Gopal Rai intently as he waited for the answer.

'Yes, Lala ji has committed to be a core member provided we build a small team of investors,' said Gopal Rai.

Sri Krishn Dass leaned back further in his moodah and smiled broadly. 'If Lala ji is in, then consider me also a part of this,' said Sri Krishn Dass.

It helped Gopal Rai that the original commitment from Ram Kishan Dass carried great value in the community. This was because Ram Kishan Dass was a man of stature in the Delhi community and had gained even more prestige after he was awarded the title of Rai Bahadur. This title had been given to him in recognition of his services as a municipal commissioner and an honorary magistrate in the city. A wealthy businessman, Ram Kishan Dass had varied business interests, including a biscuit factory and one of the earliest theatres in Delhi—the Rama Theatre in Chandni Chowk. Modern-day Delhi residents know this theatre as Majestic Cinema.

Gopal Rai now had two businessmen as his partners. Both these men were well-known and well-respected in the business community. These two were soon joined by two more men. One of these was Gopal Rai's cousin, Banwari Lall, and the other was his brother-in-law, Benarsi Dass. Gopal Rai was married to Benarsi Dass sister.

The group of five met often to discuss the proposed cloth mill. Gopal Rai had all the details about the production of cotton, the prices charged and the exorbitant profits made by the textile mills in other parts of the country. But Ram Kishan Dass wanted to know more before the venture was finalized. He decided to travel to Bombay, Ahmedabad and Nagpur to see the textile mills there himself. These cities were the main hubs of the textile industry in India. He asked Gopal Rai to accompany him.

The two men spent over four months in these cities. The trip confirmed their belief that a textile mill in Delhi was a good idea. They were also heartened by the fact that the customers in Delhi and Punjab were already buying the textiles being produced by the mills in western India. A factory in Delhi could sell to the same customers at a cheaper rate, as freight costs would be less.

'But it will require good management and lots of hard work, of course,' said Gopal Rai to Ram Kishan Dass, who nodded in agreement.

'I can be the secretary of the mill, subject to the approval of all of you,' said Gopal Rai. 'I will do all the work and manage the business and will report to the board of directors.'

Ram Kishan Dass nodded in agreement. He liked Gopal Rai and knew that he had a sharp mind. The secretary of the company operated like a COO and CEO combined. Ram Kishan Dass had no objection to Gopal Rai running the mill.

Once they were back in Delhi, Gopal Rai put together a draft business plan for the other investors. According to him the venture required Rs 7 lakh as the starting capital. This was a large amount even for the four other men, who were wealthy in their own ways. It was decided to take the plan to a larger set of people—businessmen or wealthy individuals—who would buy into the dream and also be willing to buy into the shares of the proposed mill.

Gopal Rai started working the investor market in Delhi. He spoke to wealthy men and businessmen about the proposed cloth mill. As he spoke with more potential investors, Gopal Rai started feeling more confident. The astute businessmen had not said no to him. They had not yet committed the money, but they were interested. Gopal Rai knew that he was on track and that his dream of a cloth mill in Delhi could see the light of day.

To take the matter forward, Gopal Rai decided that a meeting of interested businessmen would be useful. He spoke with Ram Kishan and got his permission to hold a potential investor meeting at the latter's home. Gopal Rai knew that holding the meeting at Ram Kishan's home would have more significance in the minds of the interested investors, given the stature of the host.

The group met at Ram Kishan Dass's house in late September 1888. It was a motley set of people largely belonging to the Marwari or bania community. Some of them were large cloth and textile traders as well. They knew each other either well or in passing. The common thread binding them all was the fact that they had money and were looking for an investment opportunity. That they were in Ram Kishan Dass's house and that he was part of the core team of the proposed mill gave each of the men in the room great comfort.

After tea and snacks were served, Gopal Rai took centre stage. He got up, adjusted his dhoti and took a moment to survey the room. He waited for that last shuffling of feet and that last cough from the audience as it, too, settled down and waited for Gopal Rai to speak.

'Lala ji and I have spent the last four months touring the various textile mills in India,' began Gopal Rai after a deep breath. He did not have any papers or written notes in his hands. He did not need any help in speaking about his dream. This was all he had dreamt of for the last couple of years. He knew that this was his moment of truth. If he was able to convince the people in the room about the mill, he knew his dream had a fighting chance of becoming reality.

Gopal Rai spoke about the fact that their trip to the textile mills had proved to them that cloth weaving was a paying business. 'Ten years ago, there were only forty-seven companies in India for textiles; now there are over one hundred,' said Gopal Rai. Of the hundred, more than half were in and around the Bombay region, he explained.

He then told his audience that, before these textile mills had been started in India, cloth used to be imported from England and then sold locally. However, since the textile mills had been set up, Indian cloth and textiles were being exported across the world, especially to England.

'We know all this, Gopal Rai. After all, we are in the cloth business,' said one cloth merchant, smiling snidely as he looked around the room for validation. Several other heads nodded. 'Tell us something we do not know.'

Gopal Rai smiled widely. 'Lala Pyare Lal ji, *thoda sabar kariye. Mein sab bata raha hoon*,' he said. 'I may not tell you something you do not know but I will tell you something that you may not have focused on. Many of you are in the cloth and textile trade. So, you will bear me out when I say that in Delhi, and even in Punjab, there is no cloth mill, yet consumption is high.'

Several heads nodded, as all of them were aware of the demand for cloth in the northern part of the country.

'Further, there is a large cotton market here, as cotton is produced in large quantities in this part of the country. There is also a large cloth market here. Now, cotton that is grown here is sent to Bombay and also to England. There, this cotton is used to manufacture cloth. This manufactured cloth comes back to our market here and is sold to people. Now think again—think about the profits that can be made if the same cotton is used to manufacture cloth here. There will be no freight charges—'

'And the labour cost is cheaper here than in Bombay,' said Lala Pyare Lal, cutting Gopal Rai short. The snide remark he had made moments earlier was forgotten.

Gopal Rai wanted to smile at the enthusiasm of Pyare Lal but kept a straight face and nodded sagely. 'You are absolutely right, Lala ji. Bombay needs to pay a worker eight annas a day to work in the factory. But here, we can get a worker at half that rate—at four annas a day.'

Now Ram Kishan Dass also added his voice to the proceedings. 'We all know that land here is cheaper than in the Bombay area. There are large plots of land available near the railway station,' he said.

By now the mood in the room was that of optimism. People were speaking to each other and over each other, discussing the various ways of setting up a mill in the area. But Gopal Rai was not finished. He gestured to all to be quiet. The room settled down again.

'The land and the workers will be cheaper here. Plus, freight costs will be almost negligible. But the engineers will have to be paid the same as they are in Bombay. If we want the best cloth, we need to pay for the best engineers,' pointed out Gopal Rai.

'But once our workers are trained I am sure we can reduce the number of engineers,' said Lala Sangam Lal, a cloth merchant.

Gopal Rai smiled a secret smile to himself as he focused on the words used by Lala Sangam Lal—'our workers'. He knew that he had at least one convert in the room.

'Absolutely, Lala ji, our workers will need to be trained and once they are up to the mark, we can reduce the dependence on engineers.' Several more heads nodded enthusiastically.

'And before I forget, let me tell you another thing,' continued Gopal Rai. By now he had the audience hanging on to his words. Many in the room leaned forward in their seats to catch what Gopal Rai was about to say.

'The quality of our cloth will be superior as well. You all know that cotton bales are pressed hard to fit as many as possible in containers for transport. The quality of the cotton is compromised due to this hard pressure. We will not need to do this here, as transport will be over smaller distances. So, the quality of cotton used to weave our cloth will be higher and therefore the quality of the cloth will also be better,' he argued logically.

'And therefore, we can sell our cloth at a higher price!' exclaimed Lala Mehtab Rai excitedly.

Gopal Rai stole a glance at Ram Kishan Dass, who was looking at the audience with an indulgent smile. He looked up at Gopal Rai, and the two men exchanged a brief, fleeting smile, acknowledging the fact that the meeting was a success.

Gopal Rai sat down to give the gathered men some time to discuss the possibility of a cloth mill. The room was full of excited chatter. Some men had stood up and were talking to each other animatedly; others had turned their chairs to make a rough circle and were discussing the business venture.

Ram Kishan Dass stood up after a while and took charge. He spoke about the fact that a limited liability company needed to be formed to take this proposal forward. 'Based on our calculations, we will require Rs 7 lakh to start this venture,' he said. A gasp went around the room as they heard the amount that was needed. In the 1880s, Rs 7 lakh was a significant amount. Unfazed, Ram Kishan Dass continued. 'We think that it would be best to set up a joint stock company with 2,800 initial shares of Rs 250 each. I propose that we form a committee of five members to draw up a prospectus for the company. I further propose that Gopal Rai be appointed the secretary of this company.'

Gopal Rai was very happy. He saw his dream finally taking shape. He worked day and night to put together the prospectus. Within a week of the first meeting in late September, Gopal Rai called for another meeting to present the draft prospectus. Once again, this meeting was held at Ram Kishan Dass's house.

'We will call this company Delhi Cloth and General Mills, and it will undertake the spinning of cotton and the weaving of cloth,' began Gopal Rai. The gathering broke out into applause at the name of the proposed company. The fact that the company was being called Delhi Cloth Mills gladdened the hearts of all in the room, as they were all Delhiites. A temporary board of directors was elected, and Ram Kishan Dass was unanimously elected the chairman. Gopal Rai had already been named secretary of the company.

The prospectus was presented to the gathering. Gopal Rai had put together a detailed paper. The prime focus of the prospectus was to get people to buy the company's shares. Therefore, it was necessary to go into the details of the proposed company. However, Gopal Rai first appealed to the patriotism of the people.

He started the prospectus by pointing out that the cotton mills in other parts of the country were contributing significantly to the welfare and economy of the country. He further pointed out that Delhi and the area around it had no cloth mills and that the establishment of a large cloth mill here would enable Delhi and its people to also contribute to the development of the country. It may have been a long shot, but Gopal Rai was aware of the fact that personal allegiance was being transferred from the self to the nation, especially after 1857. Duty towards the country was a new sentiment and businessmen were beginning to see that self-interest and national interest could coexist. They were also smart enough to understand that if they did so, their commercial endeavours would take on a new dignity.

The prospectus then went on to detail the investment plan of Delhi Cloth and General Mills. Of the Rs 7 lakh that was needed as the initial capital, Rs 5 lakh would be used to buy land, get the building up and install the machinery. The factory would have 15,000 spindles and the engine used to run the spindles would be of high power so that it could continue to be used when the factory expanded in later years. The remaining Rs 2 lakh would be kept to cover running expenses and for stocks.

Gopal Rai wanted the prospective buyers of the company's stock to be aware of the superior quality of the material that would be produced by the company. He pointed out in the prospectus that the new cotton spinning machines would spin very thin thread and would work longer than the older machines. All new machines would be imported from England and every transaction would be carried out with care, focusing on the commercials.

To enable future investors to get a sense of the business volumes and profits, the prospectus presented some rough number. It stated that the 15,000 spindles would produce 15 lakh pounds of finished goods each year—or 5,000 pounds per day—as it was assumed that the factory would work 300 days in a year. The expense per pound of finished goods was forecasted at seven annas, which included workers' pay, coal and cotton, other necessities, repairs and maintenance, commissions, brokerage to be paid and some miscellaneous expenses.

While the exact profit figure was kept blank, the prospectus gave enough indication of the profit margins, which were high. The meticulous Gopal Rai went on to say that a reserve fund would be carved out of the profits generated. This reserve fund would come in useful in times of need. The risk would be distributed across the shareholders, as it was to be a joint stock company.

Gopal Rai knew that it would not be an easy task for all the shares to be sold to the public. He knew that while the people gathered at Ram Kishan Dass's house had been enthusiastic, few would follow up their talk with money. Further, there was only one stock exchange in India at that time—the Bombay Stock Exchange, which had been established in 1875. Even though the number of joint stock companies in Delhi and

Punjab had been growing, there were less than ten companies with a capital of Rs 1 lakh or more. A large company with an initial capital of Rs 7 lakh would be an exception in the market.

Gopal Rai was, however, a man driven by his dream, and he did not allow any doubts to take root in his mind. He worked hard and spoke with merchants, businessmen and other wealthy people; he spoke to friends and the extended family. Meanwhile, the prospectus was printed in English and an application form for the purchase of shares was attached to the back of each prospectus. This form was to be returned with a Rs 25 deposit against each share applied for.

Shri Ram was four years old by this time and was already closer to his uncle, Gopal Rai, than his father. Gopal Rai, too, looked upon Shri Ram with great love. He also believed that Shri Ram had come into the family bringing good fortune. Thus, in spite of all the difficulties that he sensed lay ahead, he had faith that his dream would fructify.

Every day when he went home, Gopal Rai spent time with Shri Ram and talked to him about his dream. He talked about the mill contributing to India's development. He also talked about his own vision for the cloth mill—how this mill would just be the first of other, even larger mills.

The four-year-old toddler may not have understood all that his uncle was saying but he could hear the passion in his voice. It was this passion that drove Shri Ram once he joined Delhi Cloth Mills as a young adult in 1909. DCM was fuelled by the passion of both the uncle and the nephew.

5

Shri Ram Joins DCM

THE company—Delhi Cloth and General Mills Company Limited—was formally registered in March 1889.

Such had been the excitement in the market about DCM that even before the company was registered, more than 2,000 of its shares had been sold. Only six months had passed between the first meeting in September 1888 and the registration of the company. During these months Gopal Rai had taken Ram Kishan Dass and another member of the board to Bombay. He wanted them to see, first-hand, what a cotton mill looked like. He also wanted to use that visit to explore the possibility of acquiring machinery and to scout for engineers who could be employed by DCM. Gopal Rai knew that the board would want to be involved in these matters, and thus he used the visit to familiarize two members of the board with them.

Once the company was formally registered, Gopal Rai got down to the task of acquiring land and ordering machines for the mill. Though he was the secretary and doing all the work on the ground, the board had not formally agreed on a salary for him. But it did not matter to Gopal Rai. His main motivation was not money.

He continued to work without any salary or other form of remuneration. He bought forty-six bighas of land for the mill and associated offices for approximately Rs 17,000. He also signed a contract with Rajputana Railways to lay rail tracks and sidings in the mill and connect them to the main railway station. Rajputana–Malwa Railway was a metre-gauge railway line that ran from Delhi to Indore and Ahmedabad.

Gopal Rai needed a foreman before he could start the construction of the mill. During his visit to Bombay earlier in the year he had met and interviewed an Englishman called Howard. Gopal Rai got in touch with Howard and asked him to join the new company to oversee the setting up of the plant.

Work on the new mill started in October 1889, soon after its registration. Gopal Rai and the board also started the construction of a workers' colony simultaneously. By now Gopal Rai was managing all the company's affairs almost single-handedly. He was working from the early hours of dawn to late at night. To facilitate his working, he moved the company's office from Ram Kishan Dass's house to Barhwali Haveli in Kucha Mai Das.

It took over a year to construct the mill and the workers' colony. It was in early 1891 that the boilers of the mill were fired for the first time. It was a momentous occasion and the entire board gathered to witness it. A collective murmur of delight went up as the chimneys of the mill started to belch out smoke.

Inside the mill, the spinners were set in motion. Although the name of the company was Delhi Cloth and General Mills, people shortened it and started referring to it as simply Delhi Cloth Mills. This, too, was shortened and the mill came to be known as DCM.

The mill became a familiar landmark in Delhi. The local residents were curious to see it from the inside, as it was the first of its kind in north India. Gopal Rai saw an opportunity here. He allowed outsiders to visit the factory for a fee of one anna. There were many takers for this, and the visitors' fee added to the overall revenue of the company.

While the mill was being constructed, the board had laid down the responsibilities of the mill manager and the secretary of the company. The mill manager was to supervise the work of all mill workers, was to report to the board about the working of the mill and the inventories, and was to be in charge of the stores as well.

The secretary of the company had a much larger role. He had to maintain the accounts of the company and take care of all official correspondence. He was responsible for all purchases, including those of raw materials. He would also guide the mill manager on what goods to manufacture and the quantity of production. The other jobs of the secretary included arranging the board meetings and the annual general meetings. He was also responsible for ensuring that the directives of the board were carried out fully, and had to present a regular report to the board on the working of the company.

Of all the jobs he was expected to carry out, the two most important jobs of the secretary were purchases and deciding which goods to produce. These two functions needed a deep understanding of the business and maturity of decision-making as well. The profitability of the company depended on these two jobs being done well.

As cloth production began at DCM, the board realized that they needed a sales plan as well. Though the demand for their product was evident, a formal plan was drawn up. It was decided that the mill would ask cloth merchants to sell the goods on its behalf and that the merchants would get a commission for their efforts. This worked well, but Gopal Rai kept thinking about ways to increase sales. He was already inundated with work, but he looked at DCM as the fulfilment of his dream. He may not have been the owner of the mill, but he thought like one.

In September 1891, six months after production began at DCM, Gopal Rai proposed to the board that the company sell its goods directly in retail as well. He said in his proposal that this would encourage people to place orders directly with the company and the company, in turn, would save on the commission paid out to the wholesalers. The board liked the idea and defined retail as any order that was less than one bale of yarn or 100 thaans (lengths) of cloth. In keeping with this new policy of reaching the customer directly, a company shop was opened in Chandni Chowk.

This meant that the office of the secretary was now a full-fledged sales office as well. The power and authority of the office of the secretary went up dramatically. Thus, the story of DCM, going forward, essentially became the story of its secretaries.

Gopal Rai had been working tirelessly since 1888 and even though he was not very old, his energy had started flagging. He had developed a chronic disease. He had to reduce the time he spent at the office. The role of the secretary, however, had grown in terms of both work as well as the authority vested in it. The board was sympathetic but also wanted a secretary who worked full-time so as to be able to discharge the duties well. They held discussions with Gopal Rai, who suggested that a temporary assistant secretary be appointed to help him. He also argued that, by doing this, he would be able to train the assistant secretary. The board agreed with the suggestion and asked Gopal Rai to recruit this new assistant secretary.

Gopal Rai took no time in suggesting that his only surviving brother, Madan Mohan Lal, be appointed the new assistant secretary. Shri Ram was still in college and a teenager and therefore could not be named by his uncle. The only other surviving adult male in the family was Madan Mohan. Thus, it was not difficult for Gopal Rai to suggest his brother's name.

Madan Mohan was twenty five years younger than Gopal Rai and had not worked formally until then. He had been managing the family properties. The families of the three brothers (one had died earlier) lived together in Kucha Mai Das. Further, the office of the company had been moved to their family house. Thus, Madan Mohan was somewhat aware of the company and its affairs. He was happy to help his brother. Gopal Rai remained the oldest member of the family, but Madan Mohan became the dominant figure.

Shri Ram had been forced to give up his studies and fend for himself around this time. Madan Mohan could have given Shri Ram a job in DCM but chose not to. One of the reasons was that, while Shri Ram was meticulous about accounts, Madan Mohan was a little lackadaisical. He did not want his own son hovering over his shoulder and pointing out how the accounts could be kept better. Unable to find a suitable opportunity in Delhi, Shri Ram first went to Alwar and then to work with Boota Singh.

Gopal Rai finally gave up his fight with ill-health and passed away in 1906. A few days after Gopal Rai's death, the board of DCM formally appointed Madan Mohan as the secretary of the company. He was given a salary of Rs 500 a month, and a small commission from the sales of goods was added to his renumeration.

It was, however, not all smooth sailing for Madan Mohan. Besides the fact that he had not worked in any organized, structured environment before joining DCM, his interpersonal skills too left much to be desired. He was a man of strong likes and dislikes. Gopal Rai had, over the years, built cordial relationships with other stakeholders—the suppliers, the vendors, the distributors and the employees. After Gopal Rai's death, these stakeholders had assumed that the relationships would continue in the same vein. Madan Mohan chose to work differently. This affected the way the suppliers and other vendors dealt with the company. While Gopal Rai had been a workaholic, Madan Mohan was an aesthete. He found it difficult to match up to the reputation of his older brother.

To add to Madan Mohan's problems, the price of raw cotton had been going up. Though this was not his fault, it was he who had to deal with the resultant problems. The profit margins of the finished products reduced drastically. In fact, the enterprise had declared no dividend at all in 1904 and went into the red after 1905. Madan Mohan was struggling to discharge his duties well.

It was in 1909 that Boota Singh, one of DCM's largest customers, suggested rather assertively that Shri Ram be given a chance to work in the mill. Madan Mohan agreed, though reluctantly. In March 1909, Shri Ram started working with his father at DCM. Madan Mohan, perversely, told his son that he could not be paid a salary. Shri Ram had no choice but to agree. He asked to be assigned a job in the accounts department as the work there would be similar to what he had been doing at Boota Singh's company.

Shri Ram joined DCM almost anonymously. Madan Mohan kept the fact that Shri Ram was his own son a secret. Shri Ram was anyway a man of few words. With his thin and lanky physique, it was easy for him to melt into the background inconspicuously. But when it came to work, especially accounts, Shri Ram was another man altogether. He was a confident and controlled man who knew his own mind and could read numbers better than anyone else.

After he joined the company, Shri Ram found that DCM was going through a choppy time. The momentum given to local suppliers by the Swadeshi movement was petering out by 1909. Launched in 1905 in Calcutta, the Swadeshi and Boycott movements or aandolans encouraged people to buy and use goods produced in India and burn British-made goods.

As a result, there had been a sharp spike in the businesses that produced goods for the Indian market. Cloth made in India by Indian mills was amongst the biggest beneficiaries of the Swadeshi movement. But by the time Shri Ram joined DCM, the gains due to these movements were tailing off.

The problems did not end there. The cotton crop had failed in 1907, and in 1908 there had been an outbreak of malaria. Also, 1908 happened to be considered inauspicious by Hindus for weddings. The demand for cloth went down further. It was not only DCM that was affected by this downturn of business. It was believed that 1909 was the worst year in the history of the cotton industry in India. Most mills curtailed their hours of work; some stopped work altogether for a few months. But

DCM did not shut down and the workmen were paid their wages.

Along with the downtrend in the industry, there had been a change of guard at DCM. When Madan Mohan took over as the secretary, the manager of the mill was also changed. Harwood, the manager, was replaced by another Britisher named Lawson. The board of directors too had seen a change. By this time almost all the directors were new. The new directors did not have the same enthusiasm about being involved in the business as the founding directors had had. The new board met less frequently and left all the important decisions to the secretary. Madan Mohan thus continued to plod along without much guidance.

Shri Ram's early days in DCM were not spectacular. For one, he was kept out of sight by his father. In fact, some members of the board were unaware of the relationship between Shri Ram and Madan Mohan. Shri Ram was a man of few words and did not speak unless he needed to. He preferred to listen and observe—a habit he had carried into his adult life from his childhood. He overlooked the cold shouldering by his father and focused instead on learning more about the work at DCM.

His day started early. He would walk from his home in Kucha Mai Das to the DCM office, and more often than not, he was the first one in the office. He would spend some time going over the accounts before going to the mill. After walking around the shop floor as the workers were coming in, he would go back to the office.

Shri Ram would alternate between being in the office and the mill, and it was common for him to make at least nine or ten trips to the mill on any given day. The time in the office was spent on administrative matters, including purchasing raw materials, selling the finished goods, arranging for transport, dealing with paperwork and writing to suppliers and vendors. Madan Mohan had started delegating a lot of his work to Shri Ram even though he continued to ignore his son.

Shri Ram's learnings from the time he had spent running the ginning factory in Alwar had stayed with him. He understood the value of the workers in a mill. Therefore, he spent his time in the mill walking around the shop floor and talking with the workers. By this time there were a few hundred workers in the mill. Very soon Shri Ram was familiar with each of them and knew them by name. As he walked around, he asked the workers about their work, their families and even about their homes. He knew how many children each worker had and the conditions in which he lived. Shri Ram also used his interactions with the workers to find out the problems they faced in their work. The workers started seeing Shri Ram as one of them and were comfortable discussing their problems with him.

Shri Ram would be the first to reach the office in the morning and in the evening he would be the last to leave. Once again, he would walk back home. It was a long walk and would have taken Shri Ram almost fifty minutes if he walked without any breaks. But it took him much longer, as he would stop by the cloth market and visit a few cloth merchants every evening.

'*Kaise ho aap aaj*?' he would ask the owner. And then he would turn to the attendant. '*Aaj DCM ka maal dikhaya kya*? Did the customers like the cloth? Were there any complaints?'

The shopkeepers or the attendants initially had no idea that they were speaking with the son of the secretary of DCM. Shri Ram had been away from Delhi and even after returning, he had kept a low profile. The attendants, therefore, gave Shri Ram their honest feedback, not mincing any words.

Some shop owners realized that the kinds of questions being asked by Shri Ram were not the kinds typically asked by an ordinary employee of the company. Some of them asked Shri Ram who he was. To every such question Shri Ram had a simple answer. 'I am your humble julaha (weaver),' he would say in his soft voice.

The interactions with the cloth merchants and the attendants were useful, as they gave Shri Ram genuine feedback about DCM's products as well as sales policies. Shri Ram would share the feedback—the compliments as well as the complaints—with the workers and the supervisors. He would also ask them for their suggestions on how to deal with the complaints, especially about the quality of the cloth being produced.

Most days Shri Ram travelled on foot but on some days he would take the tram. The fare from Bazaar Sita Ram to his mill in Bara Hindu Rao was one anna each way. He put the saved one anna to good use on some evenings, as he would stop at the nearby halwai's shop and buy one kullarh of hot milk with sugar and a thick layer of malai or cream on top.

Shri Ram spent the better part of his first six months at DCM getting to know the mill, the workers and the customers personally. As he walked around the mill, he spent time understanding the working of the boilers; he got to know why the spindles jammed and learnt how to fix them. He also understood the importance of light in the mill, as he saw what it was like to make the cloth in the dingy, hot weaving shed. He also saw for himself, in the cloth market, how the DCM cloth looked when compared to a roll from Lancashire. He knew that sometimes it compared unfavourably and also knew that the cloth merchants thought the same.

In a short time, he came to love the business passionately. He remembered the passion his uncle, Gopal Rai, had for DCM. His uncle's stories of the early years of the company came back to him. The passion for the business started rising within him. Simultaneously, the ambition he had within him started raising its head again. The two failed business ventures had forced Shri Ram to tuck away his ambition in the far recesses of his mind. But now that he was part of a business that his uncle had dreamt of, his ambition started knocking on the closed doors of his mind. The knocking became incessant as the days went by, until Shri Ram was forced to acknowledge it.

He saw the potential of the business for sure. But he also saw how the cloth mill in Delhi was providing employment to hundreds of families. It was the most modern mill in north India at that time. Shri Ram saw DCM play a small but important part in nation-building.

The passion and the learnings from these early days stayed with Shri Ram for the rest of his life. The practical knowledge acquired by him sharpened his perception and enabled him to cut through the statistics and the jargon-filled reports of the experts in his later years.

Shri Ram's hard work and dedication did not go unnoticed. The board saw Shri Ram at work, heard the suppliers and vendors talk about him with fondness and respect, and were impressed. Some of the board members still did not know that Madan Mohan was Shri Ram's biological father; they knew Shri Ram as Gopal Rai's nephew.

By November 1909, just eight months after Shri Ram joined DCM, the board had enough confidence in him to pass a resolution stating that it would be Shri Ram who would work as the secretary of the company whenever Madan Mohan was away from work.

Though Shri Ram did not know it then, he was well on his way to taking DCM, and himself, to spectacular heights of success in the coming years.

6

Early Successes at DCM

SHRI Ram had been aware of the problems his father was facing in managing the affairs of the company. He understood the reasons for some of the problems and wanted to discuss possible solutions with Madan Mohan. But the father kept his distance from his son and did not encourage any talk about work. For some time, therefore, Shri Ram remained a passive observer as he continued to see his father struggle.

At home he was settling back into Barhwali Haveli. There were two children in the haveli now—one was Shri Ram's brother Shankar Lall and the other was Shri Ram's son Murli Dhar. There was only a six-year age gap between the two children. Shankar Lall, the older one, was happy to have a playmate at home. Unlike his elder brother, Shankar Lall was well-built and a strong child. He was already taller than most other children his age. Looking at the two brothers, it was difficult to believe that Shri Ram and Shankar Lall were siblings.

Shankar Lall saw his brother as a guardian and an elder, but he saw his nephew, Murli Dhar, as a cousin and a friend. The two children bonded in childhood, and this bond of friendship continued in their adult life as well.

Shankar Lall, as the much younger brother of Shri Ram, addressed him as Bhaiji. Murli Dhar, the younger boy, used to spend a lot of time with Shankar Lall and looked up to him as an elder brother rather than as an uncle. As is the wont of younger children, Murli Dhar started imitating all that Shankar Lall did. He also started aping Shankar Lall in addressing Shri Ram as Bhaiji. Shri Ram found it endearing and did not correct his son. Over a period of time most of the household started addressing Shri Ram as Bhaiji. In the coming years, all his sons, daughters-in-law, grandchildren and great-grandchildren—all of them—called Shri Ram Bhaiji. Even close friends called Shri Ram Bhaiji in later years. In fact, if non-family members were allowed to address Shri Ram as Bhaiji, they felt honoured, as it meant that they were seen as family.

Meanwhile, the quality of fabric being produced by DCM was falling, and it was affecting the prices in the market. What was more worrying for Shri Ram, however, was that he felt DCM's name was being sullied. After some time, he could not help wanting to do something about it. But he also knew that his father would not take kindly to his suggestions. As a way out, he asked his father to let him manage the ginning department of the company.

There were a couple of reasons why Shri Ram wanted control of the ginning department. One was that he knew ginning was the first process that the harvested cotton went through on its journey to becoming fabric. If the ginning process was not handled well, it affected the ultimate quality of the fabric. He wanted to address the quality problem right from the start.

The second reason was that thanks to his experience at the ginning unit in Alwar, he knew how the process worked.

Whether it was Shri Ram's persistence or Madan Mohan's knowledge that the ginning department had the worst record among all divisions of the business, permission was granted to Shri Ram to take over that department. Maybe it was also the fact that Madan Mohan was actually happy to get rid of a headache! Shri Ram, for his part, was happy that he had full charge of the unit.

Ginning is the process by which the harvested cotton is put through a machine that separates the fibre from the cotton seeds. The ginning process also helps remove impurities, including small stones, particles and dust from the raw cotton. The cotton fibre that results after ginning is then compressed into bales and sent to the factory, where it is spun into yarn. This yarn is then either woven or knitted into fabric. If the ginning process is not done well, the resultant fibre has impurities, which get amplified in the woven fabric.

The first problem that Shri Ram encountered when he took charge of the ginning unit was the lack of workers. Due to the terrible record of the ginning unit, no worker wanted to work there. Further, the working conditions within the ginning unit were suboptimal. The ginning process released minuscule particles of dust and fibre into the air, which made the working environment unpleasant. Shri Ram realized that, more than a technical problem, he was facing a human problem. He addressed it in human terms.

One of his first actions was the installation of several large exhaust fans in the factory. The exhaust fans drew out the small particles in the air, and the workers immediately felt the difference in the quality of the ambient air. There was an almost immediate lifting of the morale of the workers.

The next step for Shri Ram was to institute an incentive scheme linked to productivity. Giving extra money to the workers for doing their job was not something that the board of directors was happy about. But Shri Ram convinced them to give him three months to show results. 'You can stop the scheme and remove me from this role if it does not work,' he told them.

The scheme worked and it worked well. There was a jump in production quantities. Further, there was a perceptible improvement in the quality of the fibre coming out of the ginning unit. Both these factors led to better and more fabric being produced, which resulted in higher sales figures. The losses of the ginning unit turned into profits. The board was delighted.

Shri Ram was also delighted at this success. His early failures in business had made him doubt his own abilities. A part of him wanted to ignore the whispers of doubt that crept in from time to time. But the more rational part of his mind also reminded him that the two businesses he had started had failed. This internal battle would exhaust Shri Ram. But there was no one he could talk to about this. Shri Ram still felt the lacuna of not having good sounding boards. Since childhood, he had wished for companionship and friendship with peers. More than ever, he now wished that he had a few people with whom he could speak about matters of work, life and more. But he had no one. Phoolan Devi continued to be in the background, focusing on her own health and matters of the household. She could not provide the companionship that Shri Ram was looking for.

Now, with the success of the ginning unit, the shoots of confidence took root in Shri Ram. His ambition started knocking insistently from within. Shri Ram did not yet know all that he wanted to do, but he knew that he wanted to grow the business manifold. He also knew that he was ready for it.

He decided to go full throttle. He persuaded his father and the board to give him more responsibilities. The board was happy to authorize bringing the engineering, carding and spinning departments under Shri Ram's supervision and control. In each department he first focused on the workers and their working conditions. His reputation, too, had grown due to his early days of walking on the shop floor and then transforming the ginning unit. The workers responded to Shri Ram's overtures with enthusiasm. This manifested in increased productivity, with better control over quality.

The biggest transformation, however, was in the overall morale and engagement level of the workers—an indifferent and lethargic workforce became an engaged and committed set of employees. DCM started producing better-quality products. Cloth merchants started making a beeline for the factory, requesting they be appointed as agents to sell DCM products. All this resulted in bumper profits for the company.

The board was watching all these developments with delight. They started having discussions amongst themselves about giving Shri Ram even more responsibility. In each board meeting they saw the assistant secretary taking charge and giving business updates and details; the secretary did not seem to know as much. Even though the board was not very involved in the day-to-day working of the company, they knew that the business was in better hands with Shri Ram.

In 1912 the board named Shri Ram the secretary of the company. Madan Mohan became a figurehead while his son took charge of the role. It was a poignant moment for both father and son. Shri Ram had been aware since his childhood that his father did not think highly of him and had actively kept him away from DCM. The fact that the board had chosen him over his father was not lost on Shri Ram; nor was it lost on Madan Mohan. He had to admit, even if only to himself, that he may have been too harsh on his son. But such was the distance between father and son that neither was able to share his innermost thoughts with the other.

As the secretary of the company, Shri Ram slowly started consolidating more activities under his role. The board of directors had by then enough trust in Shri Ram to allow him more authority and responsibilities.

It was difficult for Shri Ram, or anyone else for that matter, to remember that merely three years ago he had been working as a munshi with Boota Singh; that he had joined DCM almost anonymously in 1909 without any authority or responsibility. And now, he was the secretary of the company, which meant that he was the one managing the affairs of the business. Besides this, he was also earning a good salary along with a commission on sales.

The shoots of confidence within Shri Ram had become a full-grown, deep-rooted tree!

As Shri Ram and DCM continued their successful journey, Great Britain and France declared war on Germany in 1914. India, too, joined the war. The government in India ordered all factories and mills to focus on the production of products required by the defence forces. While some factory owners were unhappy about this dictate, Shri Ram saw this as an opportunity. The army contracts were large and, according to the calculations done by Shri Ram, profitable. The payment conditions were favourable to the producers. Further, the railways gave priority to the shipment of materials meant for the army. In fact, on some routes the railways put most of the trains on military work, thereby reducing the trains available for civilian cargo.

Once he had made up his mind to focus on meeting the requirements of the army, Shri Ram concentrated on the army's need for tents. An unlucky set of circumstances had led to a shortage of tents for the army. The reason could be traced back to the Durbar held in 1911, where it was announced that the capital of India would move from Calcutta to Delhi. The government, after the announcement, had started moving its men and material to Delhi in 1912.

There were no office buildings in Delhi that could accommodate the entire machinery of the government. A new secretariat was constructed in haste in Civil Lines, but it could accommodate only some officers. The top-ranking officers moved into this building. The army came to the rescue of the rest of the administration. Army tents were neatly set up in government camps and the administration worked from these as they waited for the new offices to be built.

When the war was declared, the army was caught on the wrong foot vis-à-vis their tents. They needed tents for the soldiers but could not uproot the government officers. Shri Ram had analysed this situation shrewdly and had seen this as a once-in-a-lifetime opportunity to change the fortunes of not only the company but also his family. He came up with a plan that involved taking advantage of the way army contracts worked.

The army in India, even in normal times, had a large demand for products. The army also bought all its requirements centrally. The suppliers, however, were typically small-scale or cottage industries and were scattered around the country. The army had neither the bandwidth nor the mind space to deal with all these suppliers individually. It therefore commissioned agents or contractors who would consolidate the army's requirements and then farm them out to the individual producers. The army would thus work with one person who in turn would deal with hundreds of others. This job of a consolidator or a contractor was a much-sought-after one, as the commissions earned by the contractors were significant. However, it was difficult to be appointed a contractor for the army, as securing the position required considerable influence and networking within the army. But Shri Ram had just the man with the right contacts within the army—Diwan Chand.

Diwan Chand was a friend of Shri Ram from the days he had spent in Boota Singh's office in Punjab. Diwan Chand was fond of the young man and had seen his dedication and diligence. He had also observed Boota Singh's trust in Shri Ram. Diwan Chand was a government contractor and, over time, had built a wide network of contacts within the administration. He had also built inroads into the ordnance department, which was the sourcing arm of the army.

Shri Ram spoke to Diwan Chand about securing orders for tents from the army. Diwan Chand was agreeable. But Shri Ram had an even bigger, more audacious idea. He broached it with Diwan Chand.

'Diwan Chand ji, the army needs many more tents than DCM can produce. So, either the army or you will have to give the order for the shortfall to other suppliers. Am I correct?' asked Shri Ram.

'You are right, Lala ji,' said Diwan Chand. 'DCM, even if it works all shifts every day, will not be able to meet the requirements of the army. I will be left with no choice but to give the order for the extra tents to some other mill.'

'Diwan Chand ji, it is true that DCM cannot produce all the tents required by the army. But DCM can produce the yarn that is needed to make the fabric for the tents. How many other mills in this part of the country have the kind of yarn manufacturing capacity that we do, eh? And the army needs more than just tents, don't they?' asked Shri Ram in his measured voice, hiding the excitement bubbling within.

Diwan Chand looked at Shri Ram speculatively. He twirled the end of his safa as he thought it through. He understood what Shri Ram was trying to say and mentally applauded the young man for the thought.

'Tell me more, Lala ji,' said Diwan Chand, looking keenly at Shri Ram as he waited to see if he had read Shri Ram's mind correctly.

Shri Ram needed no further encouragement. He explained what he had in mind. Diwan Chand listened attentively, nodding from time to time. Once Shri Ram had finished speaking, Diwan Chand got up, smiled a satisfied smile and patted Shri Ram on his back. The two men then shook hands as a sign of agreement.

They had decided that DCM would not only produce tents in its mills but would also supply yarn to smaller weavers so that they, in turn, could produce tents. It was an outsourcing arrangement with these smaller captive units. Their agreement went one step further. Diwan Chand knew through his network that the army had large requirements for tarpaulins, webbing and dasooti, a coarse fabric, as well. Webbing was used to create belts, pouches and kits, while dasooti was used for uniforms and other rough usage. The two friends decided that they would take on the role of a buyer in the open market. They would purchase all these products and in turn supply them to the army. Due to Diwan Chand's network in the ordnance department, Shri Ram was sure that they would know of the army's requirements ahead of the other contractors.

This meant that Shri Ram and Diwan Chand would form a partnership to fulfil the army contracts. However, Shri Ram thought strategically rather than tactically. He realized that this partnership would earn him and his family huge profits, but DCM's gains would be limited to the profits earned from the sale of tents. He had grown to love the company as his own, even though he was just an employee. The role of the secretary had given him a glimpse of the possibilities of expanding DCM in the future. He also knew that the expansion would need a fair bit of capital. Further, if DCM had to expand, it had to modernize as well, which would also need capital.

The idea Shri Ram came up with was part-genius, part-mercenary. He proposed a three-way partnership between DCM, Diwan Chand and Shri Ram. Diwan Chand's role would be to get the contracts from the army. It was also expected that Diwan Chand would use his influence to source the maximum number of orders possible. DCM would manufacture tents and supply the yarn to other vendors, who would also use it to manufacture tents. Shri Ram would source the remainder of the tents along with the orders for tarpaulin, dasooti and webbing from the open market. The profits from all deals, including for the material sourced by Shri Ram, would be split three ways—50 per cent to DCM, 30 per cent to Diwan Chand and 20 per cent to Shri Ram.

Shri Ram kept the smallest part for himself. He wanted the plan to be a success and therefore was willing to sacrifice a bit for the larger good. He wanted Diwan Chand to be motivated; he also wanted the board of DCM to buy into the plan. With the largest chunk of profits going to DCM, it would be difficult for the directors to say no. Shri Ram had another ace up his sleeve. DCM would in any case earn profits on the tents it would supply to the army. A double benefit for the company.

Shri Ram presented his plan to the board. He told the board that he looked at this partnership as a means to build up the company's reserves quickly and more successfully than it would be able to via its normal business. He argued that these reserves would be needed after the war ended, to buy new plants and machinery to expand production capacities.

Even though it was an unusual proposal, the board saw merit in it and authorized Shri Ram to go ahead.

The scheme was a runaway success. The four years of war saw extraordinary profits for all members of the partnership. Records show that in the year 1917–18 the partnership yielded profits upwards of Rs 7.5 lakh. Fifty per cent went to the company and 20 per cent, or Rs 1.5 lakh (worth a few crores today), accrued to Shri Ram. And this was in just one year! The three previous years had also yielded similar profits to the three partners.

The four years of war proved profitable for Shri Ram in more ways than one. Besides the earnings from the three-way partnership, he continued to earn his salary and commissions on the sales of DCM. The fortunes of his family changed completely in those four years.

The war years were fortuitous for Shri Ram personally as well. He was blessed with two more sons, who would take his legacy forward in the years ahead. Bharat Ram, his second son, was born on 5 October 1914, and his third son, Charat Ram, was born on 1 January 1918. Murli Dhar, his first child, had been born in 1907.

Shri Ram's fortunes may have changed but Shri Ram the man did not. Even with his new wealth, Shri Ram maintained his spartan living style. He continued to dress in a simple, buttoned-up coat along with loose churidaars and a black cap. His demeanour remained quiet and unassuming. He was active but frail-looking. His deep voice surprised many people even now, given his small build.

DCM was transformed in to a large cloth mill by the end of the war. During the war years, DCM not only produced tents for the army but also cloth for the general market. The demand for cloth in India had shot up due to the embargo on imports from England. The war had played havoc with the supply lines and the import of cloth had almost stopped. DCM took advantage of this situation and increased the production of cloth for the civilian market. Shri Ram, thinking ahead, knew that, after the war, the demand for tents would come down but the demand for cloth would remain high.

The war years had been good for DCM, but it had its share of problems as well. One of the biggest problems, not for DCM alone but for the country in general, was the rise in the prices of food items. The war had affected food supply badly. Prices in the years between 1915 and 1918 were higher than they had ever been. The lower-income groups, especially the workers, felt the tight squeeze of the rising prices. Many workers left the big cities hoping that things would be better in their villages. Shri Ram did not want his workers leaving the mill, as it would adversely affect the supply to the army, which in turn would affect the profitability of the venture.

Shri Ram did have a soft corner for the workers and their families, especially as he had spent the early part of his time at DCM getting to know the workers on the shop floor. One of the actions he took, almost unilaterally, was to increase the wages of the workers. Then he got a provision store opened within the premises of the mill. Workers could buy their daily provisions from this store at subsidized rates. Another initiative was undertaken to address the needs of the workers' children— Shri Ram started a scheme for their education.

But these initiatives were not enough to stem the discontent amongst the workers. It may be noted that a large section of the workers was really a loose band of migrants who came to the city to seek work and moved often from one factory to the other. Most factories found it a problem to keep workers from moving away. DCM, in one sense, was already different from other factories, as it had a workers' colony for its staff. The provision store and the children, education scheme provided a couple of more reasons for the larger workers' group to stay loyal. To bind all the initiatives together, Shri Ram discussed the concept of a provident fund with the board. Some mills in the Bombay area had started discussing the same idea: a provident or welfare fund for their workers. The board was hesitant but approved the scheme. The implementation of it, though, took a few more years.

By the end of the war Shri Ram was a very wealthy man and was managing the affairs of DCM almost without any interference from the board. But he was still an employee. He did own company shares, but these were just twenty-one in number. Shri Ram realized that, if he wanted to grow the company according to his plans, he needed more shareholding.

Shri Ram discussed the matter of growth with Madan Mohan, who was not really interested. The older man saw no reason to expand the business. 'We have enough money coming in, so why should we do more? I am happy with the profits we are making,' he said.

But Shri Ram wanted to expand the business. The war had made him realize that the independence of India would happen sooner or later. He remembered all the discussions with Gopal Rai in which his uncle had pointed out that industry was an important part of nation-building. The sense of patriotism ran deep in Shri Ram. Further, his ambition was now raging fiercely. He foresaw the opportunities ahead. He decided to ignore the disinterest of his father and planned ahead.

Towards the later years of the war Shri Ram started buying DCM shares from the open market. The partnership scheme under which he was earning 20 per cent was generating enough cash for him to invest in DCM shares. As a result, after the war, Shri Ram had become the third-largest shareholder of the company.

Once the war ended, the military contracts also ended. Shri Ram had diverted a large part of the factory's machinery to the production of army goods. The machines and men had been pushed hard during the war years to produce more and more to meet the growing demands of the army. Thus, at the end of the war it was a pleasant surprise for Shri Ram in particular and the board in general to find out that production had gone up more than twice with the same machines and the same set of workers. But the hard push for productivity had taken a toll on the machines. The wear and tear had increased. Shri Ram spoke with some workers and realized that new machines would be needed if the production quantities were to be maintained.

When he put the proposal before the board the natural question asked was why new machines were needed.

'The war has ended, and we can go back to using the machines to produce less fabric,' said one director.

'We are used to making profits in lakhs instead of thousands now. Do we really want to go back to those days of smaller profits?' asked Shri Ram.

'But who will we sell to?' asked another director.

This was a valid question, as the assumption was that the demand for goods from the mills would go down due to the army contracts being withdrawn. Further, with the war ending, the import of fabric had started again. Shri Ram heard the board's questions and then answered them in his logical, measured manner.

'You know that during the war years the Swadeshi movement reignited the patriotic passion in all Indians,' Shri Ram began. 'You've seen as I have that people are actually burning foreign cloth and other material.'

Some of the directors nodded in agreement. It was indeed true that the Swadeshi movement, which had started in 1905, had taken a social boycott route by the time the war ended. All imports, especially of foreign cloth, were frowned upon. In fact, people would collect their garments made of foreign material and set them alight in bonfires. Made in India cloth was the flavour of the times. While Gandhi had used the Swadeshi movement to popularize handloom and khadi cloth, the fabric produced by DCM was also seen as swadeshi.

Shri Ram saw the directors were listening intently and went on. 'You also know that during the war people were careful in buying clothing and other items, as no one knew how long the war would last. Now that the war has ended there is a rising demand for cloth in the market. This demand is even bigger than the pre-war demand.'

'Now tell me, if we want to meet this rising demand, can we do it with our old, tired machines? 'I have had many conversations with the supervisors and even the workers. They all say that the machines cannot continue in the same manner.'

'The workers will say anything to make their lives easier. They want to work on the new machines for sure,' said one director dismissively, waving away Shri Ram's argument.

'Lala ji, the workers are the lifeline of our mill; the machines are the other lifeline. I believe my workers, also because I have seen the machinery myself. Come with me tomorrow morning and I will take you to each machine and explain why it needs to be replaced,' said Shri Ram passionately. He did not like it when people, especially wealthy people, looked at the workers dismissively. 'Lastly, there is also the possibility of accidents. Older machines may result in accidents, and if any one of our workers gets injured it will affect all the others as well.'

The board listened to Shri Ram and his arguments intently. Once he had finished speaking they discussed the matter among themselves. Most directors were happy to let Shri Ram run the business and take decisions. They had a hands-off approach to the business. They really did not want to walk the shop floor examining machine after machine. The directors were happy getting their dividends each year. Shri Ram knew this and therefore focused on increasing profits year after year.

In the end the board was convinced of the need for new machines. What helped the board make up its mind was the fact that the financials of the company were robust. Dividends had been between 25 and 35 per cent and, even after that, the company's reserves were plentiful.

The board gave Shri Ram permission to place a large order for new machines. An additional order was placed for weaving equipment (looms and accessories), spinning machinery, boilers and another engine. The orders were placed in late 1919 and the deliveries were expected in the first half of 1921.

The board had, no doubt, given permission for major capital expenditure, but it was aware of a problem that was facing the industry. This was the problem of higher wages. The cost of living had gone up after the war, and the workers were bearing the brunt of it. Mill workers in the Bombay and Ahmedabad regions had gone on strikes, paralysing the production in their mills. Shri Ram, with his pulse on the workers' sentiments, was aware that this malaise could spread to Delhi if proactive measures were not taken. The board asked Shri Ram to work on a comprehensive plan to address workers' welfare.

One of the first actions taken by the management was a wage hike for the workers. Wages went up by more than 50 per cent. However, even after this wage hike in 1919, which came after a wage hike in 1917, the workers were hard-pressed making ends meet. Such was the post-war inflation.

Shri Ram cut working hours from twelve to eight per day. This was the precursor to the eight-hour shift. In fact, the factory legislation of 1920 set the maximum working hours to not more than ten hours per day. DCM was already ahead of the government legislation.

The next part of the plan was to focus on the working conditions of the workers. Shri Ram, at the ginning unit, had already experienced the effect of better light and ventilation on the morale of the workers. He brought that learning to the larger mill and had several large exhaust fans installed there. There was an immediate improvement in the ventilation as there was now a continuous supply of fresh air for the workers.

Shri Ram then focused on the living conditions of the workers. Most workers lived with their families on the mill premises, in the workers' quarters that had been constructed for them. A small school and a provision shop had already been set up during the war. Now Shri Ram added an entertainment or recreation hall to the workers' colony. A large general-purpose hall was constructed, and the workers used this space to play games or to just relax. The medical facilities provided were also enhanced. Earlier a doctor would visit the mill once a week. Shri Ram changed that by putting a doctor on the payroll of the company. This way the doctor was available at all times, not only to the workers but also to their families. Further, a dispensary was set up under the doctor's charge. This dispensary provided free medicines to the workers and their families. To cap all these measures, the provident fund scheme that had been approved by the board was finally implemented in 1920. A separate fund that could be used by workers for the marriage of their daughters was also created.

All these measures were not mere acts of philanthropy, in Shri Ram's view. They were part of his well-thought-out plan to improve the efficiency of the mill and to further improve labour relations. His man-management philosophy could be described as enlightened self-interest. He knew that a mill could not thrive if the workers were unhappy. He also believed that it was the duty of the management to take care of its workers. He remembered Gopal Rai talking about the need to build workers' quarters along with building the mill, and he had seen, as a child, that DCM had built these quarters in the late 1880s.

Now, having worked for some years, Shri Ram had developed his own set of beliefs. He believed that, in any enterprise, there were three sets of people—the owner, the managers and the workers. It was the owner who had to create employment opportunities and then a conducive work environment, all the while ensuring worker welfare. A manager had to lead from the front, provide leadership to the workers and be loyal to the owner. The workers had to work hard and do their job well.

Shri Ram was a manager but thought like an owner. Thus, he had concentrated on these large-scale worker welfare programmes. He also knew what a steady job with a steady income meant to a poor worker. He remembered the time in his own life when money had been limited at home. Thus, he strived to provide for the workers to the best of his ability. The workers knew this and gave him their affection and love.

However, Shri Ram expected total commitment from the workers. He did not tolerate any slacking off at work. A worker was expected to join the mill at the bottom but was given opportunities to work his way up. Shri Ram gave an inaam or reward to workers who did well. He also instituted a chaupal for workers—an area where they could air their grievances. Each worker knew that if he had a problem he could catch Shri Ram either on the shop floor or in his office and tell him about it. The workers also knew that Shri Ram would try to find a solution.

Shri Ram had also focused on programmes around worker welfare because he had seen signs of change after the war. Trade unions had started to spring up. This was happening more in the western part of India, but Shri Ram was sure that the unions would reach the north as well. Nationalist leaders had started aligning themselves with the cause of the workers. Further, the start of the Russian Revolution during the First World War had given a fillip to the communist movement within India. Shri Ram knew that neither he nor any businessman could take the workers for granted in the changing environment. He wanted to take preventive action rather than react to an adverse situation later.

The board allowed Shri Ram to execute all the worker welfare programmes. All these efforts bore results, as not a single day's production in the 1920s was lost due to a workers' strike.

Shri Ram was concerned about worker welfare and improving their efficiency; he was equally concerned about the education of the next generation. He himself had been unable to complete his graduation, but he understood the importance of education. He believed that an educated youth would be invaluable in furthering the cause of independent India. In 1920, Shri Ram, along with his brother-in-law Sher Singh and friend Diwan Chand, set up an educational trust. The trust was set up on the auspicious day of Basant Panchmi.

The seed capital put in by the three friends was Rs 2 lakh. They called the trust Commercial Education Trust. The trust set up its first school, named the Commercial School, in 1920 in Charkhewalan in old Delhi. The school was expanded later to become the Commercial College. The college began with just twelve students and four faculty members. The classes were held in a hired bungalow at 8 Daryaganj.

This college grew and when Delhi University's North Campus was set up, moved its premises there. Shri Ram, as the chairman of the governing body, insisted on a spacious building for the college. He also ensured that a large library, students' hostel, sports facilities and staff quarters were constructed.

The college was renamed in the 1950s to Shri Ram College of Commerce in honour of the founder. In the years to come, SRCC, as the college came to be known popularly, would become the number one choice for students in India who wanted a degree in either commerce or economics.

7

Public Service Goes Hand-in-Hand with Business

WHILE Shri Ram was able to address the problems of the workers and their living conditions at DCM, the general living conditions in the old city of Delhi bothered him. Even after earning well during the war, he continued living in the family house in Kucha Mai Das. He still walked to the DCM office on some days and took the tram on others. When he walked, he had to pass through the narrow lanes of the old city. As he walked he had to hold his nose due to the foul smells coming from the open gutters and garbage dumps. He saw children playing in the same smelly lanes, and he saw their mothers struggle to get water from the municipal taps, which were few in number. Further, the water flowed in these taps for only a few hours a day. Shri Ram was able to get a doctor on call for his workers, but he saw the neighbourhood of old Delhi struggle to find good doctors. He was fond of the old city but also realized that it was short of civic amenities.

Shri Ram was a member of the Punjab Chamber of Commerce, and, due to this association, he had interacted with many British administrators of the municipal corporation of Delhi. He would go for meetings at the chief commissioner and deputy chief commissioner's houses, which were in an area called Civil Lines. The first time Shri Ram went to Civil Lines he felt he had entered another world. It was so different from old Delhi. Civil Lines was a northern suburb of Delhi and consisted of large bungalows with green lawns. There were no problems of water or electricity. Most importantly, there were no foul smells; in fact, the streets were filled with the sweet smells of the many flowers that grew not only in the gardens of the bungalows but also on the sides of the roads.

Shri Ram's visits to Civil Lines made him realize that people could indeed live a better life. It was possible for the administrators to improve the lives of the common people. He articulated his thoughts to a close friend, Pirzada Muhammad Hussain, who was a member of the Delhi Municipal Committee. Shri Ram said he wanted to do something for the city that he loved. Pirzada said that he would convey his friend's thoughts to the chief commissioner.

'I say, Lala ji, there may be an opportunity for you to be part of the Delhi municipality,' said Pirzada one day to Shri Ram.

'Eh, what do you mean? How?' asked Shri Ram eagerly.

Pirzada smiled at Shri Ram's enthusiasm. He knew that his friend wanted to be part of the municipality for the right reasons.

'As you know, the Punjab Chamber of Commerce nominates a member to the Delhi municipality. The current nominated member, Griffiths, is going back to England. So, here is your opportunity to be nominated,' explained Pirzada.

This was a heaven-sent opportunity, and Shri Ram worked on the members of the Punjab Chamber of Commerce. In May 1920 he was nominated by the chamber to represent them on the Delhi Municipal Committee.

It was a historic day for Shri Ram when he attended the first meeting of the committee as a councillor. As a new member, he was welcomed with garlands. A man of slight build, he was almost smothered by the number of garlands around his neck. It surprised him that he had never been felicitated in this manner, even after all the good work he had done in the mill and for the mill workers. It gave him his first insight into how the world looked at people with power. As a member of the Delhi Municipal Committee, Shri Ram was perceived to be powerful and part of the 'administration'.

'Now I understand why all these people are waiting to garland me. If they think I can do something for the city, I must make sure that I do something that will make the lives of all the people living in the city better. After all, I don't see myself leaving this city. I love Delhi,' thought Shri Ram as he stood patiently, greeting the line of people with garlands in their hands.

His opportunity came soon after he was nominated as a councillor. He found out that the municipality wanted to increase the water tax for the people of Delhi. Shri Ram found it odd that the proposal to increase the tax had no supporting workings. He wanted to know more about the proposed tax.

But he was a new councillor and did not know the ways of the municipality.

He met with a couple of old councillors and asked them about the details of the proposed hike in tax. His colleagues were of no help at all.

'Lala ji, for as long as we've been here, we have seen that any proposal presented by the secretary to the committee is passed as is,' the older councillors told Shri Ram. The secretary was an Englishman who was also an Indian Civil Service officer.

'That may have been the case till now,' said Shri Ram, 'but if I were to put forward a counter proposal with facts and logic would you support it?'

'Yes, yes, of course, Lala ji. If there is logic to your proposal we will of course support it,' they assured Shri Ram.

That was all Shri Ram wanted to hear. He got down to work. He met with the municipal engineers. During the discussions he had with the engineers, the latter were impressed by Shri Ram's logical arguments and searching questions. They gave Shri Ram access to various files and data.

Shri Ram was in his element when he had to solve a problem. He examined the files and the data. He wanted, to get the details on the amount of tax to be paid for water; how much water was consumed by the city, where the water was supplied, how many areas had water pipes, how many pipes were installed in the city and so on. He worked after office hours to find the answers to all these and other questions.

The answers he got were illuminating. According to the data and the analysis he had in front of him it was clear that a large amount of water was wasted. Shri Ram realized that if the wastage of water could be arrested then the water being supplied by the municipality was enough to meet the needs of the people. Further, there would be no need to increase the tax at all.

Armed with this data, Shri Ram went for the committee meeting. As the councillors settled down around the table and the officers took their seats behind the councillors, the secretary started the proceedings. After the routine matters, the secretary took up the matter of raising water taxes.

As the secretary looked to move on to the next item on the agenda, sure that he had the approval of the room, Shri Ram stood up. The secretary looked at him, annoyed, as he was not used to interruptions in his meetings.

'What is it, Shri Ram?' asked the secretary a bit curtly.

'It is about the proposal to increase the water tax, Mr Secretary,' Shri Ram began.

The secretary cut him short and told him that the proposal would be passed.

'No, sir, I think not. You see, I have some details here that I would like to present to you and to the committee,' Shri Ram said, then sat down and opened his file.

The secretary looked around the table, annoyed. But he saw that everyone was looking at Shri Ram with anticipation. The secretary had no choice but to wait for Shri Ram to speak.

Shri Ram spoke. He spoke with logic and with facts. He presented the analysis he had carried out based on the data of the municipality itself. Point by point he rebutted the proposal. The other councillors sat spellbound, listening to the flow of logic and numbers. They had never heard anyone speak with such authority and with such mastery.

The secretary, too, was impressed. He could not argue with either the logic or the facts presented by Shri Ram. Rather than reject the proposal, the secretary proposed the formation of a subcommittee to examine the matter in detail. Shri Ram was nominated to be part of this subcommittee.

The subcommittee met, discussed the proposal and then proposed that no new tax be raised on the people of Delhi for water. It was also decided that the subcommittee would discuss any further tax proposals as and when they came up. Shri Ram was made a permanent member of this committee.

Shri Ram was happy he had won the day with logic and facts; he also got a sense of satisfaction at having done something for the public good. Philanthropy and community service went hand-in-hand for Shri Ram. He knew he would not spend his hard-earned money on building temples for various gods, even though he did visit temples often. He promised to spend his money on building temples of education so that future generations could go there to better their lives.

8

Shri Ram Takes Control of DCM

AFTER the First World War ended, the DCM board was faced with a problem of plenty.

The four years of war had resulted in unprecedented profits for DCM. Even after generous dividends were paid out to the shareholders, new machinery was ordered and the workers' welfare schemes were implemented, there was a balance of nearly Rs 10 lakh in the company's bank account.

The board would have ideally liked to declare a higher dividend or bonus to distribute the large profits, but it had to keep the public sentiment in mind. The war years had seen some businessmen and industrialists make hefty profits, and the public saw this as war-time profiteering. The board wanted to avoid any talk of them profiteering from the miseries of the war. As was becoming habitual, they turned to Shri Ram for his advice. Shri Ram did not disappoint; he came up with an innovative solution.

He suggested that the company's capital be reduced by 80 per cent—from Rs 7 lakh to Rs 1.4 lakh. He explained that this could be done by reducing the face value of a DCM share from Rs 250 to Rs 50. Due to this reduction in face value, the shareholders would receive Rs 200 for each share they held. The total cost of this exercise would be Rs 5.6 lakh. Even after this there would be enough funds left in the accounts of the company.

This was actually a cleverly disguised scheme to give the shareholders a super-dividend without calling it so. A reduction in the face value of the shares would not be big news in the market, and the common man would not understand the technicalities of it. Even the workers would not understand the impact of this scheme. Shri Ram knew that he and his father held 444 shares of DCM. They had bought 330 shares during the war years, utilizing the profits from the military contracts. To be precise, the shares were bought by Shri Ram, as Madan Mohan was content with his shareholding. Shri Ram wanted the company to grow and expand; Madan Mohan was happy to let it remain a small but profitable company. Even then, with their 444 shares, the refund scheme would have netted them Rs 88,800.

At the shareholders' meeting in February 1921, which was called to discuss this plan, the scheme was approved wholeheartedly by all. The shareholders were delighted at this windfall. In the meeting it was also decided that the share of Rs 50 would be split into five shares of Rs 10 each.

However, fate played a trick at this time. Before the refunding of the shares could start, in April of the same year the DCM mill caught fire and, along with the spinning mill, was completely gutted. All the material inside the sheds within the mill premises was also lost in the fire. There was panic amongst the shareholders, as they knew that the plant and machinery were not insured fully. The share price of DCM stock fell drastically. Within a day it went from Rs 1,000 per share to less than Rs 600 per share.

Shri Ram was aware of the consequences of these alarming events. There was one recurring thought going through his mind. He wanted to protect the name of DCM at all costs. By now he and his father were the largest shareholders of DCM—with 444 shares, they had ten more shares than the rest of the shareholders put together. Shri Ram therefore saw himself more as an owner than an employee. In the twelve years he had spent at DCM, Shri Ram had developed a strong emotional attachment with the mill and the workers. Looking back, he realized that his bond with DCM had started when he was three or four years old. It was then that Gopal Rai had talked passionately to Shri Ram in the front courtyard of the haveli about DCM and his dreams for the company.

Shri Ram did not want his uncle's dream to be sullied. In fact, it had become his own dream. Now that he was the largest shareholder of the business there was much more at stake for him. He was thirty-seven years old and was already well known in industrial circles. It had taken him three years to become the secretary of the company, and it had taken him another nine years to become the largest shareholder. No one even remembered the quiet, timid man who had walked into the accounts office as an unpaid apprentice in 1909.

As the largest shareholder, Shri Ram felt duty-bound to address the potential reputational risk in the market due to the fire. He announced that the mill would be rebuilt and would be ready in less than three months. He also announced that he was ready to buy DCM shares from anyone who wanted to sell. The market was surprised at his confidence. The fall in the share price was arrested, as there was hope in the market. The shareholders also gave their approval for the expenditure to rebuild.

Now that Shri Ram and his father were the largest shareholders, it was easy to understand their control over the business. However, even before they owned such a large number of shares, they were able to exert disproportionate influence over the affairs of the firm. Their low shareholding did not come in the way of Shri Ram's control of the company. One of the main reasons for this was the fact that not more than twenty or twenty-five shareholders ever attended the DCM shareholders' meetings. This allowed Shri Ram to push resolutions through. The shareholders were also happy with the company's performance, which was reflected in the share price and dividends. Shri Ram saw this as a vote of confidence that he was running the company efficiently.

Now, with more shares in hand, Shri Ram was able to have his way on almost all issues. Further, no other shareholder came forth to challenge or rival Shri Ram. In fact, the difference between Shri Ram and the next largest shareholder increased once the chairman of the company, Sheo Pershad, who owned 307 shares, passed away. After his death, Shri Ram passed a resolution to abolish the post of chairman. Further, the long-serving directors were also encouraged to retire. Within a short span of time, Shri Ram, for all practical purposes, had complete control of the mill.

Meanwhile, there was the burnt mill that had to be rebuilt. As he took stock of the damage Shri Ram was told that the fire had been devastating, and the entire lot of more than 16,000 spindles had been destroyed. It was proposed, this time again by Shri Ram, that the capital available to the company be conserved to rebuild the mill. Once again, this proposal was approved unanimously, and the refund scheme was put on hold.

Shri Ram spent the next couple of months on the rebuilding of the mill. The fact that he saw himself as the true owner of the company because he was the single largest shareholder gave him new zeal and energy. Fortunately for DCM, the orders placed for the machinery in 1919 had been executed. The machines had arrived and had been waiting in the godowns of the company even before the fire. This gave him the confidence to start work immediately.

Before he had started work on the rebuilding of the mill, Shri Ram had taken stock of the market and the future of DCM. He had realized that he had a golden opportunity to modernize the mill and expand its capacity now that the entire mill was being rebuilt. He placed orders for more machines and spindles. These were more modern than the ones ordered two years ago. The fire, thus, in a way, provided Shri Ram the opportunity to give DCM a fresh start. It allowed the company to replace old machinery. It also gave DCM the opportunity to experiment and innovate with its equipment.

DCM had a new 'owner', and now it had completely new machines.

The mill resumed work in June 1921, just two months after the fire, much before the time Shri Ram had declared. It was a stupendous effort and brought to focus Shri Ram's superior organizational qualities. The new mill building had better light and ventilation; it also had modern machines. The workers' welfare schemes had already been executed. Thanks to all these factors, DCM started operations afresh with better morale and increased productivity.

This was borne out by the results of the company. This was the year when DCM started being seen as aspirational in the city. The cloth produced at DCM started edging out the competition. One of the most popular and fast-selling items in the market was the humble sheet or the chaddar. Until 1921 the mills of western and southern India were sending their sheets to the Delhi and northern markets. The mills of Nagpur, Bombay and Madras had agents in Chandni Chowk and would often undercut DCM's prices to gain market share. However, the new DCM could barely produce enough to keep up with demand. The entire production was sold off. Most of DCM's sales were through agents who were appointed directly by Shri Ram, and the secretary's office, for the short term. Shri Ram was also seen as a budding industrialist.

Along with the focus on the mill, Shri Ram, especially after being nominated to the Delhi Municipal Committee, had something else on his mind. He had seen how enthused the workers had been when he had established a school for their children. As he walked occasionally to work from Kucha Mai Das, he would feel sad watching the young children play on the dusty and dirty streets. There were no good schools in the area, and the children whiled the day away chasing each other through the streets. Shri Ram believed that the children deserved better. Since he himself had been unable to complete his graduation, Shri Ram laid great emphasis on the importance of education. His thoughts on the matter were further spurred when he found out that his friend, Raghubir Singh, had started an educational institute in 1920. Raghubir Singh was the son of Rai Bahadur Sultan Singh, who was a director on the board of DCM. It was through this association that Shri Ram and Raghubir Singh became friends.

Mahatma Gandhi had already given a call to all Indians to think of national education. The aim of national education according to him was the inculcation among young people of the values of patriotism and similar social and cultural values. Raghubir Singh, who was a businessman and philanthropist, wanted to set up an education institute that would combine the best of ancient Indian tradition with the needs of the modern times. The school he started was called Modern School.

Modern School started in Daryaganj and was a coeducational school with a focus on building better citizens for India. It was also the first private and coeducational school set up in Delhi after the capital of the country shifted to the city. Shri Ram had already set up a trust for Commercial College. He wanted to do more for children's education.

Shri Ram was also influenced by the leaders he met. Sultan Singh's house was a hub for national leaders. As Raghubir's friend, Shri Ram, too, started meeting people other than businessmen and traders. His circle of acquaintances started expanding. Shri Ram, since childhood, had wanted to have a social network. Now that he was a successful businessman he realized that his frail frame and slight build did not come in the way of people wanting to be his 'friends'.

In all the excitement of new acquaintances, Shri Ram did not forget his work, which was only increasing. He would leave for work early in the morning, even before his sons left for school. He would return late at night. His neighbours rarely saw him. Some of his neighbours, when they did meet him, told him that he had developed a formidable reputation. Some even joked that unruly children were told by their mothers that Lala Shri Ram would come to get them if they did not mend their ways! Shri Ram found this hilarious.

It was not that he did not like children. But he believed in the virtues of hard work and discipline. Therefore, he appeared stern to people.

His two younger sons, Bharat Ram and Charat Ram, went to Modern School in Daryaganj. They went to school in a tonga. The tonga-walla was an old man who liked his bidis. The young boys had not seen anyone in their family smoke and were fascinated by the concept and act of smoking. They were tempted to try it.

One day, the two young brothers lit up a bidi and started smoking. They were not used to it and ended up coughing. But worse was yet to come. Word reached Barhwali Haveli that Shri Ram's sons had started smoking. By the time Shri Ram returned from work, word had even reached him. He was livid.

'I heard you were smoking today. Is this true?' asked Shri Ram as he stood glowering down at his two sons.

Bharat Ram and Charat Ram knew that they had done something wrong. They also knew that lying would get them into more trouble. They stood quietly for a while, hopping from one foot to the other, uneasily stealing glances at each other, trying to gather the courage to speak. They knew their father and his anger.

'Why are you quiet? Has the bidi burnt your tongue? Tell me!' shouted Shri Ram angrily.

The two boys made up their minds.

'Ye-ye-yesss, Bhaiji, we did ask the tonga-walla for a bidi,' said the older boy hesitatingly.

'But, Bhaiji, we did not like it at all and will never ever have it again in our life,' said the younger one in a rush.

Shri Ram was quiet, but only for a while. The two boys thought that telling the truth had relieved them of punishment.

But it was not to be so.

Shri Ram took a horsewhip and started whipping the young boys. The boys cried piteously, but it did not stop Shri Ram. He was extremely angry. He could not understand how the young boys could have indulged in this vice. A strict disciplinarian, Shri Ram could not bear it if anyone stepped out of line.

By this time Chando Devi, Shri Ram's mother and the boys' grandmother, had come out into the courtyard. She ran to her son and tried to grab his hand to stop the beating. But Shri Ram just pushed her hand away.

Seeing her grandchildren crying piteously, Chando Devi started wailing.

'*Tu hatyara hai! Tu maar raha hai in bechaare bacchon ko! Bhagwan ke liye ab bas kar!*' cried Chando Devi.

Shri Ram stopped and looked at his sons, who were crying in pain. He did not have to say anything to them. They understood that there was no room for moral slip-ups in Shri Ram's world.

But there was another side to Shri Ram when it came to his sons. Every year the family would go to Kashmir in the summer. Shri Ram and his three sons would travel to Srinagar in their Chevrolet car via either Jammu or Rawalpindi. Phoolan Devi usually gave these summer holidays a miss as her health did not allow her to travel. Thus, father and sons had time to bond in the sylvan surroundings of Kashmir. It was here that the sons got an opportunity to see the softer side of their father. It was difficult for Shri Ram to display his affection openly, and he kept his distance from his sons. But he cared deeply for them and wanted them to have the best in life, including education. The sojourns in Kashmir built bonds of a lifetime. The sons never took their father for granted and were a bit afraid of him even when they grew up. But they, too, cared deeply for him.

It was around this time that Shri Ram decided that he needed to move out of Kucha Mai Das. Much as he loved his family house, Shri Ram realized that it was time for him move into a neighbourhood that was more in keeping with his new-found status. He was now a man of significance. He also needed to socialize with the cream of the city. This included not just Indian businessmen but also government officials, who were mostly Britishers. He needed to interact with them, as running a business required many permissions and certificates.

Kucha Mai Das was not the right place to entertain these officers and other businessmen. The lane was narrow and dirty. Further, there was a busy temple at the end of the lane—Chaurasey Ghantey ka Mandir. All passers-by would ring the bells, leading to a constant cacophony of sound. Cows lived on the pavement. The locals fed the animals there, and the area stank of cow dung. There were also quarters for Muslim artisans close by. These artisans hammered silver into thin sheets through the day and into the evening. The incessant banging was not conducive to entertaining burra sahibs.

As he pondered over moving out of Barhwali Haveli, Civil Lines kept coming to his mind. Ever since he had started visiting the senior members of the Delhi Municipal Committee in Civil Lines, Shri Ram had loved the neighbourhood. Now he explored the area with the notion of living there himself.

Shri Ram was shown a bungalow on Rajpur Road in Civil Lines. This was the toniest area of Delhi. Shri Ram approved of the bungalow, and the family moved there. However, Madan

Mohan refused to leave the haveli. The Civil Lines bungalow was on rent. Madan Mohan, a traditional man, could not live in a house that was not owned by the family. So, he stayed behind in Barhwali Haveli. It was only in later years, when Shri Ram built large bungalows on Curzon Road, that his father agreed to move out of Kucha Mai Das.

The shift to the new house also meant a change in the worldview of Shri Ram. He had begun to see a future for himself more clearly. His ambition was no longer at the back of his mind. It was at the forefront, and he wanted to do even bigger things.

Shri Ram and his family moved into a bigger house, but Shri Ram took the smallest room as his own. His room housed only his bed, a chair and a table. Other family members requested him to move to a bigger and better-furnished room, but Shri Ram stayed adamant. He did not need anything more than what he had in his room.

He also had a limited number of clothes. He did not see the need to keep buying clothes. And as and when he did buy a new kurta or a new pyjama, he ensured that he gave away one of his old ones. Thus, the number of clothes he had remained constant.

However, Shri Ram actively changed his way of living. He started entertaining more people, even more frequently. Very soon his home became a social hub where well-known Indian leaders and other celebrities were hosted by him. At the parties at Shri Ram's house local people could rub shoulders with commissioners, members of the Viceroy Council and other Britishers, collectively known as burra sahibs. It became a matter of prestige for the locals to be invited to Shri Ram's parties.

For Shri Ram himself it was a matter of deep satisfaction that he was in the midst of the city's social scene. He had travelled a long way from the days of his childhood when he would sit in a corner, watching wistfully as the other boys played together and ignored him completely. He rejoiced at being sought out by men, both older and younger than himself, who wanted to be in his company.

Shri Ram's way of life changed not only outwardly but also from within. He had been a thin, scrawny child and had grown up to be not very different. He had tried many concoctions of Ayurvedic medicine, Yunani medicine and even homoeopathic medicine to address his health problems, which had got aggravated due to long hours of work, especially since he had taken charge of DCM as its secretary. He now realized that no medicine could help him as much as he could help himself. He needed to make his body strong. Shri Ram was in his thirties at this time and knew that he had many years ahead of him when it came to work. He needed to focus on his health because an unhealthy man could not put in the effort required to build a business empire.

With this aim in mind, Shri Ram started getting up early in the morning. Come summer or winter, Shri Ram would wake up at 4.30 a.m. and go for a brisk walk on a set route, which was almost 5 km long. He found companions even for his early morning walks. He would then return and have a bath with cold water, even in the winter months. A short prayer and a cup of tea that he made for himself in his room, and Shri Ram was ready to face yet another day.

9

DCM Has a Second Mill

DELHI Cloth Mills and its products had become very popular after 1921. Shri Ram was firmly in control of the business affairs of the mill. The board of directors was largely fine with the proposals presented by Shri Ram. One such proposal was to establish a bleach and dye unit within the mill. The other proposal was to increase the capacity of the existing mill by increasing the number of spindles to 24,000 and the number of looms to 750. Both these proposals were passed by the board without too much bother.

By 1924 the bleach and dye unit was running well. The increase in the number of looms had led to an increase in cloth production for the market. But Shri Ram was not satisfied. This was a bit of a surprise, even to himself, as the mill was growing in reputation and stature almost every day. DCM products were seen as superior in the market. But Shri Ram wanted more. His confidence had soared after the successes of the past few years. The hesitations of his childhood were forgotten. He allowed his personal ambition to start growing within himself.

It was in July 1924 that he presented an audacious plan to the board. 'I want to grow the mill much larger. We have 750 looms currently, and I want to increase the number to 1,250. And I want to almost double the number of spindles—from the current 24,000 to 40,000,' Shri Ram told the board.

'But why, Lala ji?' asked one board member. 'We are doing so well, and wherever I go, people compliment me on being part of DCM. Why can't we continue to do what we are doing? After all, we are all making a good profit and the workers are also happy.'

Before Shri Ram could answer, another board member piped up. 'And where is the room in our mill just now, Lala ji? Even if we approve your plan, you will not be able to fit all the new machinery in the current space. Surely you don't want another factory, do you?' he asked almost incredulously.

Another member who was more focused on the finances and dividends of the company was more vocal. 'I say, Lala ji, for all this capacity expansion you are proposing, you will have to use the capital of the company, right? So how will we get our dividends? I don't want to give up the dividends for expansion. We are doing well,' he said assertively.

The other members now joined in and started talking amongst themselves, shaking their heads vigorously from time to time, as if wondering at the impossibility of the plan and the reduction of their dividends.

Shri Ram listened patiently to the babble of voices in the board room. He sat quietly, waiting for the board members to stop talking. Soon the room realized that Shri Ram was waiting for them to quieten down. As the room went silent, Shri Ram stood up and spoke quietly but assertively. 'Of course we will have to build a new mill to accommodate the new looms and spindles. Of course there is no space for further expansion in the current mill. But we have to think big if we want to stay relevant in the future. And don't worry about the dividends,' he said.

The board again broke out into conversation, this time a little excitedly. They were excited about the growth but also had apprehensions. Most of the men were older than Shri Ram, and maybe that was one of the reasons for their discomfort with this aggressive growth plan.

'Lala ji, all this will require money, won't it?' asked one older member loudly. 'Where are you going to get the money from? Have you thought about it at all?'

'I have, sir,' said Shri Ram, again patiently. 'We will need about Rs 15 lakh for the second mill.'

'Fifteen lakh rupees! That is a huge sum of money, Lala ji! How are you going to get it?' asked a member of the board.

'Do you think I have not thought this through?' Shri Ram asked the board. And then he answered the question himself. 'Of course I have thought this through. Here is the plan.' He laid out the plan to the board, which was now listening intently. They knew Shri Ram's capabilities and had full confidence in him. But at the same time, they did not want their dividends to be affected.

Shri Ram explained to the board that the fire and the resultant activities had used up a lot of their surplus funds. The cash in the bank stood at Rs 3 lakh. Thus, DCM needed to raise Rs 12 lakh for the expansion of the business. He proposed that the company raise its capital from Rs 7 lakh to Rs 10.50 lakh and the rest be drawn from the reserves, profits and loans.

The board members deliberated amongst themselves for a bit and gave their approval. But the proposal needed the approval of the other shareholders as well.

A shareholder meeting was called. This was held at the Bara Hindu Rao office in July 1924. Eighty-one shareholders attended the meeting and eighteen sent proxy votes. This was the largest gathering of shareholders in the history of DCM. Shri Ram had prepared for the meeting, as he wanted to use logic to win over the shareholders.

The day of the meeting was bright and sunny. The shareholders gathered in the hall of the office. Shri Ram got up to speak.

'I know that the business is doing well. But I request you not to be complacent about our success. Most of you are businessmen yourselves, so you know that it is fatal to stand still. In business we have to either go forward or we go under.'

'Our success is like a shining beacon. There are others in the market who see us and say "we can also do this". You know that there are other cloth mills being set up. They will challenge us, and we have to proactively meet them head-on. We need to grow larger and get a larger share of the market, leaving a small piece for them to fight over.' As Shri Ram spoke, he looked around the room. The men in the room were listening intently to him. Some were nodding along as he spoke. Shri Ram smiled and went on.

'To fight the new entrants and old mills, we need to grow our business. And for this we need more money. As I see it, there are three ways we can get the funds. The first is to set aside a certain sum each year from the profits we make. The second is to take out loans for expansion. The third way is to increase our capital and sell more shares. I propose that we use all three options, but I want to tell you why I believe that the third option would be the best.'

He explained that setting aside a sum each year from the profits may not generate the desired results. The shareholders themselves, he said, wanted the profits distributed as dividends. However, even if the shareholders were convinced about the need to reduce the dividend, it would lead to another problem—that of the share price falling. Most people in the market would be unaware of the reason for the reduction in dividend and would naturally believe that the business was not doing well. Thus, they would want to sell their shares, driving down the price of the shares and affecting DCM's market reputation negatively.

Shri Ram then talked about the second option—that of taking loans. He explained that it could prove to be difficult to finance the entire expansion of the plant and machinery through loans. He reminded the room that, besides the infrastructure, the company would require increased working capital as well, which again may not be possible by taking out loans.

Shri Ram then came to his final argument. He said that the best way to raise the money would be to raise the share capital. He also felt that the shares would be more marketable if they were priced at Rs 25 against the current Rs 250. He explained that a greater number of smaller investors would be able to buy the shares.

The proposal needed the consent of all 360 shareholders. Therefore, a resolution was circulated with the proposal. It was also decided to hold a second meeting to note and approve the decision in early August.

The shareholders approved raising the company's capital to Rs 10.50 lakh and replacing the existing shares, which had a face value of Rs 250, with new shares that had a face value of Rs 25. It was proposed that the existing shareholders be offered one new share at the new face value for every two shares they held—a kind of right's issue. Shri Ram had also proposed that at least 300 shares be kept for the staff of the mill, and the shareholders approved this as well. The mill workers were delighted at this opportunity, and about 150 of them invested in the company shares. Thus, DCM now had its own clerks, jobbers and workmen as its shareholders. These employee shareholders were even more happy when, shortly after being issued, the shares of the company went up to Rs 95 and then further up to Rs 118 each.

DCM was on a roll and so was Shri Ram. This was the start of the expansion and growth of the business under the active leadership of Shri Ram. He saw the meeting of the shareholders and the approval of his plan as a sign that he could, and should, follow his ambitions. Shri Ram now focused his energies on the new mill. However, the land earmarked for the new mill had to be cleared of the existing structures—the workers' quarters. Shri Ram took the assistance of H.L. Merchant, the mill manager, and Ram Narain Khosla, the engineer, to replan the entire mill complex. The workers' quarters had to be relocated. The old mill had to continue to be operational while the new one was being built. Shri Ram was very clear that the new mill had to be technologically more advanced than the old one. According to his plan, the old mill would continue to spin and weave coarse cloth while the new mill had to have machinery that would weave finer cloth. He also introduced an electric drive for the new mill while the old one continued to be run by a steam engine, which powered the looms and spindles. Shri Ram also introduced an improved system of humidification for the spinning shed.

Shri Ram, by now, had understood the importance of maintaining the right humidity in the spinning shed. He knew that all textiles are hygroscopic—which means that they absorb or release moisture depending on the relative dryness or humidity of the surrounding air. Simply put, if the air is dry then the textile will give up its moisture, and if the air is humid, it will absorb moisture. The change in moisture content affects the properties of the yarn and textile. A low relative humidity will cause the yarn or the textile to be thinner, less elastic and more brittle. Too much dryness will also cause a reduction in the weight of the yarn. As yarn is sold by weight, this would result in more yarn being needed for the same weight. Even a small amount of weight loss in the yarn can have a significant impact on the overall production and sales figures of the mill.

Therefore, Shri Ram wanted the humidity levels in the new spinning shed to be just right. The new system that he installed was able to keep the relative humidity levels between 60 and 66 per cent. Further, the ideal temperatures for the spinning process are around 31 to 33 degrees Celsius. Shri Ram installed steam pipes so that they could keep the temperature at these levels, especially during the winters. The mill also had overhead water pipes with sprinklers, which worked as a fire safety mechanism. The basic machinery was sourced from England.

It took a year to complete the new mill. Shri Ram was actively involved in the supervision of the construction. He would visit the construction site after walking the shop floor of the first mill. His brother Shankar Lall, a young man by now, was being inducted into the business by Shri Ram. Shankar Lall was charged with visiting the construction site and spending time with the supervisor to learn about mill construction.

One morning, as Shankar Lall was walking to the construction site, he saw a bunch of workers standing, almost hiding, behind a large tree and chatting. He stopped and continued to observe the group. Unaware that Lala ji's brother was watching them, the workers continued to chat and laugh at jokes that presumably were being cracked.

After a while young Shankar Lall could take it no more. His young blood boiled at the sight of this lackadaisical attitude of the men. In his hot-headedness he marched up to the group and slapped one of the workers hard. The group was stunned. The person Shankar Lall had slapped was the head mistri or the raj, the supervisor of the workers and a trained, skilled artisan.

The raj was even more stunned than the rest of the group. It was not the slap per se that stunned him but the fact that he had been slapped in front of his workers. This was an indignity that he did not like.

The next day when Shri Ram was on his daily rounds of the construction site the raj went running to him and fell at his feet. He was sobbing as he held Shri Ram's feet.

Shri Ram was surprised, to say the least. He could not understand why the head mistri was sobbing like a child. He bent down, took the raj by both shoulders and got him to stand up. Even when standing the raj kept his head down and continued crying.

'*Arrey bhai, kya hua? Kya baat ho gayee jo itna ro rahe ho*?' asked Shri Ram in his customary measured manner.

'Lala ji slapped me in front of my workers,' sobbed the raj, still unable to meet Shri Ram's eyes.

'Lala ji? I did not slap you. What are you saying?' asked Shri Ram, perplexed.

The raj started crying even more loudly.

'No, no, no, Lala ji, not you. You would never slap me, I know. It was the chhote Lala ji who slapped me. I know it was my fault but to slap me in front of all those people?' the raj said in a rush.

By now a group had gathered, round Shri Ram and the raj. They had heard what the raj said. There was sudden pin-drop silence. Everyone waited to see how Shri Ram would react.

Shri Ram was in a quandary. On the one hand it was his brother Shankar Lall who had slapped the raj, and on the other, there was the indignity borne by the raj. He also realized that everyone was waiting to see what he would do. He thought for a moment with his head down and his hand on the raj's shoulder.

Once he had made up his mind, Shri Ram looked up, dropped his hand from the raj's shoulder and then looked around at the gathered workers.

'All of you gathered here have heard what the raj said, and what he said is indeed true. His self-esteem has been hurt, and he has suffered an indignity. Now, you all are like the panch in a panchayat. So, you should decide how justice is to be delivered,' said Shri Ram as he looked at each one of the gathered people.

Now, each of them wished he was any place but there! How could they tell Lala ji what to do? It was a delicate matter. Some fidgeted while others shuffled their feet. No one met the eyes of Shri Ram, who kept standing there calmly, one hand back on the raj's shoulder.

After a while, when no one spoke, Shri Ram took a deep breath.

'If all of you are hesitating to take a decision on what to do, then I will have to do it myself. And all of you will have to agree,' he declared.

The group released a sigh of relief. They would not have to make a decision on this matter. They stopped fidgeting and waited for Shri Ram to proclaim his decision.

Shri Ram removed his hand from the raj's shoulder. He turned slightly so that one side of his face was facing the raj. 'My younger brother Shankar Lall slapped you in front of many people. I am his elder brother and there are many people here as well. Please slap me in front of all these people now,' he told the raj.

The gathered people wished once more that they were any place but there. They were embarrassed. The raj, on the other hand, was contrite. He had stopped crying, but now he started wailing loudly. He fell at Shri Ram's feet once again.

'You are like my bhagwan, Lala ji. I am like your child. It was my mistake, and I got the punishment for it. I should not have brought it to you like this. Please forgive me,' the raj cried.

A couple of the gathered people came forward and gently pulled the raj to his feet. He kept his head down and his hands folded. He kept repeating, 'I am sorry, Lala ji, please forgive me.'

Shri Ram patted him on the back, ruffled his hair and then continued on his walk through the mill. He had defused a potentially explosive situation. But he had not done it only for effect. He believed intrinsically that the workers were the backbone of the mill. He decided to have a word separately with Shankar Lall and caution him against such hot-headed actions.

The new mill was inaugurated in January 1926 by E.R. Abbot, the chief commissioner of Delhi. He had been presented with a silver key, which he used to open the new mill. It was a matter of great celebration for all the employees of DCM. Over Rs 10,000, a significant amount in 1926, was spent on sweets and food for the workers. The new mill also provided employment to 300 new mill workers.

The new mill lived up to the promises Shri Ram had made to the shareholders. After the first year of operation, it had added substantial profits to the business. In fact, the directors stated in an annual report that it was fortunate that the new mill came up when it did, for had it not, profits for that year would have been less than half of what they were!

Shri Ram felt a quiet sense of satisfaction as he observed DCM and the other mills in the region. He saw that the other mills were implementing some of the changes and new initiatives that he had introduced in DCM. He had already introduced a bleaching and dyeing unit in the early 1920s, and now, some years later, other mills were introducing the same. DCM, through its second mill, had started producing finer cloth; other mills were also doing this. Shri Ram did not sit back, though. Between 1927 and 1929 he added 600 more looms and 20,000 new spindles to the mill. He also, at considerable cost, replaced the old steam engine in the first mill with a new 2,000-kilowatt turbine.

The new mill increased Shri Ram's workload. Though his father, Madan Mohan, was still part of the company, he did not play an active part in the running of the mill. Age was catching up with him, and it was evident to him that Shri Ram was managing affairs better than he could. To help him with his work Shri Ram asked Shankar Lall to join the company formally. Shankar Lall was twenty-five years old by then and was ready to shoulder some of the burden of work. Shri Ram's entire family—father and brother—were now part of the company and managing the affairs of the business. Shri Ram was answerable only to the board of directors.

The fire of 1921 was a distant memory. In the eight years after the fire DCM had risen like a phoenix from the ashes. By the end of the 1920s DCM had grown to be one of the biggest and most modern mills in the entire country. Its 1,850 looms and 60,000 spindles were much ahead of the national average of 550 looms and 30,000 spindles. Even in the United States, the home of large-scale enterprises, 70 per cent of the mills had fewer than 30,000 spindles.

After Madan Mohan hung up his boots and retired from DCM, Shri Ram was fully in charge of the company. He did not draw a salary but earned over Rs 1 lakh a year from the commissions on the sales. And then there were the dividends that were paid out annually. But his main motivation was not money; it was seeing the business grow. He wanted DCM to grow even bigger and become better.

Shri Ram had been working almost non-stop for twenty years. Now he believed it was time to take a break.

10

Shri Ram's First Overseas Trip

SHRI Ram left for a tour of Europe in April 1929. It was to be an eight-month-long trip. The foreign holiday was his first trip overseas and also his first long vacation. During the twenty years he had been at DCM he had only taken occasional short breaks to go to the hills. However, he told everyone that it was going to be a working holiday for him, as he would travel around Europe to look at textile mills and factories there. It was fortunate that Shankar Lall was by now settled into the company as the assistant secretary. Thus, Shri Ram was able to leave the management of the day-to-day affairs in his brother's charge.

When the mill workers learnt that Shri Ram was going to be away for eight months, they were happy that he was finally taking a much-needed break, but they were also apprehensive about how the business would fare in his absence. The mill workers had a special place in their hearts for Shri Ram. They organized a concert for him at the mill as a going-away party. Some of the mill workers also prepared speeches. Shri Ram learnt of the contents of some of these speeches a day before the concert. He realized that the workers had apprehensions about his absence. He decided to address those apprehensions in his own thank-you speech.

He sat up till late at night preparing his speech. Instead of using a new sheet of paper or a notebook, Shri Ram tore out some scraps from a pocketbook and scribbled his speech on them. It had been Shri Ram's habit since his childhood days to tear off small scraps of paper from notebooks and write down his thoughts on them. Though he could now afford plenty of new notebooks, his old habit from the days when money was not readily available to him continued.

Once, a clerk had complained about his supervisor in a letter addressed to Shri Ram. The letter was on a sheet of foolscap paper and had only four sentences written on it.

Shri Ram read the note intently. The clerk had accused his supervisor of wasting resources. Shri Ram was angry and summoned the clerk as well as the supervisor to his office. As they stood in front of him, Shri Ram noted that the clerk was confident while the supervisor was puzzled, as he did not know the reason for the summons.

'Do you both know the meaning of wastage?' Shri Ram asked them. Then he addressed the clerk. 'Wastage was your complaint, was it not?'

The clerk replied immediately. 'Yes, Lala ji, that was my complaint,' he said, almost with glee.

Shri Ram saw red when he heard the answer. 'If you understand the meaning of wastage and complain about others wasting resources, then are you an idiot that you indulge in wastage yourself?'

'No, no . . . Lala ji, I am ve – very care – careful in—' stuttered the clerk in fear.

'Then what is this, eh?' Shri Ram waved the complaint letter in the air before slamming it on the table.

The clerk and the supervisor were both afraid now. The supervisor could read the letter and saw that it was a complaint against him. The clerk was afraid because he did not know what he had done wrong.

When he saw that both men were silent Shri Ram cooled down a little. 'You keep an eye on others and complain to me in case you see wastage. But why did you have to waste a full sheet of paper if you had to write only four sentences? Look within yourself before you complain about others. Understood?' Shri Ram addressed the clerk.

Then he addressed the supervisor. 'Be careful, as even a little wastage by you can result in large losses. I am overlooking this for now, but remember that I will not in the future.'

Both men folded their hands and asked for forgiveness. Shri Ram had a temper, but it was like a volcano—it erupted and then calmed down within no time. By now his temper had cooled. He told the men to be careful in the future.

So it was that Shri Ram went for the concert with the main points of his speech written on scraps of paper, which were tucked safely into his pocket.

The concert was a success and so were the speeches by some of the workers. And then it was time for Shri Ram to speak. He got up, adjusted his cap and went to the mike. Though he had scribbled down his speech, he did not need to look at it. He knew what he was going to say, and he spoke from the heart.

'My heart is full,' he began with a catch in his voice. He reminded the workers that he had been associated with the mill for twenty-four years—years that seemed to have flown by. 'I have, during all this time, worked with one objective and that is to make our mill a model mill; a model mill from every point of view—efficient in production, satisfied staff, low costs, good working conditions and a healthy atmosphere. But we cannot rest on our laurels. We need to keep moving forward and stay ahead of the competition.' The workers clapped enthusiastically when they heard this. Expansion of the business meant new opportunities for all of them.

Shri Ram waited for the applause to die down. 'You are clapping, and I am happy that you are. But the growth of DCM has been possible only because of you. I am merely your leader. As they say—*lade fauj aur naam sardar ka*—the army fights but the captain walks away with the accolades. It is you all that are responsible for the efficient production and the healthy atmosphere. What have I done? I have merely tried to address grievances as soon as they have come to my notice,' he continued.

In the speeches made by the workers some had made reference to the absence of strikes at DCM. This was a significant point as, over the years, several mills had seen workers going on strike, and many workers were forming trade unions. DCM had not been a part of this. But the workers, in their speeches, brought up these two matters and also their wish to form a union in the future. Shri Ram addressed this as well.

'I feel that workmen have a right in extreme cases to take joint action, but it is a remedy for which employers and their employees both should not allow an occasion to come,' he said. He told the workers that he would ask the managers to be cognizant of the issues faced by them and to react without delay.

Shri Ram also laid out his desire to grow the business further. 'I feel we ought to put up a new mill, if not every year, at least every second year,' he proclaimed. He then told them that was why his holiday would be a working holiday, as he planned to study the latest machinery in European mills.

And he was true to his word. His trip to Europe turned out to be more of a working trip than a holiday. He spent most of his time visiting and studying textile mills and the management techniques employed there. At the back of his mind were always thoughts of DCM and which new techniques he could introduce there.

Shri Ram found his trip to Europe quite enlightening. He was enamoured by the discipline, oneness of purpose and patriotism displayed by the people there. This prompted him to contrast Europe with India, which was still under colonial rule. Shri Ram was sad when he saw the progress that Europe was making across industries and technology; sad because he felt that India was being left behind. It made him even more determined to grow DCM bigger and better. His trip also made him realize that he needed to expand and diversify the business. He could not depend only on cloth manufacturing to make DCM one of the biggest businesses in the country.

Shri Ram returned to India towards the end of 1929. The world was in the Great Depression by then. It had started with the Wall Street crash in November 1929 and had quickly spread across the world. Even though India was not a significant part of the world economy, the Depression affected the stability of her economy. DCM, thankfully, was not impacted by the

Depression. In fact, Shri Ram came back to India with plans to set up a third mill.

The foundation for the third mill was laid in early 1930, and that same year the mill started production with 20,000 spindles and 500 looms. Shri Ram also started the third shift of workers. The mills were now running twenty-four hours a day. This generated more employment for workers and brought down production costs as there was no downtime in the mills. The third mill concentrated on producing newer types of material—sheeting, shirting, saris, towels, dhotis and voiles, to name a few. These were the types of material that were in demand hours a day the middle classes. DCM thus started competing with the mills of Ahmedabad and Bombay.

It was only towards the end of 1930 that DCM started to feel the pinch of the Great Depression. The average realization reduced. Shri Ram understood that sales could continue but the average price was under pressure. He decided to direct the production departments of the mills to start producing even more. And he decided to focus on the coarser variety of cloth, khaddar. His strategy paid off—even in those years of the Depression, DCM increased its profit margins.

Besides tweaking the production mix at the mills, Shri Ram also looked at the sales and credit processes. He increased the number of dealers as well as the offtake by each dealer. Further, he relaxed the credit limits. DCM gave a credit of seven days to its dealers. Shri Ram increased it to two or three weeks, giving dealers more time to sell and pay the company. In addition, he introduced a bonus scheme for the dealers. Dealers who sold more than Rs 50,000 worth of DCM cloth in a year were given a cash bonus linked to their sales volume.

The reason for Shri Ram's focus on the production of khaddar was the resurgence of the Swadeshi movement. Though the movement began in 1905–06, it started to gain more traction in the 1930s. The Swadeshi movement was a call given by Mahatma Gandhi to boycott the use of foreign goods. Imported cloth was an immediate casualty. There was a groundswell of support for locally made cloth. Khadi—or hand-spun cloth—was made popular by Gandhi. Khaddar was another type of cloth that saw mass acceptance. Many political workers and leaders started wearing kurta-pyjamas made of khaddar. DCM had been specializing in the production of khaddar since the 1920s. Now, during the Depression, Shri Ram directed the mills to produce more khaddar.

It was around this time that the Federation of Indian Chambers of Commerce and Industry, also known as FICCI, was born. This was a forum for Indian businesses to speak in one voice across industries. While individual industries had their own associations, this was the first time that businesses across all sections of industry were coming together. Shri Ram was now in his forties and at the peak of his creative ability.

He was elected as the vice president of FICCI in 1929. He was surprised, as he felt that he did not have sufficient experience to do justice to the role. He mentioned this to his good friend Purshotamdas Thakurdas, who stopped him even as he was speaking. 'It is not for you to accept or reject the nomination, Lala ji,' said Thakurdas. 'It is the privilege of the president to choose his deputy. You will learn the work under the able guidance of the president of the association—Shri G.D. Birla.'

Shri Ram accepted the position with humility and promised himself that he would work extra hard to learn about FICCI and other businesses. True to his promise, he worked hard and within two years was elected president of FICCI in 1930. The outgoing president warned him that the post was no bed of roses and reminded Shri Ram that it was the highest honour that the Indian mercantile community could bestow on any individual.

Shri Ram came to head FICCI at a time when there was an upsurge in national sentiment in India. A nationalist and patriot himself, Shri Ram wanted to make FICCI nationalist as well. Mahatma Gandhi had launched a fresh wave of the Swadeshi movement. Shri Ram, as the president of FICCI, decided to back the Mahatma fully.

With its call to boycott foreign goods, especially British textiles, the Swadeshi movement led to an increase in the demand for Indian cloth, which in turn helped not only DCM but also almost all the other mills in the country. The effect of the Depression was mitigated by the support given by Indians to locally made cloth. It also roused a spirit of industrial nationalism, which was to last for many years to come. However, it also gave rise to murmurs that the Mahatma was indirectly helping the mill owners and other industrialists earn more profits. Shri Ram did not like the murmurs but could not do anything to stop them. It was indeed true that the demand for Indian cloth had gone up and the mills were making more money. But he also knew what had gone wrong with the first Swadeshi movement that had been launched twenty years earlier.

After supporting the movement, many mills had gone back on their word. They had started to sell imported cloth as swadeshi. Even if they did not sell imported cloth, some mill owners mixed imported cotton yarn with indigenous yarn and continued to call it swadeshi. Shri Ram knew that if the movement was to be successful the mills would need to be disciplined.

He helped set up an organization called Swadeshi Prachar Association. He asked the association to draw up three lists—one of all Indian mills that did not use foreign yarn, one of the goods manufactured by them and one of their selling agents across the country. This, Shri Ram hoped, would spread the word amongst the people who mattered in the swadeshi supply chain. Shri Ram also asked the association to release advertisements in nationalist media on the benefits of swadeshi.

The list of mills using only indigenous yarn proved useful. The products of these mills were stamped as genuinely swadeshi. The association also requested the managing agents of these mills and their family members to wear only swadeshi fabric. Dealers were asked to deal with only indigenous products. But Shri Ram was not happy with these measures; he wanted more and wanted to counter the charge of profiteering.

Under Shri Ram's leadership the mill owners undertook a pledge to restrict their profits to not more than 8 per cent. Shri Ram's stature and power of persuasion won the mill owners' trust. Almost all Indian mill owners agreed to his proposal. In fact, some foreign companies as well agreed to restrict their profits.

Shri Ram had been supporting the Swadeshi movement and the Congress party. In return, he expected the Congress to consult FICCI when it came to formulating economic policies for the country. Of late he had started resenting the manner in which the Congress was declaring its economic policies and views on economic matters in an unilateral manner. He believed that the formulation of economic policies did not come under the mandate of the Congress. Shri Ram believed that any economic policy could be articulated publicly only after it had been discussed with the industry federations.

Shri Ram persuaded Mahatma Gandhi to inaugurate the annual meeting of FICCI in April 1931. In his speech Shri Ram made his grievances known.

'It has happened time and again that the Congress had committed itself to certain economic ideas of far-reaching effects without consulting the business community,' he said to the audience, but looking at the Mahatma. 'Economics and commerce is our field, and we could be of real service to the country and the Congress. We would therefore suggest that, in the future, in all matters pertaining to economics, the Congress, before making up its mind, will allow us to offer it our suggestions and, if necessary, have discussions with our members.'

He saw Gandhi nodding discreetly, but Shri Ram was not finished.

'If a doctor or a lawyer has earned lakhs of rupees, he is not called a capitalist by the Congress and in fact is welcomed into the Congress,' he continued. 'But if a merchant or a trader has earned even a few thousand rupees, the Congress calls him a capitalist and looks at him with great suspicion and almost disgust. We are therefore finding it difficult to enter the Congress and have no aspirations to take charge of any division of it.'

Mahatma Gandhi listened intently to Shri Ram and then got up to reply. He told the gathered businessmen, traders and merchants that they should regard themselves as trustees and servants of the poor. He urged them to work towards the benefit of the toiling millions and to work honestly to earn their pennies.

DCM earned more than mere pennies. In 1931 it made a profit of over Rs 11 lakh. This was almost 40 per cent more than the profit made during the preceding year. The shareholders were given a dividend of 35 per cent in addition to a preference share with a 4.5 per cent interest. DCM mill workers and staff were also given a bonus. A total of Rs 40,000 was distributed amongst the workers and staff as a bonus.

Shri Ram had been working hard at DCM, and with the added responsibility of FICCI his work hours had increased even more. This took a toll on his health. When his tenure as the president of FICCI ended in April 1931 he was unable to attend the meeting at which he was to hand over the charge to his successor. It was left to G.D. Birla to pay tribute to the work done by Shri Ram during his tenure as president of FICCI.

'We wish that Lala ji had been here today to receive our thanks. Those who saw him working could give testimony to his patience and his ability to work extremely hard. He worked so hard that he very nearly collapsed in the committee meeting. His health was so very poor that we all very much wished him to take a complete rest, but he did not like to shirk his duty,' said G.D. Birla in his thank-you speech.

11

Diversifying into Sugar

THE year 1931 saw a bumper profit at DCM in spite of the Great Depression. Shri Ram was happy but was also concerned about the state of the workers and their desire to form a union. The workers had touched upon this before he left for his trip to Europe. A union had been formed while Shri Ram was away. In 1930 there had even been a strike at DCM.

It was the strike that had disheartened Shri Ram. He had always believed that since he looked after his workers well and kept an open-door policy at work, the workers would unhesitatingly come to him in case they had a grievance rather than resort to a strike. But he was not a man to dwell on negative thoughts. Through negotiation, he was able to persuade the workers to come back to work. But the incident got him to think more deeply about the problem.

While in Europe Shri Ram had seen, first hand, the various schemes companies had launched to communicate with their workers. The workers, too, discussed their problems freely with the managers on various platforms. He now thought that the time was right to start a structured communication process with the workers. He started an in-house weekly magazine called *Gazette*. It contained messages from Shri Ram to the employees; it also gave space to the workers to air their grievances. He wanted to communicate directly with the workers, bypassing the union leaders.

After the profits of 1931 the shareholders were given a generous dividend. The workers too were given a bonus. The bonus, however, came with a condition: they had to remain loyal to the company and not engage in anti-mill activities. If they were found violating that condition the bonus would be recovered from their salary.

But Shri Ram continued to be restless. In fact, ever since he had returned from Europe his mind had been in a churn. He wanted to move beyond cloth manufacturing. He knew that the growth at DCM would not be easy to maintain. The tent business in Kanpur was in decline and had to be shut down. Lala Diwan Chand, Shri Ram's partner in the tent business, had died. Further, Japan had worked the exchange rate of the yen vis-à-vis the rupee in such a manner that over 500 million yards of Japanese cloth was imported into India, the high import duty notwithstanding, leading the general public to prefer the imported fabric.

Shri Ram realized that he had to diversify DCM's business. The business cycles in textiles were very sharp. He had the foresight to see that he would have to diversify his risks to make DCM's revenue and profits steady. But he also had a puritanical work ethic. Thus, a whole range of industries were ruled out, which included tobacco, alcohol and construction. Further, Shri Ram knew that a large-scale business venture would be profitable only if its products reached the masses.

Besides steadying the revenue cycle, there was another reason for diversification. Shri Ram wanted to grow his sphere of influence in industry. He wanted to be seen as an all-round industrialist—not only as the head of a cloth mill.

It was the government that helped Shri Ram make up his mind while he was looking for areas for diversification. To give an impetus to the sugar industry in India, the government passed the Sugar Industries Protection Act in April 1932. This act banned the import of sugar into India.

Three days after the act was passed Shri Ram called for a meeting of the board of directors. They met at Shri Ram's residence. While the directors knew that Shri Ram wanted to discuss business ideas in general, they had no idea about the specific plan that would be presented.

As the men settled down Shri Ram began speaking. 'As you know we recently had to close the Kanpur depot of DCM because the orders for tents from the ordnance factory had dried up. This affected the revenues of our company, as the orders were significant for us.' As the others in the room nodded in agreement, Shri Ram reminded them that if the prices of raw cotton went up by even a small amount, or the production of finished goods exceeded the demand, the fortunes of the company were affected adversely.

'Risks of the business must be distributed,' asserted Shri Ram. 'We must look at industries other than cloth. When choosing a business, we must also be sure that the demand for that product will remain constant.'

'What you are saying makes sense, Lala ji, but what other business can we do?' asked one of the directors.

Shri Ram smiled. 'Seth ji, the government has shown us the way. They have made it easy for us to choose an industry,' he said.

A murmur went around the room as the directors turned to each other and wondered how the government had made it easy. Shri Ram watched this with a small smile on his face. Finally, he told them about the new import restriction on sugar. 'As you know, sugar is always in demand, and it is a vital commodity. It will be a good business to start,' he said.

The board conferred for a few minutes amongst themselves. But Shri Ram was by now the de facto boss of the business. The board was content to let him take all the decisions. But they were also happy that Shri Ram honoured the governance process and ensured that no decision was taken without a discussion with the board.

The approval to add a sugar mill to the DCM portfolio was given to Shri Ram. The board also told Shri Ram to take all such actions as were required to get the sugar mill up and running in the shortest time possible. Shri Ram thanked the board and then requested the required changes to be made to the Memorandum of Association to enable the broadening of DCM's activities. This resolution was also passed with ease.

The approvals in place, Shri Ram moved with lightning speed. He wanted the mill to be ready for the next sugar cane crop, which was typically ready for crushing by November, which was barely six months away.

After the approval the first step was to look for a suitable site for the sugar mill. Shri Ram knew that the location would be an important factor in the profitability of the mill once it started production. The main reason was the fact that sugar cane, the raw material for the production of sugar, is bulky and perishable and thus the mill needed to be in a location where the sugar cane could be transported easily. The two states near Delhi that were major producers of sugar cane were Bihar and Uttar Pradesh.

As he scouted for a suitable site for the mill, Shri Ram honed in on a small village called Daurala. The village was about 52 km from Delhi and 12 km from Meerut. It was served by a railway line and was surrounded by cane producing areas. The villages around Daurala could be a source for the labour that would be needed for the sugar mill.

Shri Ram started the process of buying land for the mill. But he ran into an unexpected problem. The villagers looked upon the making of sugar as an activity that flouted the religious sentiments of the Hindus. Sugar is vegetarian, no doubt. But the production of sugar involved a step in which bone sulphate or bone char was added to the raw sugar solution. This was added to remove impurities and give the final product a white colour. Bone sulphate is made from the bones of cows and buffaloes. The Hindu villagers, who held the cow to be a sacred animal, did not want to be part of any activity that involved the cow.

Shri Ram had a problem on his hands. He did not want to set up a mill in an environment that would be hostile. He wanted the support of the villagers, as they were the ones who would supply the mill the raw material and labour and then be the consumers of the product. Shri Ram knew that if he were able to speak with the villagers, he would win them over. But he did not have the time, as he was busy with the DCM mills in Delhi.

As he was looking for a solution, he remembered his friend, Chaudhry Mukhtar Singh of Meerut. Mukhtar Singh was an advocate and a local leader. He had been a member of the governing body of the Imperial Council of Agricultural Research and had been on the Sugar Committee formed by the government to look into the case for protection of the sugar industry. Thus, he had in-depth knowledge of the agricultural landscape in general and of the sugar industry in particular. To Shri Ram's mind, Mukhtar Singh was the ideal person to bring in as his key man for the sugar mill project.

Shri Ram told Mukhtar Singh that if he could bring around the villagers, he could join the sugar mill as the general manager. The salary offered was significantly more than what the lawyer made in his profession. To sweeten the deal further, Shri Ram promised him a commission income of 5 per cent on the profits made by the sugar mill. Mukhtar took the deal.

Using his knowledge of the business and of the people in the village, Mukhtar Singh went to work. He spent time with the villagers and brought them around in a relatively short time.

Shri Ram was so sure of Mukhtar Singh's ability that, even while the talks with the villagers were in progress, the DCM engineers had been told to work on the blueprint of the sugar mill and to make a list of the machinery that would be needed. The orders for the machinery were placed in mid-April 1932, even as Mukhtar Singh was on the job of getting the land for the mill organized. The machinery was ordered from Stork Werkspoor of Holland. It was a large order amounting to GBP 36,000. Most such contracts had a penalty clause built in by the buyer. Under this clause the supplier had to compensate the buyer in case of any delay in the supply of the equipment. Shri Ram, however, built a reward clause in to the contract. If Stork Werkspoor were able to supply the machinery before the agreed time DCM would give it a cash reward. This contract was finalized between the two parties within two hours.

Work on the sugar mill started in August 1932. Shri Ram ran into another problem at this point. The rules at that time did not allow work on industrial chimneys at night. This rule could have derailed Shri Ram's plans of catching the next crushing season in November. He met the collector of Meerut, P.W. Marsh, and requested him to relax the rules so that work could continue without interruption.

Marsh was a seasoned bureaucrat and knew the consequences of bending the rules for a rich and influential industrialist. But he did help Shri Ram. 'I cannot give you permission, which is against the law. But go ahead. At most there will be a penalty. We will consider the matter when the time comes,' he told Shri Ram with a smile and a wink.

Work was carried out at night under headlights!

Shri Ram took it upon himself to supervise the construction. He would go to the site in Daurala every day. He would leave Delhi in the early hours of the morning and would get to the mill site before sunrise. There was an old neem tree on the site. A charpoy would be placed there for Shri Ram. A fresh sheet would cover it every day. This became his office. Shri Ram would sit there and observe the construction. He would even distribute the daily wages to the workers himself. At the end of the day, his office would be closed by folding the sheet and putting away the charpoy.

Shri Ram's presence acted as a catalyst, and the workers were energized to work harder. His presence also instilled a bit of fear amongst the supervisors, as they could not afford to be lax. The mill was finished in a record time of under two months.

Even as the mill construction was going on, Shri Ram had started work on the workers' quarters. DCM, in Delhi, had these quarters built for the workers right in the beginning, and it was a key reason for the good worker-management relationship. Learning from that experience, Shri Ram spent over Rs 1 lakh getting workers' quarters constructed for both married and unmarried staff. Further, once the work had started on the mill, Shri Ram started a free dispensary and put a full-time doctor in charge of it. The dispensary was available to all workers, their families and even to people in the areas around. This dispensary played a big role in building further positivity amongst the villagers about the upcoming sugar mill. Shri Ram also spoke to Mukhtar Singh to plan for a school for the children of the workers as well as the children from the nearby villages.

Shri Ram and Mukhtar Singh had many a mini-conference in the open 'office' at the mill site. The two men would sit under the neem tree and talk about the working of the mill. In one such conversation Mukhtar pointed out that he had heard the cane farmers in the area complaining about poor yields. Shri Ram realized that the Daurala mill could make a difference in this as well. He told Mukhtar Singh to explore ways in which the mill could provide the farmers with better quality seeds. He also told him to work out how more water could be provided to the farmers. Sugar cane is a water-intensive crop. Mukhtar Singh promised to conduct a feasibility study on the digging of tube wells. Shri Ram also asked him to get in touch with agricultural experts who could come regularly and hold workshops with the farmers to educate them on better ways of farming.

Along with the factory, there was another construction project that Shri Ram was working on at this time. It was a personal project—building two homes for the family. The family was living in Civil Lines, in the rented bungalow. Madan Mohan continued to live in the haveli in old Delhi, as he did not want to live in a rented house. Shri Ram had been on the lookout for a suitable plot where he could build his own house.

In the late 1920s Delhi was in the middle of hectic building activity. Soon after the British had proclaimed Delhi to be the new capital of the country at the Delhi Durbar in 1911, the Delhi Town Planning Committee had been formed. Edwin Lutyens was appointed as the consultant to draw up the master plan of the new capital. Many British officials had moved from Calcutta, the earlier capital city, to Delhi. In the absence of proper houses most of them were living in cramped quarters in Civil Lines. These and other British officers, for the next two decades, were focused on the making of the new capital. The construction work had been interrupted by the First World War and resumed after the war had ended. The new city was finally inaugurated in February 1931.

Shri Ram was keeping track of these new developments. He saw that Connaught Place was being developed as the main commercial centre of the city. He also saw that it was going to be the showpiece of Lutyens' Delhi. Civil Lines, Shri Ram foresaw, would no longer be as important once Connaught Place was ready.

As per Lutyens' master plan, the central business district of Connaught Place had radial roads branching out from the circle. One of these roads was Curzon Road (now known as Kasturba Gandhi Marg). Large plots of land were available to people who wanted to build their houses there. Shri Ram knew of some businessmen and other wealthy people from old Delhi who had bought plots for their homes on the radial roads. He decided to do the same.

Shri Ram bought over six acres of land on Curzon Road in the early 1930s. The plot numbers were 18 to 22, but in later years the address of the Shri Ram house came to be 22 Curzon Road. He planned to build two bungalows, one for his father and brother and brother's family, and the other for his family. He got the plans ready for the new bungalows and gave orders for the construction to start.

The bungalows, however, took much longer than the sugar mill to construct. The mill was ready in a couple of months, but the bungalows took a couple of years. Shri Ram was in no hurry to finish the construction of the bungalows, as there was no deadline. He just wanted them to be the best they could be. While he himself was a frugal man, he wanted the bungalows to be large so he could entertain his friends and associates there.

The mill was ready in no time. Once ready, it had a crushing capacity of 500 tonnes a day. The commissioner of the Meerut Division, P.W. Marsh, formally inaugurated the mill in February 1933 even though the mill had been operational for a few months by then—it had produced over 15,000 maunds of sugar by the inauguration (one maund is approximately 37 kg).

Shri Ram, at the inauguration, reaffirmed the benefits of the mill to the farmers of the area. He said that the purchase price for cane at the Daurala sugar mill had been higher than before. At that price, he reminded the gathering, the farmers had made almost 200 per cent more in profits than when they had sold gur. He added that the farmers did not have to wait more than a couple of hours for their full payment from the sugar mill. Shri Ram also thanked Mukhtar Singh for his contribution in getting the sugar mill up and running. Shri

Ram told the farmers that, while he himself was a capitalist, Mukhtar Singh at heart was a socialist and that the farmers had a friend in him.

The sugar mill in Daurala got off to a flying start. In the first year itself, it contributed almost 42 per cent of the profits of the entire DCM Group. This was also the time when the sugar industry had exploded in India. Many leading businessmen, including G.D. Birla, K.C. Thapar and Jamnalal Bajaj, had started sugar mills. Such was the proliferation of sugar mills in the country that it became a common joke that wherever there was a sugar mill there would be the three Ms—machchar or mosquitoes, makhi or flies and Marwaris!

But this dream ran into the obstacle of a shortage of cane within a year. By 1934 the sugar cane market had become a sellers' market. Sugar mills were hard-pressed to find the raw material—sugar cane. The mills had to resort to getting cane from places as far as 300 km away. This increased the cost of raw material for the factories. Further, even after paying the high prices the mills found that they had inferior product on hand. The transportation over long distances, often by rail, resulted in the juice in the cane drying up. Several sugar mills could not cope with the situation and shut down.

Shri Ram was made of sterner stuff. Instead of reducing the production capacity of the mill, he increased it from 500 tonnes per day to 800 tonnes per day. He also bought 500 acres of land adjacent to the sugar mill and converted it into a cane farm. This farm ensured that a part of the raw material requirement of the mill was met by the produce grown there. The cane farm was also used as a demonstration farm for the sugar cane farmers of the area. Experiments with new varieties of sugarcane were conducted on this captive farm. The farmers flocked to the farm to check out the high-yield varieties of cane and to learn about scientific methods of growing cane. Over the next couple of years, the farmers took to growing newer varieties of cane, which increased their yield per acre. It turned out to be a win-win situation for both parties—the farmers got more money for their produce and the mill was assured of higher quantities of quality raw material.

The sugar mill at Daurala had alternating years of good and bad profits. The years of good profits encouraged Shri Ram to modernize the factory. He hired a Dutch agricultural chemist as his advisor. Based on the advice of the Dutchman, Shri Ram had the manufacturing process of sugar tweaked. The new process enabled the factory to produce demerara and icing sugar as well as candies, syrups and squashes.

However, the problem of the fight for sugar cane continued.

Sometime in 1934 the United Provinces (now Uttar Pradesh) government had set up a tramway service between Daurala and Mawana—a small town devoted to the cultivation of sugar cane and only 40 km from Daurala. The tramway had been set up to offer better connectivity to people commuting between the two towns and to ferry sugar cane to the mill in Daurala. However, within no time the government lost interest in running the tramway.

Shri Ram sensed an opportunity and thought it through. He bought the tramway service from the government. With the captive tramcar service, the Daurala sugar mill was able to easily source quality sugar cane from Mawana. Shri Ram also wanted to set up a sugar mill in Mawana, but it took a few years before his dream could be achieved.

12

A Wedding in the Family and a New Mill

SHRI Ram was known as one of the country's best industrial minds by 1934. The diversification of DCM's business had indeed helped Shri Ram in being seen as an all-round industrialist. Other industrialists and even the government sought his advice on matters of industry. In fact, the government invited Shri Ram to lead a delegation to Kabul in early 1934. The delegation was a reflection of the government's desire to increase trade with Afghanistan.

Shri Ram went with the delegation but was underwhelmed by what he saw in Afghanistan. When he contrasted Afghanistan with the countries he had visited in Europe, he was left wanting. As he travelled within Afghanistan he saw that, outside of Kabul, there was virtually no industry at all, and the country was largely medieval and focused on agriculture.

A bit disheartened, Shri Ram returned to India but soon got caught up in arranging the marriages of both his sons—Bharat Ram and Charat Ram. As always, he took the advice of his close friend, Padampat Singhania.

Shri Ram had first met Padampat Singhania at FICCI in 1930. He was introduced to Singhania by another friend, Purshotamdas Thakurdas. Though Singhania was fifteen years younger than Shri Ram, both took to each other as if their friendship were a continuation from a past life. They had similar values and aspirations. Their political views were also the same. Both wanted India to be a great industrial nation. They also had similar views on Hindu religious practices and what was 'proper' and what was 'improper'. Both agreed on the benefits of arranged marriages and the use of horoscopes.

'You are a young chhokra compared to me,' Shri Ram would often tell Singhania while patting him on the back fondly. But he still went to his friend for advice on almost every matter—how to increase the output of the spindles, where to put up a sugar mill, how to tackle sticky labour problems and how to train his sons for business.

Thus, it was natural for Shri Ram to talk to Singhania about whom his sons should marry. Singhania advised him to first get his elder son's view on the matter.

Bharat Ram was attending St. Stephen's College at the time, after finishing his schooling at Modern School, Delhi. Bharat Ram had had to convince his grandfather to let him go to college. Madan Mohan was of the view that there was no better education than getting trained in the family business.

However, Shri Ram ruled that his sons needed to study and get a college degree.

When his father brought up the topic of marriage, Bharat Ram, as was the norm in those days, maintained a respectful silence, mumbled some incoherent words and kept his head down. Shri Ram took this as his consent!

Finding a bride for his son turned out to be a bigger problem for Shri Ram than setting up a new factory.

By now the two bungalows had been constructed on the six-acre plot on Curzon Road. As it happened, one of the bungalows was much larger than the other. Thus, they came to be known as badi kothi and chhoti kothi.

Shri Ram moved his family into the two kothis. Thankfully, his father, Madan Mohan, also agreed to move to Curzon Road. The badi kothi was given to Madan Mohan, Shankar Lall and his family. Shri Ram took the smaller bungalow. The chhoti kothi was small only in name. It was a typical Lutyens' bungalow and had twelve bedrooms, two courtyards, sprawling gardens and a swimming pool. In this big house, Shri Ram occupied a twelve-foot-by-twelve-foot room with an attached bathroom on the ground floor. It was a tiny room compared to the other rooms in the bungalow. It had a bed, a table, a chair and a fridge. There was also provision for Shri Ram to make his own tea in the morning. The room opened onto the front veranda. It was a long veranda, spanning the entire frontage of the kothi. At the other end of the veranda was Shri Ram's secretary's room, which gave Mr Khanna, the secretary, easy access to his boss. Shri Ram was content in this small room and ran his family and businesses from here.

The badi kothi was much larger. It was a grand, palatial Lutyens' style mansion. It had a large courtyard in the middle.

There was a large ballroom and a dining room with a horseshoe-shaped dining table that could seat sixty-four. The bungalow was built as a rich man's house to showcase the success of Shri Ram.

Shri Ram did not have any knowledge about the type or brand of furniture to be bought. His objective was simply to have the best of everything. He requested an acquaintance who was knowledgeable about these matters to guide the team working on the kothis. As a result, the furniture at the Shri Ram house was from Waring & Gillow, a luxury furniture firm in Britain. All cutlery was from Mappin & Webb: a hundred-piece set, in sterling silver, complete with oyster forks—this when only vegetarian food without onion and garlic was served in the house!

It was the practice at that time for the ballroom of any large mansion to have portraits of ancestors adorn the walls. However, Shri Ram was different—he did not have any well-known ancestors. So he commissioned a Bengali artist to paint twenty-four large paintings. Each painting depicted a scene from Hindu mythology. These panels adorned the walls of the ballroom.

With the Shri Ram home and office buzzing with activity, Shri Ram was hard-pressed for time. But he went about looking for a bride for his son with the same meticulousness and rigour that he displayed in everything. And as he did in some business matters, he took constant advice from Padampat Singhania. Going by the custom prevalent in those years, the father could have chosen the bride for his son and merely informed him about it. But Shri Ram consulted Bharat Ram on each prospective match.

Bharat Ram was twenty years old. He was an intelligent boy with fine tastes. He did not approve of any prospective match that was shown to him. He had seen how different his parents were from each other and that their interests did not overlap at all. He had not seen his mother and father indulge in any form of discussion or in any meaningful conversations. Bharat Ram wanted to marry a girl who would complement him and be a true partner in all aspects of his life.

Shri Ram was getting increasingly worried at his son's rejection of every potential match. He confided in Padampat.

'Bharat's engagement is a source of great worry for me,' Shri Ram told Singhania. 'I have found beautiful brides for him and rich ones, but he has rejected all of them. He says he wants a girl who will be cultured and be a true companion in life.'

Singhania took the initiative and suggested the daughter of a prosperous businessman in Bombay. He knew the girl personally and told Shri Ram that the girl was a griha Lakshmi—one who would bring good luck and wealth into the family.

Shri Ram liked what he learnt about the girl and the family. He wanted to travel to Bombay to meet them. But as luck would have it, his father, Madan Mohan, was taken seriously ill at this time. Shri Ram was torn between his duty as a son and his love for his son. He had almost made up his mind to go to Bombay when his father chided him for neglecting him in favour of his sons. Shri Ram was used to harsh words from his father, but somehow the almost accusatory words from Madan Mohan now, at this stage, made him uncomfortable. Shri Ram was torn with guilt—he knew that his father would not have any good words for him no matter what he did; at the same time, he wanted to do his best for his own son.

In the end guilt won, and Shri Ram cancelled his visit to Bombay and stayed with his father.

Madan Mohan passed away a week later. Shri Ram was devastated at the loss of his father. He was surprised at the strength of his own emotions, considering the strained relationship he had had with his father. Shri Ram was also relieved that he had cancelled his trip to Bombay. He knew he would not have been able to deal with the guilt if he had been in Bombay when his father passed away.

Shri Ram also took his father's death as a divine sign of disapproval for the Bombay alliance. Singhania, who had suggested the match, tried to reason with his friend.

'I say, Bhaiji, isn't this a bit drastic? Why are you not going to Bombay?' asked Singhania.

'I had decided to go to Bombay and meet the girl and her family, but then my father died,' replied Shri Ram.

'Oh, come on, Bhaiji, you cannot be serious? What is the girl's fault in this?' Singhania asked, throwing his arms wide open in exasperation.

'Maybe nothing, but I am superstitious about such things. So I would rather let it be,' Shri Ram replied, simply but firmly.

After the final rites for Madan Mohan were over Shri Ram returned to the job of finding the right girl for Bharat Ram. A proposal from Raja Jwala Prasad, a respected zamindar, came to Shri Ram. Jwala Prasad also invited Shri Ram and his sons to come to his bungalow in Nainital so that his daughter Sumitra and Bharat Ram could meet.

Shri Ram did not go but sent both his sons to Nainital to meet with the girl's family and to have a look at her. Sumitra was a great beauty and was eighteen years old. She also had a strong mind of her own. When she met Bharat and Charat Ram, she decided immediately that she wanted to marry the younger brother. She said that it was love at first sight for her!

Both Shri Ram and Jwala Prasad hit the roof. Charat Ram was younger than Sumitra, and the elders put their foot down against the relationship. But Sumitra was made of sterner stuff and threatened suicide if she was not allowed to marry Charat Ram.

Jwala Prasad's son, Dharamvira, who was a senior ICS officer, took it upon himself to solve the problem. He got his sister married off to another ICS officer. The marriage lasted all of a couple of days. Sumitra refused to consummate the marriage and ran away from her husband's home. Her father refused to take her back and so, again, it was left to Dharamvira to solve the problem.

He got Sumitra to enrol in Banaras Hindu University, where she studied Hindi literature. Charat Ram, also smitten by the young girl, took to visiting her often in Banaras.

In the meantime, the quest for a bride for Bharat Ram continued. Another proposal came from Hissar. Shri Ram liked the photograph of the girl and approved the particulars of the family. The father of the girl was Brij Mohan Lal, a barrister and a zamindar. Shri Ram wanted to take the matter forward. But he did not want to risk sending his two sons to the girl's house! He therefore invited the girl and her family to the chhoti kothi.

Sheila, the girl, came to Delhi along with her family. They spent half a day at the chhoti kothi. Sheila was sixteen years old and charmed the entire Shri Ram family, including Bharat Ram. She had many interests, ranging from music to drama to collecting old jewellery and saris. She also knew ballroom dancing. The proposal was finalized by both families with alacrity.

Shri Ram was proud of his choice of bride for his son.

Bharat Ram's wedding was celebrated on a large and lavish scale. This was the first wedding in the family after their fortunes had turned. Murli Dhar had been married seven years earlier. Shri Ram had got his eldest son married to a traditional, conservative girl named Swaroop Devi from Patiram Kucha in Chandni Chowk. She had settled well into the life of managing the household, and the family. For all practical purposes she was the matriarchal head of the household as Phoolan Devi continued to live in the shadows. Her health had not improved; fits of epilepsy had only increased in frequency. But she persevered in the kitchen. She had shrunk into a frail woman who looked much older than she really was.

Swaroop Devi prepared with great excitement for the wedding as she was happy that another girl closer to her age would come into the household. Her wedding had not been grand, but since that time Shri Ram had become one of the wealthiest men in India.

The wedding of Bharat Ram gave Shri Ram an opportunity to showcase his new status to all. He took a small but elegant baraat to Hissar. The entire town of Hissar talked about the baraatis for months thereafter. They had made for an impressive sight. They may have been few in number, but they were high in status. Some of the foremost industrialists of India were part of the baraat. The wedding took place in the summer of 1935. The baraatis were dressed in simple white achkans and dhotis. The achkans were simple, but they were adorned with bejewelled buttons, each of which was worth a considerable fortune!

The new bride was brought back from Hissar in a Rolls Royce. The car belonged to a friend of Shri Ram who had almost implored Shri Ram to use it. Once back in Delhi, the new bride had to go through more wedding rituals. She had to get used to the new household, where the women had to cover their heads when coming out to meet others.

Shri Ram did not forget the workers at the time of the wedding. While he could not take all of them to Hissar with him in the baraat, once the wedding party had returned to Delhi, Shri Ram invited the entire workforce to his home for dinner. The lawns of the two kothis were prepared for the wedding feast. A shamiana was put up and the entire place was decked with flowers. The air was filled with the smell of marigold and rose. A shehnai-wala was hired to play the instrument in the background.

The workforce of DCM was a large one and thus could not be accommodated at the Shri Ram house all at one time. The wedding feast carried on for five days, with the workforce coming in batches. All family members personally served food to the guests. Sheila, the new bride, also joined the family in serving food.

Sheila's father, Rai Bahadur Brij Mohan Lal, was a friend of B.K. Nehru, who lived in Hissar as well. B.K. Nehru went on to be the Indian ambassador to the US and the Indian high commissioner to the UK. B.K. Nehru had married a Hungarian girl called Foli who was renamed Shobha after her marriage. Foli, though a foreigner, could pass off as an Indian girl.

Not long after Bharat Ram and Sheila's wedding, Nehru and his wife came to Delhi for a visit. They dropped into the Shri Ram house as well. While Nehru spent time with the men in the main room, Shobha went inside the house to call on Phoolan Devi.

Phoolan Devi was conservative and orthodox. She observed all rules of chhoot-chhaat. But she took a liking to Shobha, not realizing that the latter was a foreigner. When Shobha offered to help Phoolan Devi with her lunch the older lady readily agreed. In the evening Phoolan Devi told Sheila about the guest. '*Aaj ek aisi achchi Kashmiri Panditani aai thi. Usne mujhe bare pyar se khana khilaya. Woh wahi Nehru waallon ki bahu hai,*' said Phoolan Devi in all her ignorance and innocence. (A very nice Kashmiri Pandit girl visited me today. She even fed me my lunch lovingly. She is part of that Nehru family.)

It is another matter that Phoolan Devi would have been shocked if she had known that the Nehru bahu was a mlechha! Sheila kept a straight face and agreed with her mother-in-law.

Once the festivities of the wedding had ended, Shri Ram refocused on the business. He had started a new mill before Bharat Ram's wedding. The successful foray into sugar did not make Shri Ram lose sight of new opportunities in textiles. By 1934 the textile industry was back on track. The demand for cloth had picked up, and textile mills were making profits again.

Shri Ram wanted to expand the cloth mills. But this time, instead of adding capacity to the existing mills, he looked to Punjab.

The thought of setting up ginning, spinning and weaving mills in Punjab had entered Shri Ram's mind a couple of years before Bharat Ram's wedding. He had realized that Punjab had almost no big cloth mills and their demands were met through the mills in Delhi and beyond. A network of canals had turned the semi-arid parts of Punjab into greenhouses. The province had large tracts of land where cotton was cultivated and the cotton grown here was amongst the finest in Punjab. It was a prosperous province and that meant that there was a strong market for cloth. A mill in Punjab would allow his Delhi mills to focus on the eastern markets—United Provinces and Bengal.

His idea was further solidified during a conversation with the representatives of the cotton growers of Punjab. This was during a negotiation for the Indo-Japanese Trade Agreement in 1933. Shri Ram was an adviser to the government for this delegation. The representatives of cotton growers told Shri Ram that a cloth mill in Punjab would be beneficial to the cotton growers of the agrarian state. Another meeting, this time with Sir Herbert Emerson, the governor of Punjab, helped Shri Ram make up his mind. He chose Lyallpur as the site for his mill in Punjab. Lyallpur was a canal colony—serviced by the canal system—and was in the heart of the cotton tract.

Shri Ram started buying land in the area and soon had acquired fifty-three acres—enough for work on the mill to commence. Even before the construction of the mill had begun, Shri Ram had placed an order for 20,000 spindles and 500 looms along with 96 ginning machines. Construction started in March 1934 and, by October, the mill was ready for trial production.

The work had been carried out speedily. But Shri Ram had ensured that no corners were cut. However, there was one area that Shri Ram had overlooked in the haste to set up the mill. It was in securing approvals in accordance with some government regulations. But Shri Ram remembered his experience of setting up the sugar mill and the advice given by the collector of Meerut. He decided to carry on and then ask for forgiveness.

At the inauguration, he turned to the chief guest—Sir Herbert William, governor of Punjab—and apologized.

'If in the process of hasty accomplishment of our plans, we have transgressed any rules and regulations, we sincerely apologize to the authorities concerned and assure them that these first offences will be the last,' said Shri Ram in a contrite tone but with a smile on his face. Sir William smiled as well and nodded.

Regular production started at the Lyallpur mill in December 1934. This mill was the most modern in India at that time. It had both heating and cooling within the premises to deal with the weather. It had a sprinkler system to deal with fires, if any. As with the other factories, the Lyallpur mill too had workers' quarters. There was a school, hospital, swimming pool, playgrounds and even a cinema in the workers' colony.

The factory workers were not the only ones Shri Ram focused on. He offered 40 per cent of the shares to the people of Lyallpur. These were lapped up quickly by the Punjabis and earned their cooperation in the setting up of the mill.

Lyallpur became a model industrial factory for Indians. C.D. Deshmukh, the then governor of the Reserve Bank of India, visited the factory and was impressed. 'I have yet to see an industrial unit of such importance so thoughtfully conceived, so thoroughly organized and so considerably operated,' he noted in his commendation.

Lyallpur remained close to Shri Ram's heart. He tasked his eldest son Murli Dhar with overseeing the Lyallpur mill. But Shri Ram remained connected with the mill and the workers, visiting Lyallpur at least once or twice a year. The main reason for his visits was not to take an account of the mills but to make his employees feel his presence. As with the workers in all his mills, he treated the workers at Lyallpur with warmth—almost like family members. As a result, everyone at the mill looked forward to his visits and offered him the warmest gratitude and respect. And Shri Ram did not disappoint them. During each of his visits he would make it a point to have an informal lunch with both junior and senior members of the staff. He would use this occasion to apprise himself of their welfare and that of their families and their problems, if any.

Some of the managers suggested to Shri Ram that he use a small plane to travel from Lahore to Lyallpur. Most industrialists used that mode of transport. But at every such suggestion Shri Ram would smile wryly and remind them that his money was hard earned, and he did not want to waste it!

On some occasions he would visit the factory almost unannounced. One summer the mill had heard that Shri Ram had come to Lyallpur from Delhi. They were sure that the next morning he would visit the mill. There was an air of excitement amongst the workers as they worked to spruce up the mill.

The sweeper of the mill was busy sweeping the path leading up to the gate of the mill. Outside the mill, the sweeper noticed a middle-aged man wrapped in a thin chadder loitering on the pavement, as if waiting for the dust raised by the jhadoo to settle down. As the sweeper kept sweeping, the man walked up tentatively to the gate and tried to look inside. The sweeper continued sweeping, keeping one eye on the man. But when the man tried to enter through the gate, the sweeper came running.

'Where do you think you are going?' he said angrily to the man. 'Don't you see that the mill is being cleaned? Our Lala ji has come from Delhi, and we are expecting him any time. Get out of here and go and stand there if you want to,' the sweeper thundered and pointed to a spot near the far wall of the mill.

The man started walking back slowly without saying a word. The sweeper returned to his sweeping, ensuring a clean path for his Lala ji.

After some time a cry went around the mill. 'Lala ji has arrived! Lala ji has arrived!' the workers said in excitement.

The sweeper too put his broom aside and joined the bunch of people waiting to catch a glimpse of Shri Ram.

A group of men walked up the path to the mill. Amongst the managers was a man dressed in a crisp white achkan and churidaar pyjama. This was Shri Ram.

The sweeper rushed forward to pay his respects. As soon as Shri Ram turned his head towards him the sweeper started shaking with fear. He recognized Shri Ram as the man he had shouted at earlier. He fell at Shri Ram's feet crying. 'Forgive me, Lala ji, forgive me. In my ignorance I said all those harsh words to you,' he pleaded.

Shri Ram just smiled and pulled the sweeper to his feet. 'Why should I be angry with you, eh? On the contrary, I am very happy. You are a diligent worker, and you were doing your job well. Come on now, stop crying,' said Shri Ram as he patted the sweeper on the back.

Lyallpur, unfortunately, went to Pakistan after the partition of India. It became Shri Ram's gift to the new country. He continued to guide the development of the mill even after 1947. The Lyallpur mill was the first and the biggest of its kind in Pakistan. It became a training ground for workers and other technicians in that country. Some people say that if Lyallpur was described as the mother of the Pakistani textile industry, then Shri Ram could be called the father!

13

Acquiring Bengal Potteries

SHRI Ram's trip to Europe in 1929 had broadened his view of the business. He had come back with the firm conviction that he needed to grow DCM's cloth and textile business but also to diversify in order to build a truly large business empire. Now, some events in India contributed to another change in his worldview. India was going through a political and social churn. Mahatma Gandhi had launched the Civil Disobedience movement. The Salt March was the first act that saw passionate public participation in the Non-Cooperation movement.

The British government, as a peace offering and to discuss constitutional reforms in India, had organized a series of Round Table Conferences between 1930 and 1932. The first one was held in November 1930 and went on till January 1931. The Indian National Congress did not participate in this Round

Table, as many of its leaders were in jail due to their participation in the Non-Cooperation movement. Though many reforms were discussed and agreed upon by the participants, nothing much happened on the ground in terms of execution. In fact, the Congress Party decided to carry on with its Swadeshi and Non-Cooperation movements. The first Round Table was universally seen as a failure.

The British government realized that it needed the Congress Party to be an active participant in any future conferences if any decision, on India's future were to be made. As a way to get out of a tricky situation, Lord Irwin, who was the Viceroy of India at that time, invited Mahatma Gandhi for a series of talks. The British government released Gandhi from prison, as he had been arrested after the Salt March, to enable him to participate in the talks with the Viceroy. Eight meetings were held between the two men, but the Irwin-Gandhi Pact, as it was called, also failed.

Shri Ram was a supporter of the Congress. And he was a patriot. He was upset when the Round Table Conferences failed. He was further saddened and upset when Lord Willingdon, the new Viceroy of India, issued a series of ordinances that led to the virtual imposition of civil martial law. Gandhi was arrested again, though the protests by the people against the British government continued. The Viceroy dealt with these protests with a heavy hand and a heavier stick. All this added to the discomfort of Shri Ram. He had been touched by the mass upheaval against the British. In a sense the Non-Cooperation movement had pulled Indians out of a quagmire and had given them self-respect and thoughts of self-reliance. At the back of Shri Ram's mind was the thought that he, along with other industrialists, should actively get involved in businesses that were hitherto not handled by Indians. He had already decided that he needed to diversify to grow his business empire and the Daurala sugar mill was part of this plan.

An opportunity to handle a business that was considered difficult to manage by Indians came Shri Ram's way in the early 1930s. This was the business of ceramic pottery. Shri Ram looked at this as further diversification of his business.

Though he did not know it at that time, Shri Ram's journey to the ceramics business had started when he was working with Boota Singh in Lahore. Madan Gopal Bhagat was a relative of Boota Singh and was about ten years younger than Shri Ram. In spite of the age difference the two boys had struck up a friendship, which only grew deeper as the years passed.

While Shri Ram had moved to Delhi to join and work at DCM, Madan Gopal had continued his studies in Lahore. He wanted to earn a degree in law and join the legal profession. However, he was destined to become a ceramics expert.

Madan Gopal's father had started a ceramics factory called Eureka Pottery Works in Lahore. By 1915 the ceramics factory was floundering, and Madan Gopal's father asked him to drop his studies in law and study the science of ceramics instead. Madan Gopal was able to get a scholarship to the Technical School at Stoke-on-Trent in England. It took him three years to get the highest technical diploma, which enabled him to work in Limoges, France.

Limoges is a city in southwest-central France. It is an ancient city but came into its own in the late eighteenth century when kaolin was discovered there. Kaolin is used in porcelain and is also known as China clay or porcelain clay. It is the purest type of clay known. Once kaolin was discovered near Limoges, the city became a centre for the porcelain industry. In a short time,

Limoges' porcelain became world famous and was known as the best in the world. It was in this town that Madan Gopal worked for a year. Along with his technical knowledge he now gained experience in factory operations and the manufacturing of porcelain.

Madan Gopal hoped to use his knowledge and experience to make his father's ceramics factory profitable again; but by the time he returned to Lahore, Eureka Pottery Works had shut down. Madan Gopal worked for a short while at Gwalior Potteries. He ended up at the Forman Christian College in Lahore, where he started a ceramics section. But his heart remained in industry.

On a visit to Calcutta in 1933 Madan Gopal had a chance to visit Bengal Potteries, which was the oldest and biggest ceramics factory in India. It had started in 1895 but by 1933 the company was in the red. The woes of the company continued as the communists gained control of the union and instigated the workers to go on strike. This affected the share price in the market—a Rs 10 share was trading at less than 50 paise.

Madan Gopal walked into this Bengal Potteries. Colonel Peart was the general manager of the company. The two, Madan Gopal and Colonel Peart, took a round of the factory. Madan Gopal's heart bled at the sight of the expensive kilns lying almost waste. He spent a couple of days at the factory and then told Colonel Peart that the sorry state of the company was due to a lack of technical knowledge and indifferent management.

'So, is there no hope for Bengal Potteries then?' asked Colonel Peart.

'No, no, I am not saying that. I am merely explaining why the factory is in this condition,' replied Madan Gopal. 'Of course, the factory and the business can be revived by someone who has the technical knowledge and can manage the factory.'

Colonel Peart immediately offered Madan Gopal the job of managing the factory.

Madan Gopal was at heart a ceramics industry man. His heart leapt with joy at the thought of running a large factory. He knew that he would be able to turn around the fortunes of the company and that he would run it successfully. But he also knew that he had no money to buy the business. It was then that he went to Shri Ram, who by then was one of the top industrialists of Delhi.

Shri Ram listened to Madan Gopal as his mind whirred in excitement. Since the time he had started thinking of diversifying into industries that had traditionally not been managed by Indians, he had not been able to find a suitable business. He could see now that this was the perfect opportunity. He was neither disheartened by the business being in the red nor worried about the workers' strike and go-slow movement. He was encouraged by Madan Gopal's enthusiasm and confidence.

Madan Gopal was indeed enthusiastic. 'Lala ji, you know how we Indians love to drink our tea,' he told Shri Ram. 'All of us—rich and poor—drink copious amounts of tea. And to drink tea you need mugs, cups and saucers, don't you?'

Shri Ram nodded.

'And these are things that the masses will buy. But if the right technology is used there is no reason why Indian pottery cannot be as good or even better than imported pottery. And that is what the richer people will buy,' Madan Gopal concluded.

Madan Gopal's enthusiasm was infectious. Shri Ram decided to throw in his lot with Madan Gopal. He told Madan

Gopal, 'You are a man after my own heart who believes "My centre is giving way, my right is in retreat; situation excellent, I shall attack!" You and I think alike, MG.'

In his mind Shri Ram had already run the checklist he used to judge any business. Would it fulfil an essential need for the country? Could it hold its own against foreign competition? Could it be run by Indians without undue reliance on foreign technicians? He checked off each of these three points and gave Madan the go-ahead.

It was a revolutionary decision by Shri Ram. In those times, most businessmen did not trust outsiders with their money. They invested in a new business and wanted to remain in the driver's seat. But Shri Ram had decided to put his money on a technical expert who would run the business. It was a decision taken ahead of the times—invest in a sound idea and leave the running of the business to experts.

Once Shri Ram had decided to invest in the business he moved fast. The old directors of Bengal Potteries were asked to resign, and a new company called M/s Shankar Lall Bhagat was formed to take over the management. The new directors were Shri Ram, Madan Gopal and one Bishan Agarwal, who was the brother-in-law of Murli Dhar. Madan Gopal took charge as the general manager of the company. The original share capital of Rs 10 lakh was written down to Rs 2.5 lakh. Thus, in 1934 it was as if Bengal Potteries was reborn with new parents. The proud parents were, of course, Shri Ram and Madan Gopal.

The new owners were proud indeed but were inundated with the problems of their new child. The quality of the products manufactured by Bengal Potteries left much to be desired, as did the behaviour of the workers. Compounding this was the problem of finance.

The first problem that Shri Ram addressed was the matter of finance. Since Bengal Potteries had been a loss-making unit, the share capital had been written down. Shri Ram increased the share capital to Rs 6 lakh and started the process of bringing in fresh capital. Even though Bengal Potteries was still not out of the red, the fact that Shri Ram had taken over the company galvanized the investing community. Applications for shares started pouring in. Purshotamdas Thakurdas and Padampat Singhania, Shri Ram's good friends and noted industrialists themselves, also applied for and received shares of the company.

Meanwhile Madan Gopal hit the ground running in his new role as the general manager. It was not an easy task, as he was met with the hostility of the workers. The workers, under the influence of the communist union leaders, heckled Madan Gopal whenever he visited the works. 'Look at the Punjabi intruder,' they yelled; 'Go back, outsider,' shouted others; 'Madan Gopal sahib, why are you wasting your time and money here? Many have come before you and we have sent them all back,' advised some others.

Madan Gopal went to Shri Ram with this problem and sought his advice. Shri Ram firmly believed that not only Bengal Potteries, but any company could survive and prosper only if it had the goodwill of the workers. His philosophy was to meet the demands of the labour but to stop if they took the shape of blackmail. With the experience of dealing with many workers for many years Shri Ram suspected that the demands of the workers at Bengal Potteries were more in the nature of blackmail.

He sat with Madan Gopal and discussed the matter with him. 'It will be essential to have our own trusted people here—people who are experienced in the pottery industry and who are strong labour masters. You've worked in Gwalior Potteries before, haven't you, MG? Surely there are some people there who you think will be loyal to you and will be efficient. See if you can get them to join this company,' said Shri Ram.

Madan Gopal took this matter on priority. He reached out to the right people in Gwalior Potteries. By this time word had spread about Shri Ram's interest in Bengal Potteries. Such was his reputation that everyone who was approached by Madan Gopal agreed willingly to join Bengal Potteries. Madan Gopal fired the mischief mongers in the factory along with the ringleader of the union.

As these changes were being made by Madan Gopal, Shri Ram ensured that the workers felt the impact of his personality and philosophy. By addressing the problem of the workers Shri Ram was also addressing the problem of the quality of Bengal Potteries products.

He knew that the problem of quality could not be addressed and resolved without the cooperation of the workers. He also knew that the quality of Bengal Potteries products had to be better than the competition for it to be taken seriously by the overseas market; within India the products had to be good but not expensive. For all this he needed the workers to change their mindset and attitude towards the new owners and towards their work.

He left the technical details of production quality to Madan Gopal. He focused on what he did best—on the people. He looked at all matters raised by the workers and studied them in detail. And then he confounded Madan Gopal when he recommended a wage hike for the workers who worked well. He also suggested that the working conditions be made more comfortable.

Madan Gopal was aghast at these suggestions. 'But Lala ji, these workers are giving us trouble and you want to reward them with a wage increase? he spluttered.

'MG, not all workers get up in the morning and come to work with the thought of creating a problem. There are good workers amongst all the people there. Your job will be to find them and reward them with a wage hike. With my experience I can tell you that sooner rather than later, other workers will follow suit. Of course, there will still be some troublemakers. Once you identify them, get rid of them immediately,' counselled Shri Ram.

Madan Gopal acted on this advice and was surprised at the speed with which the workers responded positively. But the problems of quality continued. And so did the pressure from Shri Ram.

When Shri Ram had started working at DCM he would spend some time each day talking with the cloth merchants in old Delhi and comparing the quality of his cloth with that of the competition. He did the same for Bengal Potteries. He went to various ceramics exhibitions and gave his feedback to Madan Gopal.

'I went to see an exhibition yesterday, but I found that the Gwalior Potteries products were much better—especially the toys, cups and saucers,' he wrote to Madan Gopal. He also asked for samples of products from the factory and then sent back his feedback my mail. 'The WC basins and the Indian-style pans that you sent as samples are too small and have no flushing arrangement. These need to be whiter in colour, bigger in size and must have flushing arrangements,' he wrote. And then soon after, he wrote to Madan Gopal again. 'I showed to some of my friends the teapot samples you had sent. They complained about the colours and the roughness of the teapots,' he said. 'So long as the quality of our goods is not up to the mark, difficulties about the sales will continue. You could look at smoothening the surface and improve the colour. Meanwhile you could look at some designs like painting of lines which could help.'

Madan Gopal rose to the occasion and handled the pressure from Shri Ram with more focus on production. He saw that the tunnel kilns in the factory needed work before they could be operated. Tunnel kilns comprise a set of kiln cars that pass through a hot tunnel. The kiln cars carry the product. The temperature of the kiln rises as the cars pass through it and then cools down towards the end. The tunnel kiln is used for large volumes of products and gives excellent consistency.

Once Madan Gopal got the tunnel kiln working optimally, production increased. He also worked on the quality and design of the products. Simultaneously he pruned down the costs and decreased the selling price. The market started taking note of Bengal Potteries.

Applying pressure to improve production and quality was not all that Shri Ram was doing—he had set himself the task of meeting senior government officials to secure orders for the electrical goods made at Bengal Potteries. He met Sir James Pitkethly of the Indian Stores Department and was able to get an order for ceramic insulators. He met Sir Thomas Ryan, director general of the Post and Telegraph Department, who was impressed by both Shri Ram and the products of Bengal Potteries.

The government orders helped improve the overall sales of the company. Within a year, Bengal Potteries made a profit of over Rs 1 lakh and declared a dividend of 6.25 per cent. This was a proud moment for Shri Ram, as the company had been able to declare a dividend after eleven years of losses.

The orders from the government were welcomed by Bengal Potteries but they also had Shri Ram worried. He knew that he could not depend on the government orders, as the senior officials could change from time to time. So, he strongly recommended to Madan Gopal that he look at some 'bazaar products'—products that were more retail in nature. Shri Ram also looked to tap the distant markets. Soon Bengal Potteries products were available in Peshawar, Burma, Bombay and Madras as well.

The strategy of focusing on retail products and distant markets paid off within a couple of years. In 1935 the overall revenue was divided almost equally between the government and bazaar products. However, by 1937 the bazaar products were contributing 80 per cent of the sales revenue. 'I am happy that we have succeeded in making our works independent of government business, which was at one time our mainstay,' Shri Ram said in a board meeting in 1938. Bengal Potteries was on a roll.

Madan Gopal, however, had quiet misgivings about the chatter in the market. He was upset when people said that Bengal Potteries had been turned around because of Shri Ram's money and influence. He felt that his hard and back-breaking work had gone unnoticed by the market. In fact, he even wrote to Shri Ram about his feelings.

'If only money and influence were the things required, this place would have been snatched up by some other party long ago. In the past history of this concern when they had two lakhs of rupees with them, an ICS officer as the managing director, the best of technical advice and a market in which prices were nearly four times what they are today, things were not so cheerful. Not that I am trying to blow my trumpet, but I only desire to bring to your mind my share of the work in building up this concern,' wrote Madan Gopal.

Shri Ram saw that he needed to do more than provide advice and criticism. He had realized some time back that the constant pressure from him was affecting the relationship between the two men. But he also knew that he had a duty towards the other members of the board and the shareholders. Now he felt that it was time to reassure Madan Gopal.

'I know that my telling you every time about these things might someday make you lose your patience,' Shri Ram wrote to Madan Gopal. 'I do not underrate the value or importance of your work, nor have I anywhere claimed the credit for myself, not only in the matter of the pottery, but anywhere else. I always admit that all my credit is due to my colleagues. But I cannot agree that the position of the managing agents or finance, including capital and loans, plays no part in the success of a concern whether in the way of reducing interest charges or in creating confidence amongst sellers and buyers.'

The matter rested there, as by this time (1938), the demand for ceramic products had increased across the country. However, most of the plant machinery was old and bordering on obsolete, which had started to affect the quality and cost of the products. To add to the troubles, cheaper imported ceramics had started coming into India. Shri Ram saw that steps had to be taken to decrease the cost of production and increase the quality of goods. He also realized that using the latest methods along with modern machinery was needed to set things right.

Shri Ram therefore asked Madan Gopal to go to Europe and the United States to study the latest production techniques. Madan Gopal left in the summer of 1938 and visited as many ceramic factories as he could across the various countries. He was impressed with a German firm and placed an order for the latest type of tunnel kilns and gas producers. After Madan Gopal returned, three new kilns were fired and the plant modernized. The new plant was a resounding success.

Delighted, Madan Gopal wrote to Shri Ram. 'I have the highest regard and respect for your views and your keen intelligence and observations in all matters concerning industry,' he said. 'I do not think I could care for the views of anyone in the whole of India so much as I do for yours.'

14

A Strike in DCM Breaks Shri Ram's Heart

AROUND the time that Shri Ram was working on the Bengal Potteries project, there was a major development that affected DCM in general and Shri Ram personally.

There was a strike in DCM in 1934. This came as a shock to Shri Ram, as he felt betrayed by the workers. 'Strikes were unthinkable in this mill,' he said to the directors of the board. 'You all will remember that we had founded a company union in 1929,' he added. The union formed by the company had the support of the workers and Shri Ram had said that any activity relating to the organization and the workers should be handled by the company union. Any activity by any worker outside it would be seen as a breach of contract and the company would consider dismissing such employees.

Delhi, in early 1930, was going through a glut in the labour market. Many mills in Ahmedabad and Bombay had decreased production. The worldwide depression had found its way to India as well. The mills in the west had started firing workers. This resulted in many skilled workers, especially weavers, migrating to the north. Delhi was an attractive destination for many.

Meanwhile, around 1931 all building activities related to the infrastructure in the new capital, Delhi, were stopped by the government. This led to a large number of unskilled labourers also looking for jobs, which had become scarce due to the economic slowdown.

Simultaneously, another situation was developing. This was reported by the Royal Commission of Labour in India in 1931. As part of their report, the commission pointed out that the spread of communism had affected the workers in many cities. The commission further pointed out that many of the strikes at mills were a result of the communist leaders and organizations instigating the workers.

The mill workers in Bombay had responded to a call for a general strike in April 1934. The call to strike was given by the All-India Textile Workers' Council. From Bombay the strike spread rapidly to other cities. Delhi, too, responded to the call to strike.

The workers of DCM went on strike in April 1934. About 6,500 workers struck work. Outsiders, too, got involved. The strike was led by Harihar Nath Shastri of Kanpur, who was a firebrand member of the All-India Trade Union Congress. The Delhi Labour Union also got involved.

Shri Ram was sent a list of their grievances as their reasons for striking. One of the reasons was the wages paid to them.

The workers claimed that they were being paid much less than the prevalent market rates. Another reason was the housing and working conditions of the workers, which they claimed were suboptimal. The workers further claimed that they were faced with hardships because they were forced to pay 8 annas per month to the cleaners of the machinery. They also claimed that the management was overworking them as the weavers were each given four looms to tend to instead of the earlier two looms.

Shri Ram was baffled when he listened to the reasons. He had good reason to believe that the allegations and claims made by the workers had no legs to stand on. But the workers were in a militant mood and listened to no placatory talk by the management of DCM. Trade union leaders such as Raghbir Singh, Satyavati and Farid ul Haq also joined the striking workers. These leaders were quick to whip up their passions. They asked the workers to think about the fact that the shareholders were paid a 45 per cent dividend, but the workers were paid low wages.

Matters took a serious turn when the striking workers and leaders resorted to violence. There were over one hundred workers and other people injured in the violence, some even seriously. There were 500 workers still at work in the mill, even at this time. But after the violence, work at the DCM factory came to a standstill.

The workers then took out a procession, shouting slogans against the mill and Shri Ram. The march culminated at Queen's Garden (now called Azad Park) behind the Town Hall in Chandni Chowk. The trade union leaders made fiery speeches to the workers.

While the trade union leaders were addressing the workers at Queen's Park, Shri Ram was addressing the non-striking workers at the mill. Though these workers had not joined the protestors, they were not at work either. The trade union leaders had threatened the non-striking workers with dire consequences if they went back to work.

Shri Ram knew this, and his speech was placatory and forward-focused. He told the workers that the wages at DCM were above those at other mills. He requested them to return to work. He assured them that they would be given full protection.

The next day Shri Ram went further. He put up a notice at the mill gate informing the workers that if they did not resume work by the end of day, they would be replaced by new recruits. However, if the workers, even the striking workers, came back to work the past would be forgotten and forgiven.

This strategy worked. Workers started to trickle back to work. In a week almost 70 per cent of the workers were back in the mill. The threat of fresh recruitment was rolled back. He even gave out silver medals to workers who had risked their lives to run the mills during the strike and gave gold ones to the workers who helped get the striking workers back to work.

The mill started humming with activity once again. But Shri Ram was extremely upset at what he believed was a betrayal. He could have used the triumph over the trade unions to browbeat the workers, especially since they had betrayed his trust. But he was pragmatic enough to know that there was nothing he could do with a bunch of surly workers. Their cooperation was essential if he wanted to grow the business.

Shri Ram wanted to send out the message that he took the grievances of the workers seriously. He told them that he would get an impartial inquiry into the matter.

Shri Ram instituted an inquiry committee and persuaded the principal of Jamia Millia Islamia to head it. Dr Zakir Hussain thus headed the inquiry commission and was assisted by Deputy Mal Jain. Dr Zakir Hussain later went on to become the third President of independent India.

The management of DCM gave the inquiry commission their full support. They placed their records and other material in front of the commission. Any information sought by the commission was promptly provided by the management. On the other side, the workers were represented by Raghbir Singh and Fazle Karim, who was the secretary of the Delhi Labour Union. The commission also met with the office bearers of the DCM union and examined their records as well. Further, Zakir Hussain and Mal Jain visited the shop floor and paid surprise visits to the staff quarters where they met and spoke with workers across all levels.

After a thorough and detailed investigation, the two-man commission presented its report to Shri Ram. 'An overwhelming mass of evidence forces us to express as our considered opinion that the strike of April 1934 was not a genuine strike to seek redress for any real grievance or disability, nor one to improve the economic conditions of the workers. It was differently conceived, and we think we would not be far wrong in saying that it was an attempt by a few discharged men to use the Bombay strike as a pretext for a sympathetic stoppage of the working of Delhi Cloth Mills,' the report said.

The report then went into the details of each grievance and gave their considered opinion about it.

The first matter was the wage dispute. 'We consider these demands to be unjustified and doubly so during the present period of economic depression,' the commission said. 'The authorities of Delhi Cloth Mills have been able to establish conclusively that the general level of the wages paid to their workers is higher not only in comparison with the local mills, but also in comparison with wages in the other important industrial centres in the country. It is only in a few sub-sections of the spinning department that only Ahmedabad and Bombay pay slightly higher wages which they too have lately sought to reduce. On the other hand, the wage level in winding and warping departments is practically double that obtaining elsewhere; and the normal working hours of the mills are nine instead of ten in all the other mills in the country.'

The next matter was the set of complaints about the living and working conditions of the workers and their families. 'We are sorry to note that quite a number of these grievances were imaginary and almost all unduly exaggerated,' the report said. 'The workers' quarters are marked by their cleanliness, their cemented roads and drains, electric lights, ample supply of filtered water, open spaces, common meeting places, loudspeakers and provision for physical exercise and outdoor enjoyment.' The two members of the commission also noted that they were impressed by the DCM management's interest in the workforce. 'We feel that so far as welfare work is concerned the DC Mills may well claim to lead the way for other concerns in the country.'

The other two matters were also dismissed by the commission. Zakir Hussain and Deputy Mal Jain found that the deduction of 8 annas from the wages of the weavers was in fact initiated by the weavers themselves. And the complaint about each weaver having to manage four looms instead of two was found to be a non-starter. 'We think,' the report said, 'with improved machinery and material an efficient weaver should be able to attend not only four but even six, eight or even more looms.'

The workers' strike jolted Shri Ram out of his comfort zone. He had been alarmed anyway about the rise of the leftists within the Congress and their disdain for businessmen. He also felt let down by the Congress, especially as he had contributed to the cause of the political party as well as to the causes held dear by Mahatma Gandhi. In fact, soon after Bharat Ram's wedding, Shri Ram had taken his son and daughter-in-law, Sheila, to meet with Mahatma Gandhi, who was visiting Delhi.

'I want you to bless the children, Gandhi ji. They are just beginning their life together and need all your good wishes and blessings,' said Shri Ram.

Mahatma Gandhi was, as usual, sitting on the ground at his spinning wheel. He looked at the newly-wed couple. The new bride was wearing a silk saree with a gold border and was decked in jewellery. As they bent to touch the feet of the Mahatma to seek his blessings, Gandhi gestured for them to sit down in front of him. He started talking about the work he was doing, especially the Swadeshi movement. He even quipped that the Swadeshi movement was helping companies like DCM, as more Indians were buying Indian-made textiles. He then talked about how he was unafraid and unashamed of begging people for money for his cause. He then looked at the young bride and said, 'Do you know that my thirst for begging is simply unquenchable? I do not mind taking ornaments either.'

The young bride understood Gandhi's message. She looked at her husband and father-in-law. Both of them, too, had received the message. The two men nodded at Sheila. She looked at her arms, which were laden with gold bangles. One by one she took them off and offered them to Gandhi, who accepted them with thanks.

Since he had supported the Congress in the Swadeshi movement, Shri Ram had expected the party to make it easier, not more difficult, for businessmen. And then the incident of 1931 came back to haunt him.

In the early 1930s members of the Congress had been collecting money for the party. In 1931, Shri Ram was paid a visit by Bhulabhai Desai. He met Shri Ram and told him that Sardar Patel wanted a contribution for the Congress. Shri Ram readily agreed and promised a sum of Rs 25,000. Bhulabhai Desai went back to Sardar Patel but returned in haste with the message that the contribution was too little and that the Congress expected more. Shri Ram told Desai that the business was experiencing difficulties due to the Depression and even the sum promised was more than he could afford. Eventually, Bhulabhai Desai came back and told Shri Ram that if he failed to give Rs 1 lakh as his contribution there would be a strike in his mill. Never one to succumb to blackmail of any kind, Shri Ram stood up and told Desai to go back and tell Sardar Patel that even the offer of Rs 25,000 now stood withdrawn. 'Let there be a strike in my factory,' he added.

With the matter of the workers' strike behind him, Shri Ram decided to change, drastically, the way DCM was managed. He was already the largest shareholder of the company. But he still reported to a board of directors. Now, he wanted to manage the affairs of the company and its various businesses differently. Towards this end he constituted a managing agency to manage the business.

The managing agency system had in fact evolved in the second quarter of the nineteenth century in India. The system was adopted by London as an efficient way to manage joint stock companies operating in the Indian subcontinent, especially where the shareholders of the companies had no first-hand knowledge of the business. The system worked as follows: the managing agency operated essentially as an entrepreneur. When the managing agency saw a business opportunity, for example a cotton mill, it raised venture capital from friends and associates of the managing agent or promoter. The shortfall in funding, if any, was borrowed from a bank. With the funds in hand, the managing agency bought the mill and set it up to operate. Once the mill and the business were running successfully, the managing agency sold its majority shareholding to the public. However, the managing agency signed a long-term management contract with the company, which gave it the right to continue to manage the business. The proceeds thus derived were invested in some other business, say, a sugar mill. Typically, a managing agency made key decisions on behalf of its operating companies and the decisions included the products to manufacture, which markets to target and where to get the raw materials from.

The advantage of the managing agency system was that it enabled the agency to control and run several business enterprises with a small financial stake in each. A managing agency's ability to raise capital from the bank and the public depended on its track record and reputation. The agency earned generous commissions either as a percentage of sales or profits plus other fees.

The managing agency system was hugely popular in pre-independent India, as the British had adopted it with enthusiasm. By the First World War, the managing agencies controlled 75 per cent of the industrial capital of India and almost half of the industrial employment. And by 1954 the managing agencies accounted for 51 per cent of the share capital of all companies.

The managing agency set up by Shri Ram was called Messrs Shankar Lall Bharat Ram and Company. This was a partnership firm with Shri Ram, his brother Shankar Lall and his three sons Murli Dhar, Bharat Ram and Charat Ram as the partners.

The board of DCM met in 1937 and passed a resolution that abolished the post of the secretary. The board further appointed M/s Shankar Lall Bharat Ram and Company as the managing agency for Delhi Cloth and General Mills Company Ltd.

The managing agency signed an agreement with DCM that allowed it to manage the affairs of the company. The managers, or the agents, had far-reaching powers. The agreement allowed the agents to take charge of all property, moveable and immoveable, including books and other outstandings belonging to the company and then to preserve, keep and maintain records and account books of the company.

The agreement further gave the agents the authority to purchase lands, buildings, raw or manufactured material stores and machinery; erect buildings and machinery; and take or give on lease such lands, buildings or factories. All this was to be done on behalf of and at the expense of the company.

The agents were also responsible for the sale of the products and properties of the company. They were enabled to draw on the funds of the company in the banks and to take on loans and mortgages.

The agreement categorically said that the company and its directors would not interfere in the agents' management of the company's affairs. The company also indemnified the agents against all losses, if any, suffered by them in the discharge of their obligations to the company.

For managing the affairs of the company, the agents were paid a commission of 10 per cent of the net annual profits of the company in addition to a salary of Rs 4,000 per month. Further, the agents were allowed the use of a motor car of the company, and they were allowed to draw from the funds of the company reasonable sums of money as a reimbursement for expenses incurred in the course of business.

With the appointment of the managing agency, M/s Shankar Lall Bharat Ram and Company, and the agreement signed with DCM, the balance of power shifted completely and unequivocally to Shri Ram. He was the senior-most partner of the managing agency and acquired sweeping powers to plan and execute all aspects of business for DCM. It was almost as if he had become a virtual dictator.

A new phase began in the life of the DCM Group, as it did in the life of Shri Ram.

15

Jay Engineering and Usha Sewing Machines

HIS role as the managing agent for DCM gave Shri Ram total power over not only the cloth mill in Delhi but also over all businesses spawned by the main company, including the Daurala sugar mill, Bengal Potteries and Lyallpur Cotton Mills. The businesses were doing well and were providing employment to hundreds of workers. However, with the expansion of production, the mills started facing a shortage of trained workers. This was a problem for Shri Ram, as he knew that manpower, especially trained and skilled manpower, was key to his ambitions of expanding the businesses even further. He also realized that, as his businesses expanded, even geographically, he needed more supervisors and officers for those factories and offices.

As was typical of the man, Shri Ram looked at the problem from the point of view of the workers. He saw that it was not a problem of scarcity of men but one of a scarcity of trained men. He had a solution but knew that he had to get buy-in from the employees for it to be implemented with conviction.

He called a meeting of some of the factory supervisors and other officers in his office at DCM. He let the men settle down before speaking.

'If I ask you to recruit one hundred trained workers by next week will you be able to?' asked Shri Ram, looking around the room.

The men were perplexed. One of them gathered the courage to ask the question that was on everyone's mind.

'Lala ji, why do you want so many new workers so soon?' asked one intrepid manager.

'Forget about why I want to recruit,' answered Shri Ram brusquely, waving at the man to sit down. 'Assume I want to recruit. Will you be able to get me one hundred trained workers by next week?'

All the men in the room shook their heads slowly.

Shri Ram had known the answer and was not surprised. But he was working according to a plan.

'Why can't you recruit, eh?' he asked. 'I see so many men all around. Why can't you recruit them? Is it that they do not want a job?'

The men all spoke up.

'No no no, Lala ji, it is not that they don't want a job. It is just that we cannot recruit them because they do not have the necessary skills,' one manager said on behalf of everyone.

'Ah, so that is the problem. These men want a job, are willing to work hard but are not trained,' said Shri Ram as if the matter had become clear to him. He thought for a moment as if pondering over a problem.

'So, where can they go to get trained? Because if they are trained we can recruit them, no?' he asked.

'Lala ji, there is no one who can train them better than us,' said one manager proudly.

'Anyone who has worked with us gets higher wages outside because everyone knows that any worker at any DCM factory is trained to do the job well,' said another supervisor even more proudly.

'If you are the best teachers, are you willing to become their teachers then?' asked Shri Ram, looking around the room with a glint in his eyes. The discussion was going according to his plan.

The men in the room did not know where the discussion was going.

'What do you mean, Lala ji? We, their teachers, how?' asked one manager, scratching his head as he tried to make sense of what was being asked.

The others also leaned forward to hear the answer from Shri Ram.

Shri Ram knew that he had their interest now.

He explained that he had thought of an apprenticeship scheme. Under this scheme, untrained workers would be recruited and put through a training programme in which they would be trained across various assignments. The new apprentices would be paid a stipend while on training.

'My aim is to train people not for the job of workers but so that over the years they can also become junior and senior officers. But I firmly believe that no officer can be effective if he has not worked at the ground level,' explained Shri Ram. The others in the room nodded in agreement.

'I see that you all agree. That's good,' continued Shri Ram as he took stock of the room. 'Therefore, an apprentice will have to work as a worker for five years. And you know the best part? As part of the apprenticeship programme, once they start working on the job as workers they will also get the worker-wages. Now, don't you think this will be a good scheme?'

The men in the room were silent. It was such a good suggestion that many of them were kicking themselves for not having thought of it themselves.

But there were some sceptics as well.

'But, Lala ji, after all the effort we put in to train them, what if they leave?' asked one shop floor supervisor.

'Well, you can't force people to work with you, can you?' asked Shri Ram. 'People leave for better wages, but they also leave if they find the environment they are working in unbearable. But we at DCM are known to take care of our workers and their families. Your responsibility as the officers of the company is to make sure that the supervisors and you yourselves help make the environment conducive to workers wanting to stay on.' Shri Ram did not want the supervisors to make life difficult for the new apprentices.

The apprenticeship scheme was started in DCM for all its businesses in 1937. It got off to a slow start, as it was a new concept in the industry. But soon, word got around, and eager, raw workers began lining up. This scheme, in a sense, was a precursor to the management and graduate trainee programmes currently run by many organizations. In fact, even up until the 1970s and 1980s the trainee scheme at DCM was a coveted position in the industry. Top talent from the best universities and business schools in India were recruited into this management trainee programme.

Shri Ram's foresight and understanding of the workers back in the 1930s helped DCM attract talent for many years ahead as well. And it helped him get a better quality workforce across all his businesses.

One of the businesses that he focused on was Bengal Potteries. Shri Ram went to Calcutta often to spend time at Bengal Potteries. He usually stayed with Madan Gopal Bhagat at his home. When Shri Ram was in Calcutta in December 1937, Madan Gopal invited a visitor to meet with him. When the visitor walked in, Shri Ram exclaimed in delight.

'Ah, Bishandas, we meet again!' said Shri Ram delightedly.

Shri Ram had first met Bishandas in the late 1920s. He had gone to Calcutta to attend a Congress session and his friend, Hans Raj Gupta, had invited him to stay with him. Hans Raj Gupta was the owner of Delhi Iron Syndicate & Company and was a well-known person in the industry. The Congress session had attracted many visitors to Calcutta, and the day before Shri Ram was to arrive, Hans Raj found that his house was full. He realized that he could not offer Shri Ram a separate room to stay in. Hans Raj's friend, Bishandas Basil, heard about the predicament and offered to host Shri Ram at his own residence.

Both men had not met since then but the intervening ten or so years had not dimmed the memory that Shri Ram had of Bishandas. The man was full of restless energy and creative passion, and this drew Shri Ram to him.

Bishandas was happy to meet Shri Ram, who, by now, was one of India's leading industrialists. There was some talk of work at the dinner table during which Shri Ram realized that Bishandas was not altogether happy with the work he was doing. He asked Bishandas if the two of them could meet the next day.

'I am keen to know more about what you are doing, Bishandas. Let's meet tomorrow at leisure and you can tell me about your sewing machines,' said Shri Ram, patting Bishandas on the arm as he leaned towards the other man.

Bishandas was only too happy to meet with Shri Ram. It was indeed true that Bishandas had run into business problems. He saw this as an opportunity to seek counsel from the industrialist.

Shri Ram and Bishandas met the next day. Once they were seated comfortably, Shri Ram encouraged Bishandas to start speaking. The man needed no encouragement, and once he started talking, it was as if a dam had burst. He spoke with fervour and with passion as he told Shri Ram his story.

The story began in the early 1900s, when young Bishandas had joined Roorkee College of Engineering. He was a good scholar, and after graduating with a diploma in engineering, he went to England on a scholarship for specialized training and studies. Once he returned to India, Bishandas joined the Post and Telegraph Department in 1906 as an apprentice engineer. He soon made a mark there due to his exceptional engineering skills. Before long he was the superintendent of the workshop attached to the Central Telegraph Office in Calcutta.

One of the main duties of Bishandas' department was to order equipment. As the head of the department, Bishandas needed to sign each order. Most of the equipment ordered by the department needed to be imported, as India was not a big manufacturer. This pained Bishandas. He was an engineer by profession, had studied abroad and had interacted with numerous engineers overseas. He was sure that Indians, given an opportunity, could manufacture any equipment within

India. Thus, every time he signed an import order for a piece of equipment, the question that came to his mind was, 'Why can this not be manufactured in India?'

Bishandas loved to spend time in the research and experiment cell of his department. It was there that he would tinker with various mechanical devices. Like a child, he would take them apart and try to put them together again. He spent long hours after work examining the insides of fans, sewing machines, telephones and even typewriters. If the machine had a motor inside it, he would be even more excited to take it apart so he could understand how the motor worked. His various experiments made his hypothesis even stronger—he was sure that India could produce such equipment.

He would have started an engineering unit, but his government job came in the way. As an alternative, he persuaded his friend, Binay Krishna Rohtagi, to start an engineering company. Binay Rohtagi was a big businessman in Calcutta. He saw merit in Bishandas' suggestion and started the Scientific and Electrical Instruments Manufacturing Company in 1921. The company specialized in the repair of telephone, telegraph and railway signalling equipment.

The next decade passed quickly, but Bishandas' desire to start manufacturing equipment in India did not dim. He kept exploring the workings of various types of equipment but there was no single item that fired him up more than the others. But then a chance meeting with a friend changed that.

One of his friends ran an agency for Pfaff sewing machines. Established in 1862, Pfaff was a German brand. It was known in the market for its sleek designs and high performance. Bishandas' friend told him that India imported over 60,000 sewing machines each year. These were used by tailors, housewives, harness-makers and cobblers. Bishandas was surprised at this large number. Surely, he thought, India could manufacture sewing machines.

With this thought in mind, he asked his friend to help him buy a second-hand machine. He took the machine to his garage, which he used for his experiments. The desire to start producing a sewing machine in India ran deep in him. But he also realized that he could not do this alone. Thus, he invited four of the best mechanics in his department to accompany him home one evening after office hours.

The four men were intrigued and went along with their boss. As they entered the garage they saw a Pfaff sewing machine sitting proudly in the middle of the large table in the centre of the room. They looked at Bishandas enquiringly.

'Let us see what this machine is made of,' said Bishandas.

The four men and Bishandas took the machine apart. They carefully spread the parts on various tables and numbered each part. After a few hours the machine was completely dismembered.

'Good god, there are 360 separate components!' exclaimed one of the mechanics, his face falling.

'Never mind the number, let us see how many of these we can make,' replied Bishandas.

Each man looked at the various parts and separated the ones that he thought he could make. Within minutes the mood in the room changed. The men realized that the task of manufacturing a sewing machine was not impossible.

Bishandas' garage workshop became the place where the five men would gather each day after office hours. The workshop had a lathe, a press, a capstan, a milling and a drilling machine. These were the five bare minimum machine tools that were needed to build a prototype of the Pfaff sewing machine. The prototype would require copying each individual part.

The men worked for almost eight months. And their joint labour was fruitful. In early 1934 they had a prototype of a sewing machine that could stitch. It was 100 per cent indigenous. The men were overjoyed. They named the machine Usha, after Bishandas' daughter. The first Usha machine was presented to Binay Rohtagi, who had provided invaluable financial support during the eight months of work.

With the Usha sewing machine in place, Bishandas looked for partners for the business venture. Binay Rohtagi introduced him to Kishen Lal Poddar, another rich industrialist of Calcutta. A new company was created in November 1935 and was named Jay Engineering Works. Jai Kishen was Kishen Poddar's father and the company bore his name. The company became known as JEW.

The company continued to be operated from Bishandas' garage. The number of people working there increased manifold. Within a year the manufacturing unit in the garage was churning out two sewing machines a day. The fifty machines produced each month were sold largely through a door-to-door sales effort. The company had employed a sales manager who had a few sales assistants—mostly ladies. These ladies went knocking on doors to sell Usha sewing machines. They did demonstrations for those interested as well. The fact that it was an 'Indian' machine was used liberally in all sales talk. These were the years when the Swadeshi movement was strong, and patriotism played some part in the sales. The price difference between the Usha and Pfaff machines added to the sales pitch. The Indian machine was nearly Rs 30 cheaper than the foreign one.

Usha may have been cheaper than the foreign machines, but it was not as attractive as its foreign competitors. Usha was a homegrown machine lacking the sleek finish of the foreign ones. Bishandas was aware of this and was sure that he could produce a better-looking product with more modern production facilities. However, Rohtagi and Poddar were unwilling to put more capital into the venture. They lacked the conviction that an Indian production unit using Indian materials could churn out products that could compete with foreign ones.

'So, this is where I am at, Lala ji,' sighed Bishandas as he finished his story, looking forlorn. 'I know that we can give the foreign machines a run for their money, but I don't have the money. No one seems to believe that we Indians can do this. Even my optimism and enthusiasm are taking a hit now.'

Shri Ram leaned back into the sofa as he took a deep breath. He had listened to the story intently. More than the story he had watched Bishandas's face first light up and then slowly dim in enthusiasm as he told his story. Shri Ram was a man who understood people. He also understood business opportunities. In Bishandas he saw a man who was full of creative ingenuity, patriotic fervour and almost limitless optimism. In Usha Shri Ram saw an opportunity to do something completely new, something European-style and, most importantly, something that India did not yet produce but could be proud of once it was indeed produced. But before taking a call he needed to see the business plan.

'Bishandas, I am willing to look at Usha, but I need more details. Will you be willing to share these with me?' asked Shri Ram.

Bishandas was more than willing to share as many details as Shri Ram wanted. He saw his dream, which had been fading, suddenly start shining again. He knew that if Shri Ram got involved then the future of Usha was bright. He therefore readily agreed when Shri Ram asked him to travel to Delhi for a more detailed business discussion.

In January 1938 Bishandas visited the DCM offices in Delhi. Shri Ram had asked some of the senior executives of DCM to join in the discussions. There were two engineers—T.R. Gupta and B.D. Pathak—to discuss the engineering part of the business. Bishandas had been authorized by Kishen Poddar, chairman of Jay Engineering, to represent the company for all discussions.

The business meetings were spread over three days. Shri Ram asked Bishandas to meet with the members of the managing agency—Madan Mohan Lal Shri Ram & Company. This was a new managing agency floated by Shri Ram, and it was this agency that would be the managing agent of Jay Engineering, if the discussions progressed along expected lines.

After the exhaustive and exhausting discussions Bishandas returned to Calcutta an energized man. He knew he had had a breakthrough in the business. Shri Ram had bought into the business plan. Bishandas now needed to get the other senior partners in Jay Engineering—Rohtagi and Poddar—to agree. These two men readily agreed to Shri Ram's proposal as they were not keen to invest further in the business.

In February 1938 the old Jay Engineering was wound up and a new Jay Engineering Works was born. This was now a public limited liability company. The old shareholders were paid a sum of Rs 50,000. The capital of the company was increased to Rs 15 lakhs. M/s Madan Mohan Lal Shri Ram & Company was appointed as the managing agent of the company. It would receive 12.5 per cent of the net profits of the company as commission.

Shri Ram had no difficulty in raising new capital for the company. He persuaded his friends—Padampat Singhania, Karam Chand Thapar, Hans Raj Gupta and Madan Gopal Bhagat—to invest in this company and to join the board as directors. Singhania and Thapar were two well-known industrialists of north India. Their association with Jay Engineering enhanced the stature of the company and gave it a more national character.

Bishandas was appointed as chief engineer. Shri Ram was aware of the inventive capabilities of his chief engineer. He also liked to work on a large scale. He knew that Bishandas had experimented with fans, typewriters, water meters, railway signalling equipment and even stoves. But all these needed more space to manufacture than the garage at the back of Bishandas' house. They also needed better machine tools.

With a view to expanding the manufacturing capabilities and capacities of Jay Engineering, Shri Ram looked for land in Calcutta. He finally found what he was looking for—31 bighas of open land outside the southern part of Calcutta. With the land identified for the manufacturing unit, Shri Ram ordered machine tools. The foundation stone was laid, and work began on the construction. Shri Ram left the details to Bishandas and went off to Europe with his family.

Shri Ram was accompanied by his son Bharat, his daughter-in-law Sheila and their young son Vinay. Madan Gopal, a friend and business associate of Shri Ram, also accompanied the family. The group spent some time in the thermal spas in the Bavarian town of Bad Kissingen, Germany. However, much of the time was spent visiting factories across Europe where Shri

Ram learnt about modern manufacturing techniques. Then he went to London along with Vinay. Bharat and Sheila continued their vacation in Europe.

While in Germany, unknowingly, both Bharat Ram and Sheila ended up taking part in Hitler's Nuremberg rally. The young couple were in the town and saw a protest march with many people on the streets and waving flags. They did not realize the orientation of the march and thought it would be good fun to join the marchers. It was only later that they realized the enormity of what they had done!

Bharat Ram and Sheila were in Germany well before the war started. But the atmosphere was already tense. The couple was on a tourist bus in Berlin when they saw the bus ahead of them being stopped. As they watched in horror, men, women and children were asked to get off and were lined up in a field, where they were shot. Bharat and Sheila were terrified and hid behind the seats of their own tourist bus. They could not get out of Germany fast enough. The rest of the holiday was not as eventful for the Shri Ram family. They spent six months overseas.

In Shri Ram's absence, Bishandas was the man in charge of all operations. The new factory at Prince Anwar Shah Road was ready and operational. But the company had not seen much change in the day-to-day management of business. Bishandas, in charge of the new factory with modern machines, had set himself two objectives—to improve the quality of manufactured products and to increase production quantities. But he ran into problems and the factory was not working as envisaged.

Once he returned to India, Shri Ram quickly took stock of Jay Engineering. He realized that Bishandas may have been a good engineer but managing a large workforce was not his strong point. Shri Ram believed that the success of a factory and business was heavily dependent on the relations with the workers and the high engagement levels of the workers vis-à-vis their work.

Shri Ram decided to spend more time at the factory. He started visiting Calcutta more frequently and staying in the city for longer periods of time. His day in Calcutta would start early. He would go to the factory on Prince Anwar Shah Road and watch the workers coming in to work. He would observe their body language and overall demeanour. At lunchtime he would join the workers.

The staff knew the routine. Just before lunchtime a charpoy would be put under a tree. A fresh white sheet would cover the charpoy. Shri Ram would sit in the shade and wait for the workers to trickle out of the factory. While some went straight for the food, others came and sat around the charpoy. Some sat cross-legged while others hitched up their pyjamas and squatted on the ground.

Shri Ram talked to them simply, in a language they understood. He asked them about their work and about the problems they faced. He also repeatedly told them that Jay Engineering was as much the workers' property as it was his. He talked about India and how industrialization would help not only India but also all Indians.

The workers would nod as they listened. Some talked about the work while others gave suggestions. One man, carried away by the informal atmosphere, piped up with a comment that made everyone laugh. '*Kala aadmi, kaali masheen, gorey ko nikaal do*! (We are black people; the machines like us are also black; we get on better with the machines than with the white man. Turn out the white man)!' he said. The simple sentiment drew cackles of laughter from everyone. Shri Ram also laughed loudly.

Then, turning serious, he told the gathered men, 'A machine does not distinguish a Hindu from a Mussalman. Neither is there low caste and high caste in front of a machine. We are all equal in the eyes of the machine.'

The men nodded in agreement.

'You think that you are humble workers and carry no weight in the scheme of things?' he asked.

'Lala ji, of course we are humble workers. Why do you even ask this question?' said one worker.

Shri Ram waited patiently as the others nodded and murmured in agreement. 'You all work with the machines, correct?' he asked the gathered men. Then, without waiting for their answer, he continued, looking intently at all of them, 'All of you know that the smallest, humblest screw or nut taken out from the machine can bring the biggest machine to a complete standstill.

'You think of yourself as humble workers? In reality you are like that mighty screw or nut. The nation itself can go to ruin if the workers in it come to a standstill. Our motherland will suffer. Therefore, it is our duty to be true patriots and work honestly and with dedication to ensure that our motherland prospers.'

The workers saw merit in the logic and nodded sagely.

Shri Ram was not finished. 'You work with your hands and that is the biggest puja you can perform. India needs more people who work with their hands for the betterment of the country. The last thing we need is more babus.

Naam liya karo, kaam kiya karo (take the name of God and do your work).'

Shri Ram not only sat and talked with the workers but also took care to single out good workers and reward them. Some he patted on the back in front of all others; others he rewarded with cash from his own pocket; he even gave radio sets and cameras to exceptional workers. The workers developed an affection for their Lala ji. But more importantly, they developed a sense of ownership in Jay Engineering. The workers believed Shri Ram when he told them, 'This is your factory, I am only a custodian.' The motivation level of the workers rose, and it was reflected in the output.

Besides the workers Shri Ram also met with senior officers of the company. Once during each of his stays in Calcutta, the senior officers were invited to dinner by Shri Ram. The pre-dinner talk revolved around the work and business. Shri Ram would set the ball rolling. He reviewed the progress as well as the failures of the business. The officers listened intently as Shri Ram praised some officers and critiqued others. Shri Ram then gave the officers an opportunity to talk about the problems and difficulties they faced.

Once the business talk was over everyone moved to the dinner table. The talk at the dinner table was on matters other than business. After dinner, Shri Ram would request a few officers to accompany him to the movies—usually Indian films with a religious or social theme.

These initiatives by Shri Ram bore fruit. Simultaneously, Bishandas focused on production. The two strategies worked well in tandem, and Jay Engineering started to turn out more and better-quality machines. Bishandas also started producing hurricane lanterns and water meters.

The sewing machines and hurricane lanterns needed a robust distribution system. Jay Engineering did not have a large sales force that could service the small and large retail stores across the country. Shri Ram realized that distribution was one of the main factors that could propel sales. He did not believe it was viable to build a captive sales force. Jay Engineering was a manufacturing company, not a sales distribution one. He looked around for solutions.

Shri Ram thought back to his early days at DCM. He remembered the sales agents he had appointed in north India. He wanted to adopt the same system for sewing machines and hurricane lanterns. Rohtagi, one of the early investors in Jay Engineering, showed interest in taking on agencies for the company. Shri Ram was only too happy to deal with a known person. Rohtagi was given the territories of Bengal, Uttar Pradesh and Punjab. The western region was proving to be a bit of a challenge till Shri Ram was told about M/s Bell & Company. This was a reputed firm based in Bombay that had a distribution network for imported sewing machines. Shri Ram signed Bell & Co as a distribution agent for the entire western region.

The agents were paid a commission of 20 per cent of the sales along with an incentive of Rs 5 per sewing machine sold. As part of their agreement, the agents were required to have showrooms where Usha sewing machines were displayed. Further, the showrooms had to have facilities for demonstration for those customers who wanted to see the machine in action. The agents were also required to recruit a trained mechanic to address customer complaints, if any. Shri Ram understood that the agents could not penetrate deep into the smaller towns and villages. Thus, he allowed the agents to appoint sub-agents in the hinterland and upcountry towns. The agents were free to set the commission for the sub-agents, which, in any case, came out of their 20 per cent. Shri Ram also understood the importance of advertising, as the foreign machines, especially

Singer, were promoting their brands. Thus, Shri Ram offered a commitment to advertise the sewing machines, which would help the agents sell them more easily.

The water meters did not require either advertising or the use of a distribution agency. This product had a different customer segment. The largest buyer of water meters was the Government of India, through its Stores Department. Smaller buyers included the various municipalities and corporations around the country. Shri Ram targeted the biggest buyer. He invited the chief controller of the Stores Department, R.N. Targett, to visit Jay Engineering. As he went around, escorted by both Shri Ram and Bishandas, Targett liked what he saw. He saw workers with happy faces who seemed to be fully engaged in their work. Targett was also happy with the quality of the water meters. At the end of the visit, he placed a large order. Soon after his visit, the Calcutta Corporation and other local bodies followed Targett's example and placed orders for water meters.

'Lala ji, you have worked your magic once again,' said Bishandas one evening as the two men drove back from the factory. 'When I told you the story of Usha I had not even dreamt that one day we would be running India's best manufacturing factory. Thank you, Lala ji, for your support.' Bishandas folded his hands and bowed his head.

Shri Ram patted Bishandas on his back and took his hands into his. 'You are the one with the dream, Bishandas. I merely enabled your dream. But I have also learnt a lesson here—which is to always follow my gut. You will also do well to remember this. And lastly, remember too that hard work never goes to waste,' Shri Ram said, looking fondly at the engineer.

16

DCM Turns Fifty

THE year was 1939. DCM was now fifty years old. Shri Ram had been running DCM almost as its sole proprietor since 1937, when he had become the managing agent of the company. He wanted to use the fifty-year milestone to further put his stamp on the company and on the group. He decided to hold a two-day celebration for the golden jubilee, involving all workers and their families.

Shri Ram wanted a chief guest befitting the occasion. Doreen Maud Milner, the marchioness of Linlithgow, was the wife of the Viceroy of India at that time. The second marquess of Linlithgow, Victor Hope, had been appointed as the Viceroy in 1936 and continued in the position till 1943—making him the longest-serving Viceroy of India. The Viceroy was the senior-most government position in British India. The marchioness, for all practical purposes, was the First Lady of India.

Shri Ram invited the marchioness to be the chief guest at the golden jubilee celebrations. She accepted the invitation. In addition to having a sterling chief guest, Shri Ram wanted to create a souvenir that would serve as a reminder to people, even after many years, of the golden years of DCM.

'The souvenir has to represent all that is DCM,' instructed Shri Ram, addressing the team working on the document. 'As you all know, DCM is the first big company of its kind in Delhi—'

'Lala ji, DCM is probably the first of its kind in all of north India, not only in Delhi,' piped up a manager enthusiastically, forgetting that Shri Ram did not like to be interrupted.

But Shri Ram overlooked the interruption, looking at the manager with an indulgent smile.

'Yes, Tiwari, you are absolutely correct. And remember, DCM is not only the biggest company but also one that takes care of its workers. All this must be covered in the souvenir. Because remember, long after we are all gone and forgotten, the souvenir will still be read by people in the years to come,' Shri Ram said.

The team nodded and promised to bring out a world-class souvenir that would be remembered by all.

The souvenir was released by the marchioness and was presented to everyone in attendance. The souvenir had a purple cover, and the outline of the Qutab Minar was embossed on both the front and back jackets. The image of the Qutub signified that DCM was Delhi's first large company and thus was as much a landmark for the city as the Qutab Minar.

The souvenir had many photographs. The first page had photos of the directors, and one of the inside pages had a photo of Shri Ram and Shankar Lall, his brother. The two brothers were photographed along with Shri Ram's three sons—Murli Dhar, Bharat Ram and Charat Ram. The men were all dressed in achkans and churidaar pyjamas.

Shri Ram wanted the photos to chronicle the life of the DCM Group. He wanted people who saw the souvenir even in later years to understand the ethos and philosophy that was DCM. One of the photos was of a sugar cane farm at Daurala—the site of the sugar mill. The photo showed two men—one Englishman and one Indian—standing in the sugar cane field. The sugar cane was almost twice as tall as the two men. The Englishman was photographed in the typical sola topee. Another photo of the field showed a tractor pulling a plough. In those years there were no rubber tyres and thus the tractor and the plough were all metal, including the wheels.

Shri Ram also wanted people to remember the work the group had done for the workers. He instructed the people working on the souvenir to include photographs of the akhara, gymnasium, swimming pool, shower areas and theatre for the workers. There were photos of workers taking showers, swimming, diving and even grappling in the akharas. The photographer had even caught three workers, wearing only langots, sliding down the slide that was installed in the gymnasium! The hospital run by the company was also showcased. One of the photographs depicted a ward with some of the beds occupied. Shri Ram was not too happy with the patients caught on camera.

'Did you ask them to pose for you?' he asked the photographer with a laugh when he saw the final souvenir.

'Why do you ask that, Lala ji?' asked the photographer.

'Because see how uncomfortable they look tucked up inside the blankets on the hospital beds!'

Notwithstanding the uncomfortable-looking patients, the souvenir was appreciated by all those who saw it. They especially appreciated the section on relations with staff. It was proudly pointed out in this section that DCM had rented and furnished a bungalow in Mussoorie for its officer employees. These employees could stay there for up to fifteen days to recuperate or take a break.

After the souvenir was formally released by the marchioness, she stood up to address the gathered people.

'I like to be associated with an enterprise at once so successful and so human which, having started in 1889, has steered a course of uninterrupted progress and prosperity. Prosperity not only for the owners and shareholders but for the workers in their charge,' said the marchioness.

And then, interestingly, she talked about DCM being a family business. 'In addition to the business ability, the success of this firm is due in my opinion to the family tradition and the handing of its affairs from father to son or from brother to brother,' she said.

In one broad stroke the marchioness named DCM a family business. She then spoke further about the advantages of a family managing a business.

'It means that the close personal touch which is so valuable an asset to both employer and employee is maintained. Unless the personal interest is there, the tendency is for the worker to be looked upon as a machine. The workers, if they feel that their employer is interested in them as human beings and is anxious to promote their welfare, will give of their best. During my first winter in Delhi, I was shown over the works and taken to the houses, the hospital, the school, and in fact I saw the welfare scheme in every detail, and I can truthfully say that I have never seen better in any country,' the marchioness said, speaking in glowing terms.

Shri Ram was delighted at the public endorsement by the First Lady of the country. The marchioness ended her speech, reiterating the role of the family in the business.

'In conclusion, I would like to wish the brothers, Lala Shri Ram and Lala Shankar Lall and all members of their family long life and prosperity. I congratulate them on combining the most up-to-date machinery and maximum of human feelings.'

Soon after the golden jubilee of DCM in 1939, the political environment in Europe started to change drastically and rapidly. The Second World War began and Indian industry was dragged into it as well. However, the war turned out to be beneficial for some businesses. The Indian cotton mill industry anticipated an immediate boom as it remembered the years of the First World War. And indeed, some of their anticipation crystallized. As soon as the war started, the cotton mills were able to sell their accumulated inventory of cloth. DCM, too, was able to clear its godowns and reap the benefit of high sales revenue.

As the war progressed the demand for cloth from the defence services went up. Simultaneously, the demand for cloth, from Singapore to South Africa, also went up. This high demand led to an increase in prices in the Indian market. The demand from the Indian government did not slow down either. Thus, a large number of cloth mills in India moved to working in two shifts. The cloth industry was booming, and labour was back in demand.

The government was focused on the cloth mills as it did not want production to falter—the war-driven requirement for cloth was rising almost every day. The government realized that the labour shortage could lead to problems in production and took some steps to pre-empt any threat of a production slowdown. These included a nudge to the mills to pay a war bonus to the workers. The trade unions were given funds to publicize and promote higher production by the workers. The government also looked at the interests of the mill owners and shareholders. The cost of alterations to plant and machinery was allowed to be treated as a revenue expenditure. The government also opened up a channel of communication between itself and the mills so that any bottlenecks in production could be highlighted quickly. Strikes and lockouts were banned.

All these measures led to a boom not only in production but also in profits. The cloth mill industry was on a roll. DCM, too, rode the boom.

Shri Ram's other business, Jay Engineering, also saw an increase in revenues. Once the war started, Jay Engineering was ordered by the government, under the Defence of India Rules, to switch to the production of items for the defence services. Jay Engineering started producing pressure gauges, vaporizing tubes, stoves and components for fighter aircrafts. The orders from the defence services kept coming and the factory needed to work round the clock to meet these orders. This led to higher profits no doubt, but it almost killed Usha, as only a handful of sewing machines were allowed to be produced.

Bengal Potteries in Calcutta also saw an upswing in revenues. The orders from the defence services kept the revenue board ticking, but Madan Gopal focused on the production of insulators. It was a product line that had proved lucrative for the business even before the war. The profits kept rising but the dark clouds of labour shortage kept hovering on the horizon. There was a labour shortage in general because most mills and factories were working overtime. Calcutta, in particular, saw an impending labour shortage due to the threats of Japan bombing the city.

Notwithstanding these problems, Bengal Potteries continued to churn out better revenues and profits each month. However, Shri Ram was sure that the boom was short-lived and would last only as long as the war. He was in Delhi, and he put his thoughts in a letter to Madan Gopal, who was the general manager of the works.

'I would personally prefer your giving more attention to the bazaar goods insomuch as with the stoppage of the war we will be faced with great difficulty in selling these goods as we will have to face foreign competition in addition to creating the market for the goods which we are now supplying to the government,' Shri Ram wrote with his customary foresight.

Shri Ram was also concerned about Madan Gopal, as he had seen the general manager working extremely hard and almost round the clock. When the war started Madan Gopal worked to get four new automatic kilns commissioned. Setting up the new facility and getting it to work at full capacity meant that Madan Gopal was working non-stop. Shri Ram realized that this was taking a toll on the younger man. The preferred mode of communication for Shri Ram was the letter. He wrote another one to Madan Gopal.

'You have been very unfair to yourself,' stated Shri Ram in the letter. 'You need a big rest. The blessed affairs of the world will go on a little better or a little worse. After all I am the senior member of the managing agents firm and if, as a friend, I cannot induce you to take rest, I can as a partner of this management order you to take rest.'

Shri Ram did not end the matter there. He even wrote to Madan Gopal's wife to ensure that her husband got all the rest he needed. A shrewd businessman, Shri Ram realized that Madan Gopal was needed by Bengal Potteries, especially during the war when the order book was overflowing. He preferred that Madan Gopal take some time off to recuperate rather than be incapacitated later or unable to work at optimal levels.

As the war continued, the problem of the workers became bigger. Shri Ram had already allowed a liberal dearness allowance to all his employees to handle the difficulties due to the war. But this was not enough. He wanted to do more for two reasons. One, because he genuinely had the well-being of the workers at heart; and two, because he knew that the problem of trained labour was not going to get better any time soon. He wanted a solution that would not only deal with the issue of trained workers but also give genuine relief to the workers.

With these thoughts in mind Shri Ram put forth two proposals that were ahead of their time. He told the board that he wanted a profit-sharing scheme for the workers and that he wanted to institutionalize a scheme for training different categories of employees.

The board listened to the scheme as put forward by Shri Ram in a meeting. It was an original scheme and far-reaching in its ambition. The profit-sharing scheme included treatment for sickness, life insurance, provision for dependants after death and pension in old age.

A sum of money equal to 15 per cent of the total dividend payable to the shareholders was to be set apart each year. This was to be treated as a fund for the benefit of the employees and would be called the Employees Benefit Fund. Shri Ram also proposed that this sum of money be managed by a board of trustees who would decide on the manner in which it would be invested and spent. At no instance would the money from the Employees Benefit Fund flow back into the company. The money from the fund would be used to pay the company's share of the provident fund as well as for many other employee benefit activities. Some of the activities listed out by Shri Ram included starting and maintaining hospitals, dispensaries, schools, gymnasiums, akharas and libraries for the workers and their families, and gratuities either as a lump sum or as annuities for retiring or ailing workers.

The board had no hesitation in approving this proposal. They saw it not only as an employee benefit scheme but also as a way to attract better and more talented workers to the DCM Group.

Along with this benefit scheme, an institutionalized training scheme for officers in the engineering, weaving, spinning and dyeing departments was set up. Shri Ram, in his meeting with the board, reminded the members that there was unprecedented demand for qualified and trained officers. He also reminded them that DCM had helped the government by releasing its own qualified staff to manage work in other friendly countries, including Afghanistan. He drew the board's attention to the fact that the apprenticeship scheme for workers had been successful. Many of the trainee workers were on their way to becoming supervisors. It was time, he said, for a similar apprentice scheme for officers.

There were different training schemes for different categories of officers. The qualifying requirement for officer trainees in the engineering department was a mechanical or electrical engineering degree; for those in the spinning and weaving departments, it was a degree in mechanical engineering. The training course was spread over three years, with a stipend being paid to the trainees. Each group of trainees was monitored and trained by a supervisor. The officer trainees were to be paid Rs 75 per month in the first year, Rs 100 per month in the second year and Rs 125 per month in the third year of their training. In addition to the stipend, trainees were paid a dearness allowance at the prevailing rates. Further, they were paid for any remunerative work done by them while on duty, and they were even entitled to free accommodation.

The officer training scheme was divided into several courses. Similar to a course in school or college, the trainees had to appear and clear regular tests. After the completion of the course, the trainees had to work with the company for a minimum of three years. They had to sign a bond to this effect. Defaulters, that is, people leaving the company before the completion of three years, had to refund the stipend paid to them during the training period. For those who stayed and worked with the company, the starting salary was Rs 175 per month along with a dearness allowance. This was a princely sum of money in those years.

Along with the officer training scheme, Shri Ram also introduced similar schemes for other cadres. Thus, there was the subordinate apprenticeship scheme, which selected and trained suitable candidates from amongst the workers to make them fit and ready to take on the role of a subordinate supervisor. There was also a scheme for trainees in non-technical areas of business. The objective of this scheme was to train people for administrative roles. Another scheme was for the clerical staff, which was a novelty at that time. Shri Ram wanted to focus on the rural candidates for this scheme. He also wanted to give priority to the sons of existing workers for this scheme.

Meanwhile, the war continued. With the entry of Japan into the war, the Indian subcontinent came under real and serious danger. With the fall of Burma in December 1941, Calcutta faced the threat of being bombed. These fears increased when the city saw some sporadic air raids soon after. Shri Ram did not want any harm to come to his workers at Jay Engineering. He was mulling over the options available to him when Calcutta was bombed in reality.

It was midnight of 20 December 1942 when Calcutta was woken up by the sounds of bomb blasts across the city. The Imperial Japanese Army Air Force was bombing the city. India, as a colony of Great Britain, was a de facto ally of the British Empire. The bombing damaged the infrastructure of the city. It also affected the livelihoods of its residents. Calcutta was put under a curfew and the city was 'blacked out'—street lights and all windows in homes and offices were covered every evening to make it harder for the Japanese to locate targets. Many of the bomb blasts took place in the vast Maidan—the open ground in the centre of Calcutta. It was at this time that the famous Red Road of Calcutta was transformed into a landing strip for the Allied forces. The Maidan also became a parking place for oil tankers. All this led to a mass exodus from the city. A large number of tailors also left the city. Usha lost many of its customers!

Shri Ram decided it was time to move part of the plant to Banaras. A small part of the works found a home in the temple city. It was here that Bishandas retired and handed over charge to T.R. Gupta. Gupta was a young engineer who had played a key role in DCM Delhi. He now became the general manager of the works. Gupta had always admired and respected Shri Ram and was now delighted to work with him directly. Shri

Ram, too, looked upon Gupta with both fondness and respect. The relationship that developed between them was like that of a guru and disciple. Shri Ram had only to say the word and Gupta carried it out with almost son-like obedience. And whenever Gupta ran into any obstacle he turned to Shri Ram for advice.

The association with Shri Ram influenced the way Gupta looked at work and money. Working with Shri Ram, he had seen that money was the last factor on Shri Ram's mind whenever he took a decision regarding the business; it was the industrial advancement of the country that he always thought of first. He told a friend, 'If you work with Shri Ram, money becomes a secondary consideration.' Gupta wanted to make Jay Engineering the pride of India and he vowed to Shri Ram that he would work tirelessly to make this happen.

Amongst the first things he focused on, as advised by Shri Ram, was the infusion of new workers into the factory. But here he ran into a problem. The workers were employed through contractors who charged the workers a monthly commission. The workers were unhappy with the contractors, as the latter operated more like a tough mafia than a recruitment firm. Shri Ram, who always put the interests of the workers first, advised Gupta to get rid of the labour contractors and start recruiting directly. It was not a simple task, as the labour contractors did not want to lose this lucrative business. They threatened Gupta and the workers.

Hectic discussions took place between Gupta and Shri Ram. 'Maybe we should look at renegotiating with the contractors,' said Gupta.

'Not at all. I don't like being blackmailed or threatened,' said Shri Ram.

'I know, Lala ji, but these contractors are also threatening the workers. The workers are scared. They want to work with us but don't want their legs broken by the contractors' goons,' said Gupta plaintively.

'These contractors are like leeches. They are sucking the life energy out of our workers,' said Shri Ram sorrowfully. He understood the plight of his workers and wanted to help them. 'I want my workers to work without fear. If they are not recruited directly, the contractors will continue to have a hold on them.'

'But what can we do? The contractors are a nasty bunch,' cried Gupta mournfully.

Shri Ram changed tack. His mind had been working even during this conversation. He sat up straight with a determined look on his face.

'Gupta, you know the good thing about these contractors?' Shri Ram asked his general manager.

'Huh? Good thing? Contractors?' Gupta was flummoxed.

'Yes, good thing, Gupta,' said Shri Ram with a smile. 'These contractors are only driven by money. They don't want to spend time or energy on nation-building or on things that are good for either the workers or the country. So, if money is their God, give them money. Buy them out,' he explained.

'Ah, Lala ji, I see what you mean,' Gupta said immediately.

Gupta understood and started a different negotiation with the contractors. He was able to buy them out. When the news spread, the workers were delighted. They came and thanked Gupta. They promised to work even harder to make Jay Engineering the best manufacturing unit in the country.

With the workers' problem solved, Shri Ram and Gupta focused on training them. A training school was set up within the premises of the factory. All new hires were put through a training process. The more skilled and technical jobs required a different type of worker. Young engineering graduates were hired for these jobs and Gupta took it upon himself to train them.

Shri Ram, meanwhile, focused on the plant and processes. He hired a German expert, who got down to work and pointed out machinery that was obsolete. He also suggested ways to streamline production. Gupta carried out all his suggestions. He ended up spending almost every night at the factory. But he did not complain, as he was on a personal mission to make Shri Ram proud of Jay Engineering.

Shri Ram's heart was really in technical education. He believed strongly that this education was a prerequisite for India's modernization. During his travels overseas Shri Ram had seen technical skills at work and had been impressed. He wanted to raise the technical knowledge and skill levels of Indians, as he believed that industrialized countries owed their progress to their trained manpower. Shri Ram also wanted India to move its exports from low-value commodities to value-added manufactured products.

In December 1937 Shri Ram invited some of the top chemists of the country to his home. The discussion centred on the importance of technical research and India's growth. At the end of it, Shri Ram decided to set up an institute for industrial research. The institute would focus on research to improve the efficiency and output of existing manufacturing processes and invent new ones to utilize indigenous raw materials. The areas of research identified by him included textiles, high polymers including plastics and paints, chemicals and chemical engineering, and design of instruments.

Shri Ram set aside Rs 30 lakh for the institute and worked on setting up a design and analytical team for each discipline. He also arranged for land in the Delhi University Enclave for the proposed institute. He registered it as a non-profit organization.

All formalities were over by 1940. But due to the ongoing World War there was no movement on the project. Shri Ram restarted it once the war was over. The foundation stone for Shriram Institute for Industrial Research was laid in 1947.

Raising money for the institute was not a problem. Shri Ram had himself contributed Rs 30 lakh, of which Rs 20 lakh had been spent on the building. Shri Ram appealed to his fellow businessmen to give to the institute for the sake of industrial research in the country. He realized that the institute needed to work, and be seen to work, independently for industry to take it seriously. If industry at large saw it as a captive research centre for DCM and its companies, then support would be difficult to get.

With this in mind, Shri Ram insisted that organizations such as the Council of Scientific and Industrial Research (CSIR), Delhi University and even FICCI be represented on the board. He also co-opted scientists from other institutions and had them join the board. The strategy worked. Several industrialists donated to the institute. An annual grant of Rs 2 lakh was ensured. Shri Ram also proposed that the institute would earn a royalty from giving its technology and innovations to industry.

It took seven years for the plan to be manifested in the actual institute. Shriram Institute for Industrial Research started work in 1950. The institute carried forward the belief of its founder that, for India to catch up with the rest of the world, it was essential to understand existing technology and to innovate through research.

The work that Shri Ram did in planning the institute and his strong advocacy of technical education were recognized by the government. Shri Ram was made a member of the first All India Committee for Technical Education in 1945. It was based on the recommendations of this committee that the Indian Institute of Technology, Kanpur, was formed after independence.

17

A New Sugar Mill and Foray into Chemicals

THE DCM sugar division had, like all other businesses, been affected by the Second World War. Shri Ram, however, remained bullish on sugar as a commodity. Contrary to the advice given to him by his well-wishers, he wanted to expand the capacity of his sugar mill. But, rather than expand the capacity of the Daurala mill, he scouted around to see if he could buy an existing sugar mill. He found one in Barhni in Uttar Pradesh, close to the Nepal border. The mill was called Popular Sugar Company and had started production in 1934. Over the next six years the shareholders of the sugar company and three different managing agencies had struggled with the business. None of the managing agencies were able to run the business profitably. The situation turned from bad to worse, and by 1940 the courts ordered the mill to be auctioned.

Shri Ram was, by now, an expert on sugar. Duarala had been a success, and since the opening of the sugar mill Shri Ram had learnt the intricacies of the business well. He heard of the court-ordered auction of the Barhni mill and asked his team of managers to examine the opportunity. The reports presented to Shri Ram were favourable. They showed that the mill could be turned around with some prudent manufacturing practices. Shri Ram was not worried about the failure of the three managing agencies at Barhni. The key, according to Shri Ram, was not to overpay for the assets. If that happened his plans would not be able to take off.

Shri Ram was shrewd enough to realize that if he went to bid for the mill the price would go up. He decided to send one of his trusted munims, Rampat, to the auction.

Rampat turned up at the auction site and sat in a corner quietly. No one recognized him and no one took the unassuming man sitting in the room seriously. The room started filling up with men who came dressed flashily and walked in with a swagger. Rampat chatted with the people sitting next to him. His neighbours looked at him and saw a simple man dressed in a thin muslin kurta and pyjama. They took him to be a worker who had come there to pass the time. Therefore, they had no hesitation in talking to him. Rampat found out that most of the men in the room wanted to buy the sugar mill to dismantle it and then sell it as scrap.

The bidding started. The opulently dressed men started their bidding loudly. Most of them knew each other and looked at one another with a smile as they tried to outbid each other. No one gave the man in the simple kurta-pyjama a second look.

However, the entire room turned to look at the simple man in amazement when he raised the bid significantly. A murmur went around the room as people asked one another about his identity. No one knew. The men in opulent suits were angry and raised their bids higher. They could not be seen to be outbid by a simple man. They thought that the high bids would scare him. But the simple man was made of sterner stuff and had the approval of Shri Ram to take the bidding up to a certain level. The bidding war did not last long, as the men in opulent suits could not keep up with the raised bids of the simple man.

The auctioneer brought down the hammer at the final price of Rs 13 lakh. Thirteen lakh! A buzz went around the room as the people wondered why the simple man had paid such a high price for this sugar mill. The murmur turned to amusement as they thought that the man had lost his mind. However, the amusement died down quickly when it was revealed that the actual buyer of the sugar mill was Lala Shri Ram. While the experience and knowledge of Shri Ram were well known, the people in the room still wondered if Shri Ram had indeed made the right decision.

For some time after he acquired the mill it did look as if Shri Ram had made a mistake. The sugar mill did not respond to the touch of the new owner. For one, there was not enough cane grown in the region to be used by the mill. And then the workers, tired of the fights between the owners over the past years, were disgruntled. Shri Ram tried various tactics, but none worked.

Shri Ram then asked his son, Bharat Ram, to help him with the mill. Bharat Ram, a young man in his twenties, had started work at DCM as an apprentice some years ago. He had learnt his lessons about work and the right approach to work the hard way from his father.

Even as an apprentice Bharat Ram would go to work in his car. One day he reached the office late as his car had broken down. As part of his morning routine Shri Ram used to take a round of the mill. He noticed that his son was not at work. Bharat Ram's supervisor was told to send the young man to Shri Ram's office as soon as he came to work.

Bharat went to his father's office as instructed. Shri Ram was busy with work. Bharat Ram waited for a moment and then bent down to talk to his father.

'Bhaiji, you called me?' asked Bharat Ram.

Shri Ram looked up and gestured to his son to step back from his desk. 'Why have you come late today?' he asked Bharat Ram.

'Oh, that? My car broke down and that's why I got late, Bhaiji,' answered Bharat Ram easily.

'You know that there are thousands of other workers here at DCM, don't you? They don't have cars. Yet they come to work on time,' Shri Ram said in a stern tone, and proceeded to grill Bharat Ram. 'Could you not walk to work? If a worker comes late to work he is sent back. Why should I not send you back as well?

Bharat Ram had no words. He hung his head and stared at the floor. He shuffled his feet as he waited for his father to speak.

'Bharat Ram, you know that this is the office of the chairman. There is a protocol here. You should know how to stand in front of a senior officer. You may be my son, but I cannot make any allowances on that count. In fact, you should set an example and work harder,' Shri Ram said.

Bharat Ram stood up straighter and stopped shuffling his feet.

'You will do a double shift today because you came late to work,' Shri Ram instructed his son and gestured that he could leave the room.

Bharat Ram left the room with a lesson learnt that was to stay with him his entire life.

He was now helping his father with the new sugar mill. When it refused to respond to all the new measures, father and son sat down to look at their options. One of the options on the table was a rather radical one. Bharat Ram suggested to his father that they uproot and transport the entire factory from Barhni to Mawana. One of the reasons for this was that Mawana was closer to Delhi and Daurala; Barhni was almost 700 km from Delhi. The other reason was that sugar cane was grown in abundance in the Mawana area. Shri Ram decided that it was the best option for the sugar mill.

Meanwhile the villagers in Barhni learnt of the plans to shut down the mill. They were extremely unhappy. The mill was a source of livelihood for the villagers, and many would be left jobless after the move. Further, the workers from outside who lived in the village gave the local shopkeepers good business.

The villagers carried out protests against the shutting down and dismantling of the mill. *'Dilli walon wapas Dilli jaao, yeh mill hamari hai,'* they shouted. (People from Delhi, go back to Delhi; this mill is ours.) The villagers also moved court to prevent the move. When none of this worked they resorted to violence. Two guards on duty at the mill were killed.

Shri Ram was not happy with the agitation, but he could not let the loss-making factory continue as it was. He went directly to the villagers. In his meeting with the elders and the young men of Barhni, Shri Ram promised to employ all those who were willing to relocate to Mawana. Those who did not want to move would be compensated for the loss of income. The tactic was successful in placating the villagers. Even then it took both Shri Ram and Bharat Ram a great amount of effort and tact to get the entire factory moved to Mawana.

Shri Ram's dream of having a factory in Mawana was finally fulfilled. The sugar mill in the new location responded well and was soon seen in the same light as Daurala when it came to sugar.

Shri Ram's work in the industry was being noticed by all, including the government of the day. In 1941, Shri Ram was knighted. The British wanted to recognize the industrial and administrative work done by Shri Ram. Thus, on 18 February 1941 Shri Ram was honoured with a knighthood. He, however, had mixed feelings about the award. Within his own family there were murmurs of discontent about the honour. His sons were not happy at his acceptance of the knighthood. Some members even said that he had used his proximity to the top bureaucrats to get the honour. But Shri Ram maintained throughout his life that he had nothing to do with the knighthood.

The war years were years of scarcity. The British government, recognizing the importance of industry, did everything it could to keep top industrialists happy. Shri Ram was also an astute businessman. He did not want to cause any heartburn to the government or be seen as arrogant by it. He accepted the knighthood graciously. But the timing of the honour could not have been worse. Mahatma Gandhi was on the verge of launching the Quit India movement.

Shri Ram, after accepting the honour, let it be known that he would prefer to continue to be addressed as Lala Shri Ram.

Meanwhile, the war had been raging since 1939. There was another kind of war raging within the Shri Ram household. Charat Ram had remained adamant about his desire to marry Sumitra, whom he had met in 1934. In the intervening years Shri Ram had tried to get Charat Ram to marry someone else but his son had been stubborn. Charat Ram had been brought up to always maintain decorum in front of his elders. Thus, there were no loud arguments between father and son, but the lines were drawn clearly on both sides.

Undeterred by the somewhat hostile attitude towards his intentions, Charat Ram continued his romance with Sumitra while she was studying Hindi literature at Banaras University. Charat Ram had started working at DCM in 1936. He was put under the traineeship of Ahmad Islam Khan, who was the general manager. Charat Ram worked in the foundry and also learnt the various facets of cotton trading. He was then sent to Padampat Singhania's factory in Kanpur for further training.

Charat Ram was happy being in Kanpur because it was closer to Banaras. He would visit Sumitra there very often. Shri Ram knew that Charat Ram went to Banaras often. He therefore sent his son to Calcutta to work at Jay Engineering, hoping that the distance between the two cities would dim the intensity of his son's emotions. Charat Ram had studied economics and philosophy. He also appreciated literature. For a man like him, working at Jay Engineering was a forceful induction into the world of machines and engineering. But he persevered and came to love the world of machines and technology.

By 1941 it was clear to Shri Ram and all in the family that Charat Ram's mind was made up regarding Sumitra. Moving to Calcutta had not dimmed the fires of emotion on either side. Further, Shri Ram was aware that his son was getting older. Societal norms required Charat Ram to 'settle down'. The societal pressure was felt by Shri Ram as well. Finally, he relented. He called up Dharamvira and told him that if he wanted to get his sister married to Charat Ram he should do it in the next one week.

One week's notice was not enough for a large wedding. But Charat Ram and Sumitra also wanted to formalize their relationship. So, a low-key wedding was held in 1941. Sumitra became Mrs Charat Ram and moved to Delhi.

The Shri Ram household was a vibrant one, with all three bahus living there. Each was different from the other, but each contributed in her own way to making the Shri Ram house the cultural centre of Delhi in the years to come.

Around the same time that the sugar mill in Barhni was in the process of being acquired, Shri Ram was toying with the idea of entering the chemicals business. The idea had taken root in his mind because of the opportunities presented by the war. There was an acute shortage of sulphuric acid and hydrochloric acid, which were key chemicals in the textile manufacturing process. Most of these chemicals were imported. There were a couple of Indian producers, but their units were far from Delhi.

Once the war started, the Indian manufacturers doubled their prices. On the other hand, the imports of these chemicals suffered due to the war. As a result, the prices of sulphuric and hydrochloric acid shot up in the market. The DCM textile division was a heavy consumer of both these and saw their production costs go up significantly. Further, the sporadic supply of these chemicals led to quality issues as well. There was also a growth in the black market for these products.

Shri Ram disliked using the black market and thus pondered over the idea of setting up a chemical factory. He spoke to his associates and executive team members, who examined the business opportunity and gave it a green signal. They told him that a chemical factory could produce enough to meet DCM's needs, and any surplus could be easily sold in the market. Lastly, Shri Ram was also told that the cost of the chemicals produced in-house would be significantly lower than the market rate they were paying.

The chemical division of DCM took birth as an acid factory. The chemical works started as a branch of DCM and started small. About two to three tonnes of sulphuric acid were produced every day. Within a year production had doubled to six tonnes a day. Most of the chemicals produced were sold to DCM itself, with the surplus sold in the open market. The demand for DCM chemicals was high in the market, as Shri Ram refused to take advantage of the shortage and charge higher prices.

It was at this time that Shri Ram asked his youngest son, Charat Ram, to start work with DCM's chemical division. The young Charat Ram had graduated from St Stephen's College and had started work in the textile and engineering divisions. He was posted in Calcutta with Jay Engineering. Shri Ram now called him back and gave him more responsibility. As the work of DCM Chemical Works expanded, he gave Charat Ram complete charge of the business.

Charat Ram did not disappoint his father. Amongst the first things he observed was that the scientists and other technical experts were comfortable in the chemical industry and were managing the existing products well. They also had the expertise to work on new products. Charat Ram wanted to expand and make DCM Chemical Works bigger. The problem he ran into was that sulphuric acid had limited use. Even after selling it to DCM and in the open market, there was a limit to how much DCM Chemical Works could grow by producing and selling just the acid. However, thought Charat Ram, if sulphuric acid were used to make other value-added products then the possibilities of growth opened up.

He spoke with Shri Ram and got his approval to start experimenting with new products. The scientists and other experts were given the task of identifying other chemical products that could be manufactured. One of the first products added to the line was aluminium sulphate. This was used in water purification and was also needed during the production of paper. Charat Ram found that there were ready buyers for the product—Delhi Water Works and the paper mills in Saharanpur and Jagadhari.

After aluminium sulphate, the next product that the team worked on was Turkey red oil. This was used by the armed forces in makeshift runways for planes. Turkey red oil sets in very fast and thus, in a very short period, a surface hard enough for an aircraft to land on could be made with it.

Gradually, other chemicals such as magnesium sulphate, sodium sulphate and ferrous sulphate were added to the product line. Simultaneously, the production of the acids went up significantly to 75 tonnes per day.

Charat Ram's association with DCM's chemical works was to last several decades, and he is the one responsible for making DCM one of the country's leading manufacturers of chemicals, plastics and fertilizers.

DCM's foray into fertilizers came about after a brainstorming session that Shri Ram and Charat Ram had with the team. Shri Ram began the meeting by reminding people that the war was going to end sooner or later.

'And once the war ends, our business will be affected,' asserted Shri Ram.

'Lala ji, why do you say that?' asked one manger, drawing up the courage to question his boss.

'Because, Sharma, the armed forces will not need our products any more,' answered Shri Ram.

The manager nodded immediately, as he understood the matter.

'The orders from the armed forces, as you all know, are very lucrative. But they will dry up for sure,' said Shri Ram. 'So, the thought that often comes to my mind is, what will the future of DCM Chemicals be? In fact, I often wonder if the company should be wound down completely.'

All the people in the room reacted immediately to this last comment from Shri Ram. 'No no, Lala ji, please don't even think like that,' said one.

'Lala ji, we promise we will find ways to keep the business going. Don't even think of shutting down the company,' implored another.

Shri Ram stood up and raised his hands to quieten everyone down. As he sat down again he looked around the room. 'I certainly don't want to shut down this company. All of you have done splendid work. But I also need you to keep in mind that no business stays the same. We have to change to stay relevant and profitable. Therefore, please think seriously about what we should do next,' he said.

He stood up again. 'I am leaving now, but you continue with your discussions. Hopefully some solutions will emerge from them,' he said as he left the room.

The team continued their discussions, which turned animated. They considered three options—find new product lines and expand, or keep DCM Chemicals as an appendage to DCM, or shut it down. Since Charat Ram was personally involved in the running of the chemical works, he took it upon himself to find a viable solution. He did not want the business to shut down.

After many more rounds of discussions, the team veered around to looking at superphosphate as a focus product. Superphosphate was one of the first chemical fertilizers to be made in the world, and it was first produced in the 1840s. Sulphuric acid was one of the key ingredients of this fertilizer.

Charat Ram was happy with the result of their brainstorming. He requested his father to come for a meeting with the team.

As Shri Ram walked into the room he sensed a crackling energy. He looked around and saw people sitting confidently and with smiles on their faces. He realized that the team had a viable solution to the problem.

'You asked us to find a solution and we believe that we have one,' said Charat Ram as he began his presentation to Shri Ram. 'You know that India is an agrarian economy and fertilizers are key to the development of this sector. Sulphuric acid is one of the main ingredients of superphosphate, which is a chemical fertilizer. If we start producing superphosphate at DCM Chemicals then we would be the first company in north India to make this fertilizer.'

A young member of the team could not contain his excitement and butted in. 'Lala ji, you know that north India is mainly dependent on agriculture. Think of how much fertilizer we could sell, as it will be in demand for a very long time,' he said excitedly.

Shri Ram looked at the young man with a smile, as he liked his enthusiasm. Charat Ram looked at the young man with irritation, as he did not like being interrupted.

'Anyway, as I was saying, if we start making superphosphate we will have an advantage because we make sulphuric acid here. The in-house production of the acid will help us reduce the price of the fertilizer.' Charat Ram ended his presentation and sat down.

Shri Ram liked the idea, especially the fact that his factory would be a pioneer in north India. He gave his approval, and the factory went ahead with the production of superphosphate.

Superphosphate became a profit-generating machine for DCM Chemical Works. Over time, other products were also added—a laundry soap called DCM Bar Soap, a toilet soap called Basant and phenyl, amongst others.

Before the Second World War ended, Shri Ram toyed with the idea of making alcohol at Daurala. The process was a simple forward integration for a sugar mill. He knew that Gujarmal Modi had done that at his sugar mill in Modinagar. He thought about the idea a bit more, discussed it with the general manager of the sugar mill but ultimately discarded it. He did not want to make gains through unwholesome methods.

The alcohol diversification may have been a non-starter but the foray into vanaspati was a big success. People in India had traditionally used coconut oil, mustard oil and ghee for cooking and frying. But ghee was an expensive product, and not everyone could afford it. A Dutch company called Dada & Co had seen an opportunity in the market and had started selling hydrogenated vegetable oil as a substitute for desi ghee. They even called their product vanaspati ghee! The name—vanaspati ghee—was a misnomer, as the product was not ghee in the technical sense; it was hydrogenated vegetable oil that mimicked the look and feel of ghee.

The product used to be imported, largely from Holland, by Dada & Co. Lever Brothers sold the imported product, and to reflect their ownership, they added the letter L to the name of Dada—hence Dalda. In a bold marketing move, the Levers advertised their product as Dalda vanaspati ghee. The association of the product with ghee worked and the concept caught on quickly, as Dalda had the look and feel of ghee. The biggest advantage, however, was the price of Dalda, which was a fraction of the price of desi ghee.

Shri Ram sensed an opportunity in this market. Dalda was the only brand that was available nationally. All the other vanaspati manufacturers were regional players. Shri Ram decided to set up a factory in Delhi to manufacture vanaspati. The required machinery was imported, and within months, in December 1946, the factory went into production.

Unlike some of his other businesses, the vanaspati venture had a shaky start. Due to the cost escalations of the raw materials the business was not profitable. Shri Ram had chosen the brand names Rath and Panghat for his vanaspati. The initial setbacks saw some of his friends advising him to shut down the business. But such advice was like waving a red flag before a raging bull!

Shri Ram firmly believed that the vanaspati business had a great future. He just needed to find the right solutions to the problems he faced. So he studied the vanaspati manufacturers who were doing well.

He was ready with his solutions the next time a well-wisher suggested that he shut down the vanaspati business and cut his losses.

'Look at the other vanaspati manufacturers,' he said, waving his hands around. 'They are all making money. You really think these guys are better than me? If they can make profits, then so can I.'

And he was true to his word. He had understood the problems faced by the business and had found a solution. In typical Shri Ram style, he increased the production of vanaspati. As the production increased, the cost of production per unit came down significantly. Rath and Panghat started competing in the market due to their reduced prices. And as the product was of high quality, it quickly built a loyal clientele.

Rath and Panghat became household names and continued to be so for many years.

18

Shri Ram Takes a Sabbatical

ALL these successes in business had started leaving Shri Ram cold. He had been working at DCM for almost forty years. The hard work had taken a toll on his health. Further, his wife Phoolan Devi had passed away in an unfortunate accident.

Phoolan Devi had been unwell and had frequent epileptic fits. But she had kept herself busy with pooja-paath and the kitchen. It was while she was cooking one day in 1941 that she had a fit. As she fell, her sari pallu caught fire. Before the servants and family members could reach her, the fire had grown. Although they managed to douse the fire, Phoolan Devi could not survive the trauma.

Shri Ram was in Calcutta at this time. By the time word reached Calcutta about Phoolan Devi's death, Shri Ram had left the city as per his schedule. The Kalka Mail was the fastest way to travel between Delhi and Calcutta in those days, and it was Shri Ram's preferred mode of transport.

The family was in a fix. Shri Ram was in the train and hence could not be reached. Phoolan Devi had to be cremated soon as the body could not be kept for a long time. The sons and Shankar Lall huddled together and then took a decision. A small aircraft was to be hired and sent to Allahabad so that Shri Ram could be contacted when the train stopped at the Allahabad station.

Air travel was not considered safe at that time, especially in a small aircraft. Further, no one wanted to be the one to break this news to Shri Ram. A young DCM executive, B.D. Pathak, offered to undertake the journey.

Pathak flew to Allahabad and then rushed to the station. He was just in time, as the Kalka Mail had just entered the station. By the time Pathak ran to the first-class compartment Shri Ram had come to the door of his coupe to enjoy some fresh air.

Shri Ram was leaning against the door and was watching life at the station go by. His attention was caught by a young man rushing towards the first-class section. Shri Ram recognized him as an executive from DCM. His antenna went up. He realized that something was amiss. Shri Ram waved to the young man, who rushed up to him.

'Lala ji, you have to get off the train and come with me,' said Pathak without even wishing Shri Ram.

Shri Ram's suspicion grew. Something was definitely amiss.

'What has happened? Why do you want me to get off the train?' he asked Pathak.

'Lala ji, you get off the train, and I will get your luggage from the coupe. Please let me go in.' Pathak avoided answering the direct question. 'The aircraft is waiting at the airport, and we have to go to Delhi immediately.'

'Young man, I am not going anywhere until you tell me what is the matter.' Shri Ram crossed his arms and stood at the door of the coupe resolutely.

Pathak was in a fix. He knew that the train was about to leave the station. He also knew that he had to get Shri Ram off the train. He wanted to get the luggage off the train first.

'Lala ji, you are needed in Delhi. I will tell you everything, but let me get your luggage out of the train first. You know it is about to leave. Please, Lala ji, I beg you, let me get your luggage. Please,' pleaded Pathak with folded hands.

Shri Ram stood aside as all kinds of thoughts raced through his mind. Once his luggage was on the platform, Shri Ram took Pathak by the shoulders and demanded that he be told what the matter was.

It was a moment of reckoning for Pathak. The young man stammered but conveyed the news of Phoolan Devi's death to Shri Ram. He was not prepared for the reaction.

Pathak, and everyone else at DCM, had known Shri Ram to be a strong man, an authoritarian boss. This strong man almost crumbled as he heard the news. Pathak was afraid that Shri Ram, a frail man at all times, would stumble and fall. In any other circumstances Pathak would not have had the temerity to hold Shri Ram by the shoulders. But now he did.

Shri Ram held on to Pathak for dear life. He put his head on the young man's shoulder and wept profusely. Pathak did not know how to handle this. All he could do was hold the older man as the latter wept like a child. He kept patting Shri Ram on the shoulder till his sobs quietened down.

Shri Ram wanted to know the details of the death. Pathak told him on the way to the airport. Shri Ram was quiet and reflective all the way to Delhi. Pathak sat apart from him, giving his boss the space and privacy he needed at that time.

By the time Shri Ram reached the house all preparations for Phoolan Devi's cremation had been made. The body was taken to Nigambodh Ghat, where she was cremated. Shri Ram was shaken to the core, visibly. The despair and regret showed on his face. He made no attempt to hide his grief. He felt he owed it to his departed wife. The affection and emotions he could not demonstrate in her lifetime, he did at her death.

After Phoolan Devi's death Shri Ram found that he was unable to concentrate on work for long hours. With his health poorer than before, he began thinking of retiring from active business. He wondered if his life's work was done. Hinduism actually encourages men to abandon the pursuit of wealth in later life and retire to a life of contemplation. This stage of life is called vanaprastha, which translated means retiring to the woods/forests. However, Shri Ram argued with himself, the Hindu religion also frowned upon a karamyogi, or doer, abandoning the field when the battle was only half won.

As he argued with himself, a halfway solution, almost like a compromise, started forming in his mind. He could, he thought, leave the businesses of DCM, including the sugar mills and the ceramics factory, to his brother and sons. Murli Dhar was managing the textile mills, especially Lyallpur. Bharat Ram and Charat Ram had been trained well and were firmly established as leaders in their own rights within the businesses. Shankar Lall, his brother, was there to take his place as the nominal head of the family. The only business Shri Ram wanted to spend his energy on was the engineering one. He had said in the past that Jay Engineering was his 'pet concern.' Now that this company was running into choppy waters, he believed that he was duty-bound to get it back to health.

His mind made up, Shri Ram asked his board to accept his resignation. This was not the first time that he had requested the board to relieve him of his duties. In 1942 he had requested the board to let him retire. He had told them that during his forty years at DCM he had trained many others who could run DCM successfully. He had also pointed out that the staff and managers were loyal and devoted to their work. The team had given evidence during the past years that they were able to deal with difficult situations and could adapt to changing conditions. Shri Ram had also said that due to his ill health he had been unable to carry out his responsibilities as well as he would have liked to. Considering all the above, he had said, it would be better for him to resign from the partnership.

The board had been unwilling to let Shri Ram go then. They had requested him to postpone his retirement. It was pointed out to Shri Ram that the country was passing through a difficult time. On the one hand there was the World War; on the other hand the calls for independence for India had become louder. The general thought was that India would gain her independence once the war ended. The board was of the view that it was a delicate time for the company, and the business could not afford to lose the judgement and guidance of Shri Ram. They requested Shri Ram to reconsider his decision to retire.

Shri Ram had withdrawn his resignation but reiterated his intention of retiring once the war was over and the situation became normal. He also told the board that while DCM was a stable business, Jay Engineering and Bengal Potteries needed his guidance more.

Shri Ram went back to work and soon he was pulled into a new endeavour by his fellow industrialists—the Bombay Plan. This fifteen-year plan was co-authored by a group of leading industrialists and technocrats of that time and was an import-substitution-industrialization-based proposal for the post-independence economy of India. In spite of his desire to cut back on work, Shri Ram joined the group as he was a staunch patriot. He believed that the Bombay Plan would be good for India's economic advancement in the years to come.

This plan of economic development for India, or more commonly known simply as the Bombay Plan, was drafted by J.R.D. Tata, G.D. Birla, Ardeshir Dalal, Kasturbhai Lalbhai, D. Shroff, Purshottamdas Thakurdas, John Mathai and Shri Ram. The purpose of the plan was to prepare an economic policy plan for the first fifteen years of the future government of independent India. It was feared at that time that independent India may decide to take populist economic measures in a hurry. The group feared that these measures were even more likely if the new government faced demands from politicians for the redistribution of income and wealth. The group was of the view that measures like these, if implemented, would harm India's economic development over a period of time. Thus, the group suggested that a process be set in motion before that, which would make the government and the people at large aware of the issues of development and wealth distribution. It also proposed state intervention in the economic development of free India.

The objective of the Bombay Plan was to increase agricultural output by 130 per cent, raise industrial production by 500 per cent and services output by 200 per cent in fifteen years. It planned to achieve this development through three periods, each of five years. Interestingly, the Planning Commission formed after independence also prepared five-year plans and prioritized agriculture, industrialization and then a transition to a services economy. The state intervention, according to the Bombay Plan, was for an equitable society.

When the plan was made public it was slammed by the communists, who termed the authors capitalists. On the other hand, the rightists saw the plan as a harbinger of socialism. And the centrists viewed it as a pitiable apology from businessmen who had made super-normal profits during the Second World War.

Shri Ram continued to give his support to the Bombay Plan in the various interactions he had with others. He continued to work at DCM as desired by the board but his health was a cause of concern.

In 1944, he lost sight in his left eye. Shri Ram had endured all his ailments with stoic calm and had refused to let them interfere with his work. But the loss of sight in one eye could not be overlooked either by him or his friend Padampat Singhania.

Singhania was so concerned about his friend's loss of vision that he wrote an impassioned letter to Shri Ram. 'I only wish and pray to God that he would give back your eyesight because your life is so important and useful to our country that God must restore you to normal health.'

Shri Ram, too, was concerned and had the means to go to the best doctors not only in India but also in Europe. But none of these renowned doctors were able to help him. As a last-ditch option Shri Ram went to a hakim, who gave him a nostrum. To the delighted surprise and relief of all, the nostrum worked and Shri Ram regained his sight.

But his troubles were not to end. A year later Shri Ram suffered a stroke. It was a severe one, and the right side of his body was paralysed. The stroke also left Shri Ram full of despair and low in spirits.

'I feel both mentally and physically tired,' he told a friend mournfully. 'I don't know what evil stars are haunting me.'

Shri Ram was treated by the best of doctors. This time he responded to the treatment, and he was able to use his limbs again. His body may have responded to the treatment, but his spirit was still broken. Shri Ram knew that no medicine could restore his spirits, so he sought the company of sadhus to heal his spirit.

'I am happy to say that I am both physically and mentally better,' he told the same friend after some time. 'Probably the reason is that yesterday I went to a place where some good sadhus were giving kirtan and discourse on religious and spiritual matters.'

The stroke firmed up Shri Ram's resolve to retire from active work. Once the war was over in 1945, Shri Ram renewed his request to the board of DCM to allow him to retire. The board, still unwilling to let him retire, found a middle path. As his health continued to be of concern, they allowed Shri Ram to go on a long leave of absence so he could focus on regaining it. This worked well for Shri Ram because he too had worked out a halfway solution.

Shri Ram was on leave from early 1947. But he continued to provide informal guidance to the business. The managers and other family members, who now had a freer hand in taking business decisions, proved that their training was good. The sales and profits doubled.

Once he was on leave from the main businesses Shri Ram was free to devote most of his time to Jay Engineering. The company felt the full impact of Shri Ram's personality. From the head of the company to the clerk in the office, Shri Ram engaged with them all. His mantra to all was 'produce more, make stuff cheaper and better'.

His relentless pressure started showing results. Production went up from fifty machines per month to 500 and then to 1,000. The increased production brought down the average cost of each unit. Usha was sold at Rs 140 less than the foreign sewing machines—Singer and Pfaff. He also got the team to work on the appearance of the machine. Better paint with a shine was used. He also instructed the management team to work on the after-sales customer service.

By February 1949, Usha, and Jay Engineering, were out of the woods. The company was making handsome profits once again. But this brought another kind of problem. The other industrialists took note of the profits being churned out by Usha. Some were tempted to enter the business. While Shri Ram was not bothered about the smaller entrepreneurs as competitors, he took a pause to think when he heard that the Birlas were thinking of setting up a modern factory for sewing machines and working with a foreign technical collaborator.

Shri Ram discussed the matter with his sons and asked for their suggestions. While many options were discussed, the one that caught everyone's fancy was the suggestion made by Shri Ram. He wanted to dampen the would-be competitor's enthusiasm even before they finalized their plans.

'Step up the production of sewing machines to 5,000 machines per month,' instructed Shri Ram. His plan was to saturate the market so that any new competitor would find it difficult to break through. And his plan was successful! When the Birla management examined the market situation they came to the conclusion that their money was better invested elsewhere. Shri Ram announced this good news to the workers and managers himself.

His relationship with the workers was Shri Ram's secret sauce to success. It was also his main source of strength. Shri Ram, since the early days of DCM, had ensured that he had his communication lines clear and working with the workers. The workers had also responded to this overture by their owner. This was borne out time and again, especially in times of crisis when the relationship between the management and the workers became strained. Even in those times Shri Ram could reach out to the workers directly.

Calcutta had always been the hub of left-wing trade unionism. Jay Engineering was no different. Even though Shri Ram's businesses paid better than the market rates and provided superior working and living conditions to the workers, the trade union leaders were always on the lookout to ask for more. As Jay Engineering came out of the red, the union leaders thought it was time to ask for more.

The workers of Jay Engineering were incited to ask for an additional bonus. The management engaged in a dialogue with the workers' representatives, but the matter reached a stalemate. Neither side was willing to give in. Due to the hard attitude of the workers, production had slowed down. Shri Ram was perturbed by the situation. Even though he was on long leave, he wanted to address the issue. He soon found the right occasion for it.

The management and the workers were in a meeting in the canteen. The meeting had started on an even note but soon voices were raised on both sides. The management team objected to certain remarks made by the workers; the workers got upset at being told off. Passions were running high and the antagonism in the atmosphere was palpable.

It was into this tension-filled canteen that Shri Ram walked coolly, along with the general manager and a few other senior executives. The workers and the management were almost shouting at each other, each trying to get their point of view across. In all this bedlam, it took a moment for the room to realize that Shri Ram was in their presence.

A couple of workers saw Shri Ram standing quietly by the entrance. They quickly tapped their neighbours on their arms to draw their attention and pointed to Shri Ram. As the workers started looking at Shri Ram, the management also turned around to look at what had drawn the workers' attention. As they saw their owner standing there, the management team immediately got to their feet and rushed towards him. They asked him to sit down, but he gestured that he preferred to remain standing.

The workers were uncertain how to react to Shri Ram's presence. Some of the workers who knew him, and knew that he knew them as well, were embarrassed. They sat with their eyes downcast, not wanting to meet Shri Ram's eyes in case he looked towards them. The trade union leaders and other workers, however, did not have any such qualms. In fact, they saw it as a minor victory that the Jay Engineering management had to bring out the big guns to negotiate with them.

Believing that they had the upper hand in the demand negotiations, the group took an aggressive stand. One union leader started thumping the table with his fist and shouting, 'Give us our bonus or we will burn down the mill!' The other workers took up the chant and soon the canteen was filled with the noise of workers thumping the tables and shouting the slogan. Shri Ram stood where he was and just watched the workers. As he watched without saying a word, the workers got more agitated and raised the pitch of their sloganeering.

The situation was becoming ugly. The general manager tried to get Shri Ram to leave but was brushed aside. Another senior executive whispered in Shri Ram's ear, 'Lala ji, someone may harm you. Please allow me to escort you out of the room.'

Shri Ram brushed him aside as well with a wave of his hand. He then drew up a chair and stood on it, raising his hand to gesture to the workers to quieten down so that he could speak. Some workers quietened down immediately; others took a moment or two. Soon the room was silent.

'If any of you believe that I will be frightened by your threats, think again,' Shri Ram began in a low but assertive voice. 'I am standing here in front of you. If anyone wants to slap me or hit me, here I am. Come and do your job.'

The workers shuffled their feet, looking embarrassed. Some of the union leaders stared at Shri Ram defiantly. Shri Ram was not finished speaking.

'You say you want to burn down the mill?' he asked the gathering. Getting no answer from anyone, he continued to speak. 'Go ahead and burn it down. After all, it is your own property. How can I, or anyone else, prevent you from destroying your own property, eh?'

Now, even the trade union leaders looked embarrassed. The other workers continued looking down, unwilling to even raise their heads lest they caught Shri Ram's eye.

Shri Ram knew that his words had hit home. He did not want to leave the room with a negative sentiment. He therefore changed his tone. 'Bhaiyon, Jay Engineering is your own company; it is your property. I am only a custodian. You know that it has just come out of a bad time. Give me some time to make it earn more money. After all, when it earns more money there is more money for you and for me,' he said.

The workers now raised their heads. They were no longer embarrassed. They looked at Shri Ram as he continued to speak.

'If you have any problems come to me. Don't listen to mischief-mongers who will leave you without providing you alternative jobs or even money. And always remember, hard work never goes to waste and is always rewarded,' he said. Most workers, he saw, were nodding their heads in agreement.

Shri Ram felt it was time to wind up matters. 'Has anyone got any questions for me?' he asked before stepping down from his chair.

No one had any questions. But there was a lot of chatter amongst the workers as they spoke to each other about what Shri Ram had said. As they were chatting, they saw Shri Ram walking towards them.

Shri Ram knew some of the older workers. He knew their names, and he even knew the names of their wives and children. He stopped and patted a worker here and a worker there on his back. 'How is Daya?' he asked one; 'Has Badri started going to school?' he asked another; 'You have been at Jay Engineering for some years now, Kumar Bhai. Tell me, how do you think we can improve the quality of our products?' he asked yet another worker.

The mood in the room had changed completely. The antagonism had vanished into thin air and was replaced by an easy camaraderie. The canteen, which had been filled with angry slogans, was now filled with animated chatter interspersed with laughter.

The workers went back to their work without rancour. Shri Ram had won another battle.

Meanwhile, the 1940s saw the Shri Ram houses on Curzon Road emerge as the centre of culture in Delhi. The Shri Ram household was a full one with all his sons, their wives and children living there. This was in total contrast to the lonely haveli at Kucha Mai Das in old Delhi where Shri Ram had been the only child, with no friends, in a house full of adults.

Shri Ram made up for his childhood loneliness with a vengeance! The Shri Ram home at 22 Curzon Road was always full of people. 'Blessed are the ones who get to host guests,' Shri Ram often told his family.

Shri Ram had friends of three different kinds. One consisted of his industry peers. Then there consisted of his colleagues from the different businesses. The third were the people totally unconnected to the business who had gained distinction in their own fields. He loved spending time with all of them. Shri Ram revelled in the fact that he did not have to ask people to come over and spend time with him; they did it themselves and willingly.

Sometimes when Shri Ram was in a pensive mood, he would sit alone in the veranda outside his spartan room. Closing his eyes, he would go back to the days in the haveli in Kucha Mai Das when he would cry because no boys would come to his house to play. And then, he would shake his head delicately, as if throwing those memories out of his head.

It was easy to understand that he had friends from his industry. It was the set of friends from outside the industry that surprised even him initially. These ranged from politicians to economists to artists. But then he realized that successful people want to be in the company of other successful people. And Shri Ram was amongst the leading industrialists of that time. He actively encouraged his non-industry friends to spend time at his home.

It was also a fact that the creative set of people were introduced by the younger of Shri Ram's two bahus. Sheila Bharat Ram and Sumitra Charat Ram were two different individuals, but the creative arts bound them together. Shri Ram, incidentally, was tone deaf. He was not a connoisseur of music. It was Sheila who was fond of music and other creative arts. Even as a young bride she had encouraged her father-in-law to invite various artists to the Shri Ram house on Curzon Road.

Shri Ram was a traditional, conservative and even an orthodox man. He liked his bahus to follow protocol. Every morning the bahus had to be bathed and ready before 8 a.m., dressed in crisp, starched saris, heads covered by their pallus, a big bindi on their foreheads, a string of pearls round their necks, and sit at the breakfast table. Shri Ram, after his morning walk, puja and bath, would come out of his room and enter the dining room at precisely 8 a.m. He expected his bahus to be there waiting on the family and also expected his sons to be there for breakfast. The ladies would get up and touch their father-in-law's feet. He would give them his aashirwaad and sit down for breakfast. The bahus would then sit peeling fruit and generally tending to the menfolk as they ate their breakfast.

Shri Ram also expected his bahus to be at the table when the time came for evening tea. The bahus, in fresh saris once again, would supervise the setting up of the tea. Typical Indian snacks of pakoras, samosas or laddoos would be served at teatime.

This orthodoxy did not come in the way of Shri Ram encouraging his bahus to invite various artists to their home. Sheila started the trend. Amongst the first artists who came to the Shri Ram house were Uday Shankar and his troupe. The music director of the troupe was Baba Allauddin Khan, a noted multi-instrumentalist and music teacher of the times. In fact, there was a room in the Shri Ram house that was called Baba's Room, as he stayed there for extended periods, teaching many future artists.

Baba inspired Sheila to take up sitar lessons again. She had learnt a bit before her marriage and was delighted to pick it up again. Baba told young Ravi Shankar to start teaching Sheila. As she would sit in the room learning, her young son Arun Bharat Ram would sneak in and sit quietly and listen. In later years Ravi Shankar, seeing the young boy's interest, started teaching Arun the sitar as well. Arun and his elder brother Vinay were the only ones from amongst Shri Ram's grandkids who showed an interest in music. Vinay was older and was a trained musician already. Thus, it was young Arun who was the cynosure of all adult musicians, including Baba, who took a fond liking to the boy. He even gave Arun the gold watch he had received as an award from the then President of India. It is another matter that once Sheila found out she forced Arun to return the watch and also gave him a sound beating!

It was Baba who was instrumental in setting up the Shri Ram house as the cultural centre in Delhi. Ravi Shankar and Baba used to stay at the Shri Ram house for extended periods of time. Every now and then Baba would ask Ravi Shankar, 'Robu, just find out which artist is playing at All India Radio.'

In those years, All India Radio was the only media channel available to performing artists to take their artistry countrywide. Ravi would find out and inform Baba. 'Okay, then tell them to come and perform here at home,' Baba would instruct Ravi Shankar. The artists would troop in and perform for a small audience.

This was the beginning of the popular baithaks at the Shri Ram house. Many well-known artists came and performed at these informal gatherings. Sheila was in charge of organizing these evenings. Once Sumitra joined the family, she too helped organize them.

Shri Ram himself may not have been musically inclined, but he encouraged Sheila and Sumitra to host these cultural evenings. Once a month or so performing artists who were big names by themselves would come to the Shri Ram house, the badi kothi, for the baithaks.

In the summer months these baithaks were held in the lawns. The staff would water the lawns by the late afternoon so that by early evening the ground had cooled down. White cotton sheets were spread over the lawn so that people could sit without fear of getting their clothes stained by the grass. Mogra flowers were sprinkled on the sheets for a sweet fragrance. In the winter months the baithaks were held in the big room of the badi kothi. These were serious musical evenings and thus no cold sharbat in the summer nor hot tea in the winter would be served during the performances. The people could partake of light refreshments after the musicians had finished their performances.

The baithaks started off with small audiences made up almost entirely of other musicians who lived in Delhi. But as the baithaks gained ground, people, especially from old Delhi, who were fond of music started attending these informal concerts. Each baithak had about thirty or forty people in attendance. Thus, these were intimate sessions where the audience had a chance to spend quality time with well-known musicians. Over time, musicians started reaching out to Sheila or Sumitra themselves to let them know that they would be in Delhi and to request a baithak. Being part of the baithaks soon became a status symbol both for the attendees as well as the musicians.

Shri Ram took part in the baithaks as often as he could. While he could not understand the music as much as maybe some others, he revelled in the company of the people. It gave him a great sense of quiet satisfaction to have well-known people wanting to come to his house. The ghosts of loneliness from his childhood were melting away in the crowds.

The liberal outlook of Shri Ram was also visible in his allowing the bahus of the house to indulge in creative activities. Rabindranath Tagore's niece, a friend of Sheila's, put together a dance drama based on her uncle's works. Sheila, Sumitra and a host of other amateur performers rehearsed for months and put up the show at the All India Fine Arts and Crafts Society, or AIFACS as it was more popularly known.

The khaandani families of Delhi were surprised that Shri Ram had allowed the ladies of the house to be on stage. Those were the days when girls from 'good homes' kept away from such activities. But Shri Ram sat proudly in the hall applauding his bahus. He may have allowed the bahus to perform their dance drama, but they had to be back at the dining table at 8 a.m., bathed and dressed in crisp saris, heads covered with their pallus, peeling fruit for the menfolk!

19

A Plane Crash Devastates Shri Ram

A major event during the early years of Shri Ram's leave from work was the inauguration of a new cloth mill soon after India became independent. In honour of the country's independence, the new textile mill was named Swatantra Bharat Mill. The decision to set up a new cotton mill had been taken back in 1943. But the raging World War had made it difficult to get the building material and machinery. Once the war ended, it was decided to set up the new mill in Patiala. But then, during the Partition, there was an influx of refugees, a large number of whom came to Delhi. After internal discussions a decision was taken to set up the new mill in the industrial area of Najafgarh Road in Delhi. This would enable the mill to offer employment to many of the refugees who had come from Pakistan.

Shri Ram's younger sons—Bharat Ram and Charat Ram—were given the responsibility of setting up the new mill. Charat Ram helped to design the mill, and the execution of the design on the ground was carried out by Bharat Ram. Once completed, the Swatantra Bharat Mill was the best-laid-out mill in India.

Shri Ram was content giving guidance to the business and was happy not to be involved in the day-to-day running of the business. By 1949, his brother Shankar Lall was managing the business along with Shri Ram's three sons. The eldest, Murli Dhar, was actively involved in the Lyallpur textile factory even though it was now in another country—Pakistan. He also bore a large part of the responsibility of the DCM Group. Bharat Ram and Charat Ram, the younger sons, had their own responsibilities cut out.

It was then that life dealt Shri Ram a cruel blow. A plane crash took away his eldest son and daughter-in-law in 1949.

Murli Dhar was to travel to Lyallpur, and his wife had decided to accompany him. She wanted to buy some jewellery in Karachi as their son Shri Dhar was to get married the following year. The two of them were travelling from Lahore to Karachi. A navigational error on the part of the pilot led to the plane crashing. There were no survivors.

The news reached Delhi around noon. Shri Ram was in shock but wanted to travel to Pakistan immediately. He got in touch with his friend, Ramnath Goenka, who in turn spoke with R.K. Dalmia, who was the chairman of Indian National Airways at that time. Dalmia got a plane organized for Shri Ram. Goenka, along with Desh Bandhu Gupta and B.D. Pathak, accompanied Shri Ram. B.D. Pathak was the same man who had travelled to Allahabad to break the news of Phoolan Devi's death to his boss.

Once the plane landed in Karachi, Ghulam Mohammed, the then Governor General of Pakistan, received Shri Ram at the airport. Goenka was amazed at the high esteem in which Shri Ram was held in Pakistan. There was already a huge crowd of high officials and friends who had gathered at the airport to express their condolences to Shri Ram. The plane wreckage had still to be spotted, and the group waited restlessly.

It was in the evening that the news came that the wreckage had been spotted at Jungshahi, about 160 km away from Karachi. The group boarded a train and reached the railway station near the plane crash site. The plane had crashed on a hilltop, and the wreckage was spread over a wide area. No one had survived, and some of the bodies were burnt beyond recognition. Shri Ram wanted to go to the crash site but was prevailed upon to stay back at the station.

It was a small station without a waiting room. Wordlessly, he stretched out on a wooden bench on the platform. As Pathak could identify Murli Dhar, Shri Ram requested the young man to go to the crash site along with the others. As Pathak turned away to join the group leaving the station, Shri Ram called him back. He used to wear a pashmina shawl in the winters—in fact, the pashmina shawl had become a trademark of Shri Ram's. As Pathak came towards him, Shri Ram took off his favourite shawl and handed it over to the young man. 'Please wrap Murli in this when you find him,' Shri Ram said softly and went back to lie on the hard bench.

The group could not identify anyone, including Murli Dhar, as the bodies had been burnt beyond recognition. The small group returned to Delhi, sad and broken.

Two years after the plane crash Shri Ram lost his brother Shankar Lall, again unexpectedly. Shri Ram was devastated.

Shankar Lall and Murli Dhar had been just a few years apart and were more like brothers than uncle and nephew. They were both of similar temperament as well—they had liked poetry and the creative arts. It was a difficult time for Shri Ram, but he dealt with it with stoicism. He would tell people that he must have done something wrong in his previous birth and therefore had to suffer the loss of his eldest son and brother in such quick succession.

Shri Ram could not grieve for long as the business needed his attention. With both Shankar Lall and Murli Dhar gone, Shri Ram decided that he needed to end his sabbatical and get back to work. By 1951, a little over a year after the plane crash, Shri Ram returned as the chairman of the DCM Group. His two surviving sons, Bharat Ram and Charat Ram, were thirty-seven and thirty-three years old respectively.

Although Shri Ram had returned to work, he was not his old self. Always delicate, his health had been of increasing concern to him for some years now. The trauma of losing his brother and eldest son prematurely added to his mental fragility. Even more than before, he realized the importance of enabling his two younger sons to manage the business. He also ensured that the sons of Murli Dhar were trained and given charge of businesses as well. Shri Dhar, the elder son of Murli Dhar, was sent to Calcutta to manage the factories there. Thus, even though he came back as the chairman, Shri Ram kept away from the day-to-day affairs of the business. His sons and the DCM managers took on the responsibility of running the business. Shri Ram continued to provide guidance and the overall vision.

By the time he returned to the business, Shri Ram was counted amongst the top industrialists of India. The government and other industry bodies sought his association and guidance. He had been nominated as a member in the first board of directors of the Reserve Bank of India in 1935. Now the government needed him and his business acumen in Sindri Fertilizers.

Sindri Fertilizers was one of the first big ventures of the government. It was a commercial venture set up and run by the public sector. The new government under Jawaharlal Nehru was committed to socialism, and Sindri Fertilizers was to be its early showpiece. But the company ran into problems even before it could start production. The cost of setting up the factory itself had overshot its budget twice over. There were murmurs, subdued no doubt, wondering that if public sector ventures were to be so outrageously expensive, then how could they be run efficiently and profitably.

Nehru decided to get two businessmen on the board of Sindri Fertilizers. In 1951 he invited Shri Ram and J.J. Ghandy of the Tata Group to be directors on the board. Shri Ram pondered over the invitation. And then he accepted because he saw the fertilizer business as essential for the newly independent India. Even though it was a government company, Shri Ram was determined to give his views on the manner in which it was run.

The government babus who had been chosen to run the company had their own ideas. More bureaucrats than businessmen, they tried to run Sindri Fertilizers like a government department. The board had ten members and was headed by C.C. Desai, who was a secretary in the government. Six directors on the board were representatives of the owner—the government—and represented the ministries of finance, agriculture and industry. In addition, there was a labour leader and a member of Parliament on the board. Ghandy and Shri Ram were the other two directors.

Shri Ram, even though a non-executive director, took on his task with his customary seriousness and enthusiasm. He spoke out about matters that concerned him. He told the chairman of the board that since he had given his word, he would do his best for the company. 'In fact, even if I had not given my word, once I agreed to become a director, I took it as my moral responsibility to do the best I am capable of,' he continued.

Shri Ram was determined to do his best to make Sindri Fertilizers a viable and profitable venture. But he realized that the government babus running the company saw him as an obstacle. The wily bureaucrats had made a provision in the articles of association of the company empowering the president of the union to remove directors at will.

Shri Ram found this provision odd. He scrutinized the articles of association of other public undertakings, including the Industrial Finance Corporation and the Reserve Bank of India. He found that no other body gave this power to the president.

At the first board meeting Shri Ram asked the members what the reason was for empowering the president to remove directors at will. There was silence for a minute as the board did not expect this direct onslaught. The chairman tried to downplay the provision and explained to Shri Ram and Ghandy that it was a temporary provision and that he, as the chairman, had no desire to invoke the provision as long as eminent persons such as Shri Ram and Ghandy were on the board. But Shri Ram was adamant and continued his argument even outside the board meeting. Letters were exchanged between the chairman and Shri Ram. 'It is true that much depends upon the working and the attitude of the official and the non-official directors, but there always is an underlying psychological and sentimental point of view which it is no use ignoring,' he wrote to Desai.

Shri Ram's onslaught worked. He made it abundantly clear and also brought on record that the president would not question the supremacy of the board of directors. Shri Ram further proclaimed to the board that he would look upon Sindri as an autonomous body and not as a department of the government.

Having won this small but important battle with the board, Shri Ram settled down to serve Sindri Fertilizers to the best of his ability. He worked as if it were his own firm. He went into the minutest details, scrutinized every report and questioned any item that he found odd. And he did not wait for the formal board meetings to take up these matters; he discussed them with the chairman and even the management whenever he felt it was required. He also encouraged his own staff and management to give suggestions on how to turn around the fertilizer company.

Shri Ram addressed the problem of Sindri in four ways. He wanted the cost of production to be brought down, the output increased and the market exploited extensively. The fourth point was the one he focused on in all his ventures. He wanted the company to create such conditions for the staff that all workers, foremen, executives and managers would give their best to the company. He also suggested setting up a training school for mechanics and maintenance workers. Shri Ram had great faith in the Punjabi attitude towards work and their mechanical aptitude. He wanted to bring in Sikh fitters as gang-leaders and hoped that it would infuse the spirit of hard work in the other Sindri workers. He also wanted to bring in a foreign expert to set up a training unit at Sindri.

Shri Ram's relentless efforts started bearing fruit. By 1954, three years after Shri Ram was inducted on to the board, production had gone up by one-third, which resulted in better revenues and profits. Shri Ram credited the success to the team of workers and managers of the company.

In his own ventures, Shri Ram always gave matters of staff the highest priority. He was involved in all matters concerning recruitment, training, working conditions and workers' participation. In fact, he looked at his workers as members of a large family, with Shri Ram himself at the top as the karta. (A karta is the senior-most male member in a Hindu undivided family. He acts as the head and is responsible for all the affairs of the family, including legal and financial matters.) In his own ventures he projected himself as a father figure to the workers. But he kept away from all this in Sindri. He was clear that it was not the role that he wanted in a government undertaking. So he did not get involved, unless specifically asked, in staff matters.

There was one staff matter, however, that Shri Ram had very strong views about. This was the matter of recommendations in recruitment. Shri Ram had prided himself on building a business empire by focusing on merit. He ignored all considerations of caste, race, religion or province and focused only on the ability of the person before him. At Sindri, if any applicant turned up with a letter of sifarish, Shri Ram would not allow himself to be influenced by the letter—even though the letter may have been written by the Prime Minister himself. Soon word got around that the only place Shri Ram had for a sifarishi letter was the dustbin!

While Shri Ram was busy with the affairs of Sindri and other businesses, his household had grown and was bursting with the energy of all his grandchildren. It was only Shri Dhar's family that lived in Calcutta, as he was in charge of Jay Engineering. Shri Dhar was much older than his other cousins; his father Murli Dhar had been at least ten years older than his younger brothers. Thus it was that Shri Dhar's children, Shri Ram's great-grandchildren, were closer in age to the other grandchildren. Nieces and nephews became friends with their uncles and aunts.

Shri Dhar's children visited Delhi during the holidays and joined in with their uncles and aunts—children of Bharat and Charat Ram—for the holiday fun. Gauri, the younger daughter of Charat Ram, along with her siblings—Shobha, Vivek and Siddarth—would join her cousins in many escapades. Though Charat Ram and his family lived in the badi kothi along with Mrs Shankar Lall, it was the chhoti kothi that was the scene of all activities.

In the evenings, Shri Ram would sit outside his room and watch his grandchildren play in the garden. Sellers of chooran, papad, chaat and candy floss would come on their bicycles selling their wares to the residents of Curzon Road. Shri Ram would ask the grandchildren to buy whatever they wanted to. The kids' favourite item was the gol gappa, which sold at eight for 25 paise. The children would sometimes use their pocket money, Rs 2 a week, and at other times would look to earn more money from Shri Ram.

Shri Ram would gather the children around him and give them a deal. If any child could recite a Kabir ka doha they would get Re 1. If a child plucked out a white hair from Shri Ram's head they got 50 paise. If a child could recite a passage from the Ramayana, they got Rs 2—the equivalent of their weekly pocket money. The children would gather around Shri Ram crying, 'Bhaiji, I know a doha, Bhaiji, I know a passage from the Ramayana, Bhaiji, I see a white hair!'

Shri Ram's room was at one end of a corridor on the ground floor. At the other end of the corridor was the room of his secretary, Khanna Babu. Bharat Ram's family lived on the first floor of this bungalow. When Shri Dhar and his family visited from Calcutta, they stayed on the ground floor. The elders, during the day, were all on the ground floor, leaving the children free run of the first floor.

It was here that all plans were hatched. One of the favourite antics of the children was to put itching powder on the beds of all the adults. And then they would watch in glee as the elders got up scratching various parts of their bodies.

Bharat Ram's boys would often shoot their air rifles at the various birds in the Curzon Road area.

One day the children gave twenty pieces of bubblegum to the pet monkey of Mrs Shankar Lall. The monkey became bad-tempered because it got tired of chewing the bubblegum non-stop and started scratching the people near it. But Mrs Shankar Lall refused to get rid of it as she believed it was an avatar of Hanuman.

Shri Ram was either ignorant of all these antics or was aware and ignored them. But there was one incident that got him angry. It involved his trusted secretary, Khanna Babu.

Khanna's room was down the corridor from Shri Ram's room. Khanna had a phone—phone number 42421—in his room to enable Shri Ram and any others to reach him easily. One lazy hot afternoon when all the adults were in their rooms and Khanna was away, the children sneaked into the secretary's room. They knew that Khanna Babu had a diary in which he wrote all the important phone numbers he needed.

One child was asked to keep vigil at the door and warn the others if he saw anyone coming. Giggling and shushing each other, the other children leafed through the diary. They first found the phone number of the local halwai. Then they found the numbers of various ministers in the government.

The oldest child dialled the halwai and spoke in a deep voice. He said that they were calling from the Shri Ram house and that Khanna Babu had asked him to call the halwai. The halwai was ordered to send boxes of mithai and samosas to various ministers' homes. The halwai took the orders and delivered. Shri Ram was a big man and a big customer. The halwai did not ask too many questions.

Shri Ram was enjoying his evening when minister after minister started calling him, thanking him for the mithai and samosas. They assumed that there had been some good news or a celebration at home that had prompted him to send out the mithai. Some ministers who thought they were close to Shri Ram even chided him for keeping the good news, whatever it was, a secret.

Shri Ram was perplexed. But he could not show this to the ministers. He summoned Khanna. The children, peeking down from the stairs, heard the bellow of Shri Ram. They looked at each other and giggled with impish looks in their eyes. They crept down the stairs and waited behind the door to Shri Ram's room to hear what would happen next.

'Khanna, *yeh kya hai? Sab mujhe phone kar rahe hain. Tum ne mithai kyon bhijwaai hai in sab logon ko?'* yelled Shri Ram in anger. (Khanna, what is all this? Everyone is calling me. Why have you sent mithai to all of them?)

'Bu-b-but Lala ji, I have not done anything,' stammered Khanna. He was aware of his boss' anger.

'*To kya halwai ne apne aap hi mithai bhej di hai un sab logon ko? Paagal hai kya woh? Jaao pata lagaao aur mujhe bataao*,' instructed Shri Ram. (Then has the halwai sent the mithai on his own? Is he mad? Go and find out the details and tell me.)

Khanna ran back to his room. The children giggled some more.

Khanna came back after a while having found out the details from the halwai.

'Lala ji, the halwai says that a call came from our house instructing him to send the mithai and samosas to the ministers,' said Khanna hesitatingly. 'But I did not given any such instruction. Lala ji, did you by any chance tell the halwai to . . .' Khanna trailed off as he saw the thunderous look on Shri Ram's face.

'You are asking if I instructed the halwai? Khanna, what is wrong with you? Why would I send mithai? And if I had, as you seem to be implying, why would I be asking you?' shouted Shri Ram, truly angry by now.

Khanna was not finished yet. But he did not know how to tell Shri Ram the next bit.

'Why are you still standing here, Khanna? Go away,' Shri Ram said in frustration.

'Lala ji, the halwai said that the caller did not sound like an adult. Maybe some of the childrennnnn . . .' Khanna said softly but stopped as he saw Shri Ram getting angrier.

The children knew that Shri Ram was upset. But they did not know how upset. They stayed put behind the door, some still giggling softly.

Shri Ram got up, took his walking stick and walked to the door of his room. He flung it open and saw all the children huddled together, giggling away. The children stopped giggling and a pin-drop silence ensued. Shri Ram did not have to ask them anything; the children's expressions gave them away.

Shri Ram raised his stick and hit the child nearest to him. The rest of the children started running away. Shri Ram managed to catch hold of the arm of one grandchild even as the others ran into the garden. The children, well-versed in the game of try-to-catch-me, ran in different directions.

'Khanna, go catch them,' yelled Shri Ram, trying to keep hold of the squirming child. The child managed to break free and ran into the garden.

Khanna by now had come out running and was out of breath. Shri Ram told him to chase the children and catch them. He himself also ran into the garden waving his stick threateningly. The children were more agile and ran to the far end of the lawn and hid behind the bushes. Shri Ram ran around for a bit but then got tired and went back inside the house.

He came out to the veranda, pulled out his chair and sat there waiting for the children. And when they did troop back, they did so with their heads down and faces downcast. By then Shri Ram's anger had also subsided. The children had to settle for a verbal lashing!

But they did not mind, as they had had the most wonderful afternoon.

This incident aside, Shri Ram had the greatest fondness for his grandchildren and great-grandchildren. All the love that he could not demonstrate to his sons he showered on their kids. The sons and bahus were afraid and wary of Shri Ram, but the children had no such qualms. Shri Ram kept jars filled with chooran, candy and aam papad on his table in his room. The children, every morning, would troop into his room to say 'Jai Ram ji ki.' He would ruffle their hair. And then each child was allowed to take one piece of any of the goodies from the jars.

The Shri Dhar family missed out on these daily fun events. But when they came for holidays, Ajay Shriram, and his brother and sister would join in the fun.

Shri Ram loved the cinema. The family did not go to the cinema, as Shri Ram would get the cinema to come home. The projector would be set up and the screen erected. The family would gather and watch films in the Shri Ram house. There was one movie, however, that Shri Ram wanted to take the entire family to watch. The movie was *Jagriti*. It was playing at the Regal in Connaught Place.

The family was told to get ready. Ajay was a small child and was to be left behind with the staff. But he wanted to go with everyone. He saw his mother getting ready and knew that she was going with the family. He followed her to the main room and then to the veranda, all the while holding on to her pallu. His mother, Prabha, kept trying to disengage her son from her pallu and kept telling him that he could not go. But young Ajay kept on.

By then Shri Ram had come out of his room, ready to leave. He saw that Prabha was standing in the veranda and not sitting in the car. He gestured to her to get on and not hold everyone up.

Prabha tried one last time to get Ajay to leave her pallu. Ajay did leave her pallu but then caught hold of her legs, refusing to let her go. As Prabha stood there helplessly, trying to get her child to leave her, Shri Ram walked up to the pair. He bent down, took Ajay's hands off his mother's legs and picked him up. He then put Ajay on a small table that was on the veranda and gave the child one tight whack.

'You are making us all late for the movie. Now go and play inside. Your mother will come back soon,' Shri Ram told the child quietly but firmly.

Shri Ram's anger was like a volcano. It erupted and then quietened down. He did not keep any malice in his heart. By the time the adults came back the children were asleep. In the morning when all the kids, including Ajay, went to Shri Ram's room for their daily dose of goodies, Ajay got a fond ruffle on his head and an extra aam papad!

20

The Setting Up of Lady Shri Ram College

BY the late 1950s Shri Ram was in the seventh decade of his life. After the death of his brother and eldest son he had had no option but to return to DCM on a full-time basis. But his motivation levels were low, and his health was of concern. He tried not to get involved with the day-to-day affairs of the business and to concentrate instead on some of the new ventures he was involved in. Sindri Fertilizers was one such venture, but it was not his own. The textile mill at Hissar was different—it was his own, and it had been set up at the behest of the local government.

Hissar was the home district of Shri Ram as well as the hometown of Sheila—Bharat Ram's wife. At that time it was part of Punjab and was mostly a wasteland. There was no industry at all. However, the local government was keen to get some industry started. They knew that any industry would be a force multiplier for the local economy. They turned to Shri Ram and requested him to set up a textile mill in Hissar. A textile mill was seen as a venture that would provide many jobs to the locals in one go.

In 1956 Shri Ram was seventy-three years old and of fragile health. But he could not say no to the local government. He discussed the matter with his sons, who gave him the confidence to go ahead with the venture. With both Bharat Ram and Charat Ram taking on the full responsibility, the construction of the mill and the workers' colony started. The mill was planned with 25,000 spindles, which increased as the years went by. The workers' colony had 700 houses with electricity, running water, sewerage lines, consumer cooperative stores, a primary school, a library, an auditorium, a swimming pool, playgrounds and a children's park and dispensary.

It was around this time that it was mentioned to Shri Ram that there was a need for a third women's college in Delhi. Miranda House and Indraprastha College were the two women's colleges in Delhi in 1955, but these were insufficient to take in the number of women wanting to study further.

Shri Ram wanted to set up an educational institute in memory of his wife. He thought a girls' college would be the ideal way to remember Phoolan Devi. He discussed the idea with his sons, as they were the ones now managing the business and finances. If the college had to be established it would need the support of funds from DCM. The sons liked the idea and agreed to give Rs 3 lakh to begin with.

Shri Ram applied to Delhi University to start Lady Shri Ram College for Women. He told the university that the corpus would be put together by DCM and the Commercial Education Trust, which was already running the Shri Ram College of Commerce, also in Delhi University.

Lady Shri Ram College came into being in August 1956 in a small building in Daryaganj. The building had been the hostel of the Shri Ram College of Commerce. It was subsequently that the fifteen acres of land in south Delhi was bought.

Lady Shri Ram College was perhaps the closest to Shri Ram's heart. He supervised the construction of the college and hostel buildings himself. In spite of his frail health, he would spend time at the construction site and interact with the workers. In the summer there would be an attendant with an umbrella for him. But Shri Ram would ignore it and move quickly from one place to the other, keeping a close eye on the ongoing construction. Any good book he came across would be kept aside, earmarked for the college library.

The new college building was completed in early 1958 and classes began in the new session in July of the same year. It was Shri Ram's desire that this college become the premier educational institute for women in India. He took a lively personal interest in the running and development of LSR, as the college came to be known popularly. He interviewed all staff personally, especially the faculty. As the chairman of the governing body, he was always present ahead of time for the meetings. All reading material sent to him before each meeting would be studied by him in detail.

LSR soon became the college of choice for women even though it was not in the main North Campus of Delhi University. Even today, decades later, Lady Shri Ram College is the first port of call for women seeking admission in a Bachelor's course in Delhi.

Besides supervising the development of LSR, Shri Ram was actively involved with Jay Engineering. A particular challenge had come up in 1955. Punjab had become a hub for indigenously manufactured sewing machines. Some enterprising Punjabi craftsmen had started making sewing machines in local foundries and selling them in the market at lower rates than those of Usha. Shri Ram was not unduly worried. He believed that a sewing machine was a piece of precision equipment and that local foundries were not capable of delivering the precision required.

The government, however, had other ideas. Jawaharlal Nehru was inclined to promote local small-scale industry. The bureaucrats, too, supported the thought, as the big industrialists were looked upon with suspicion by the government. To help the growth of small industry, the government proposed a monthly production limit of 10,000 sewing machines for Jay Engineering. Further, the government was proposing to permit the import of some smaller parts that would enable these cottage industries to manufacture sewing machines and needles. The government was also planning to impose a 10 per cent excise duty on Usha sewing machines.

Shri Ram knew that the Indian government had a socialistic mindset but he was unable to understand the reason for giving preference to cottage industry over larger manufacturing units, especially in relation to products that required precision. He engaged with the government and argued his case. 'To be able to export to foreign markets and to give a really satisfactory article to the consumer in this country, the quality must steadily improve at lower and lower prices. This can only be done by large-scale industry provided they are allowed to steadily increase the production and sales,' he argued. He also tried to convince the government that his desire to expand the production capacity was not to make more profits. This was a purely socialistic mindset, he said. He wanted to expand capacities in order to capture foreign markets for India.

Shri Ram was partly successful. The government did not lift the production ceiling but increased it to 25,000 machines per month. Jay Engineering was also given permission to set up a plant to manufacture sewing machine needles. While planning for the new plant, Shri Ram decided to discontinue the production of hurricane lanterns. This was one product that he believed the cottage industry could produce. It was not a precision product, and he wanted Jay Engineering to focus only on those products that required specialization.

Around this time Shri Ram asked his team to set up a separate plant for Usha fans. The fans business had grown over the years, and Shri Ram believed that it needed a factory of its own. Jay Engineering was already producing over 16 per cent of India's fans by this time, as per a Government of India's Ministry of Commerce and Industry report. And it was producing a whopping 98 per cent of India's sewing machines.

Though he fought against the reservation of the production of sewing machines and needles for the cottage industry, Shri Ram realized that the subject of small-scale industry was close to the Prime Minister's heart. Being the shrewd strategist that he was, Shri Ram decided to advocate the cause of the small sector with enthusiasm. He also saw this as a chance to collaborate with various government departments. Shri Ram drafted a detailed scheme for economic work units. His report had suggestions on how these small units could be supplied with raw materials, at what price they could sell their finished products and how their workers could be housed. He also propagated various community development programmes. One such programme was the setting up of the Usha silai kendras, or sewing institutes.

Shri Ram realized that, while full-fledged tailors were the first target of Usha sewing machines, the housewife could also be trained to use a sewing machine. He foresaw each home having a sewing machine so minor repair jobs and probably some new clothes, especially for the children, could be stitched at home. It was with this thought in mind that Shri Ram set up the Usha silai kendras. He gave his daughters-in-law the responsibility of managing them. These kendras provided training to women in all aspects of sewing. While the kendras in the cities did well, it was in rural India that they found their true calling. The village women flocked to the kendras to learn about stitching and sewing. Shri Ram even provided the Usha machines free of cost to these kendras.

Jay Engineering was so close to Shri Ram's heart that even when his health deteriorated further he would try to visit Calcutta and the factory. In what was to be his last visit to the city of Calcutta, Shri Ram insisted that he be allowed to visit the factory. His grandson Shri Dhar accompanied him and got his doctor to be present through the visit. The workers knew of Shri Ram's ill health and were touched and delighted that their boss was taking the trouble to visit them. They decorated all the buildings with festoons and painted large banners with gold paint. The banners welcomed Shri Ram and had 'Long Live Shri Ram' written on them.

Once Shri Ram reached the factory the welcome party told him that all the workers had gathered to meet him. He was also told that each worker had hand-made a garland for him and wanted to present it to Shri Ram individually. The doctor and Shri Dhar were aghast, as they were sure that Shri Ram's frail health would not be able to take the strain of a thousand handshakes. They were also worried that the heavy garlands of marigold and jasmine would put a strain on his neck. They spoke to the welcome party and told them that it would not be possible.

But Shri Ram was adamant. 'How can I not return the affection of my own people?' he asked his grandson and the doctor. 'Of course I want to meet each of my workers. You can't stop me. Let's go.' He got up as if to start the tour.

Shri Dhar and the doctor caught hold of Shri Ram's hand and pulled him down gently into the chair. 'Bhaiji, if you want, you will meet all the workers,' said Shri Dhar, 'but we will go in an open jeep.'

Shri Ram agreed. The open jeep with Shri Ram, Shri Dhar and the doctor was driven around and through the works. The thousands of workers who had gathered there put up a shout of welcome as they saw the jeep coming. Shouts of 'Shri Ram zindabad' rang through the factory and seemed to energize Shri Ram. He shook hands with the many workers who were able to make their way to the jeep and accepted the garlands they gave him.

No one, least of all Shri Ram, realized that it would be the last time that he would visit Jay Engineering.

21

Shri Ram Fights His Health, but Fails

SHRI Ram was seventy-three years old when he had an accident. He was en route to Pilani with a couple of other men in a car. The men were talking about work animatedly when the car swerved sharply. The driver had not seen a drum that had rolled on to the middle of the road. He had swerved to avoid the drum.

The passengers in the back seat were thrown against each other. Shri Ram was sitting near the window in the back seat. As the car swerved he was thrown against the car door and the other two men were thrown on top of him. Luckily for everyone the car door held and did not open—the result of that would have been catastrophic.

Shri Ram was pinned against the door by the weight of the other two men. As a result, the door handle dug deep into his ribcage. Shri Ram felt the pain but could do nothing as the weight of two adult men was on him. The car stopped, the men disentangled themselves and sat up straight, but Shri Ram knew that he was hurt. He made light of the incident and the car continued on its journey to Pilani.

Once they reached Pilani the officials wanted to send for a doctor. But Shri Ram would have none of it. He sent for a hot water bottle and insisted that he would go ahead with the scheduled programme.

The next day he made a concession to his discomfort. He decided to fly back to Delhi instead of undertaking the long ride in a car. By the time he landed in Delhi he knew that he needed to get medical help for his pain. He did not go home but went straight to Dr Sen's Nursing Home in Daryaganj.

Shri Ram's fears came true. The x-ray taken showed an injury to the spine. Dr Sen ordered his patient complete bed rest for several weeks. This time Shri Ram agreed meekly. Dr Sen encased his back in plaster, which made Shri Ram immobile.

The plaster and the forced bed rest healed his spine, but the immobility played havoc with Shri Ram's delicate digestive system. Shri Ram was not an easy patient. He complained and grumbled all the time. 'My only problem at the moment is that I have no work to do,' he cried to the visitors who came to check on him.

It took him almost a year to get back on his feet and start attending to his business and social obligations. But he had become more accident-prone.

A year after he had recovered he was in Hyderabad. He was going for a meeting, and as he got out of the car, he stepped on a bed of dry leaves. The leaves slipped under his feet, and he fell down. He tried to break his fall with his hands, and his wrist took the entire weight of his body. Shri Ram may have been frail and of slight build, but his entire body weight proved too much for his wrist, which broke. His hand, including the wrist, had to be encased in plaster, and he could not do any paperwork.

Shri Ram was in despair. He wanted to work but found his body did not cooperate. 'I wish somebody with a whip in hand would teach me how to walk again, perhaps a few furlongs on the first day, until I can do two or three miles a day,' he confided to a friend who came to visit him. 'I have lost confidence in my legs and my eyesight,' he said to another.

Shri Ram resigned from the chairmanship of DCM. He also resigned from the directorship of the Reserve Bank of India and left the board of Kirloskar Industries. But the workaholic in Shri Ram refused to release its grip, at least on Shri Ram's mind. It was the classic case of 'the mind is willing, but the flesh is weak.'

Shri Ram had known no life, since 1909, other than DCM. He had spent most of his life working to grow and expand his business. He was now restless as he could not do what he loved the most—work.

'I have made up my mind to revolt,' said Shri Ram aggressively one day to a visitor. 'My doctors want to keep me alive, but I don't know for what. I do not want to keep this physical body even one day longer if it cannot be of use to the country.'

The visitor tried to placate Shri Ram, but he would not listen. 'A person cannot die twice. If by going to Calcutta or Bombay I get a heart attack, so be it. Maybe it will be for the better. One does not have to die lying in bed; let death come where it may,' he told the visitor, who gaped, aghast at hearing this.

Shri Ram, obviously, could not go to either Calcutta or Bombay. Hardly any of his organs were functioning properly by this time. And in August 1962 the doctors discovered that both his kidneys and his prostate gland were in an advanced state of infection. This brought on a severe urinary infection. But Dr Sen, his friend and doctor, was loath to operate on Shri Ram, who was seventy-eight years old and of delicate health.

'I am fed up with life,' moaned Shri Ram to no one in particular as he lay in bed. 'I don't know how long more I have to suffer. I am getting deeper and deeper into the mud.'

By this time Shri Ram had realized that the chances of his getting better were dim. A practical and pragmatic man, he called for the lawyer and drew up a new will. He left enough for his funeral and cremation expenses and then provided for the people who had served him. Khanna Babu, his secretary, and Puran, his personal valet, were provided for generously. He also gave to the Shri Ram Industrial Research Institute. The rest of his estate he bequeathed to his sons, grandsons and their wives.

Shri Ram was being looked after at home. His sons, daughters-in-law, grandchildren and family loyalists were in attendance at almost all hours. The old man was bedridden and alternated between optimism and pessimism.

Finally, a decision was made in October 1962 to move Shri Ram to Dr Sen's Nursing Home. His sons, Bharat Ram and Charat Ram, wanted their father to be under the supervision of doctors and nurses at all times. Shri Ram was not happy with the decision, but all his objections were overruled firmly by the family.

On October 16 the ambulance came to transfer Shri Ram to the nursing home. He was running a high temperature. But he refused to get on the stretcher.

'You can do that when I am dead,' he told the attendants as he got into the ambulance himself. And then at the nursing home, he again refused a stretcher to go to the room earmarked for him on the first floor. He climbed the steps and went to the room himself.

Room Number 1 in Dr Sen's Nursing Home became Shri Ram's home. Even though he was bedridden, he dictated letters to his friends and family. Khanna Babu carried out his duties as his secretary. Shri Ram also requested a friend's daughter to sing two of Mirabai's bhajans to him every day.

The mood in the nursing home was not despondent. The family knew that Shri Ram was not getting any better, but they did not want the atmosphere to be melancholy. Both his sons, Bharat Ram and Charat Ram, had moved into the nursing home to be near their father during this critical time. All efforts were made to keep the talk around him cheerful. It was clear to everyone, however, that Shri Ram's days were numbered.

On 10 January 1963, Shri Ram slipped into a coma in the late evening. The family now knew that this was the end. But they still kept hoping for a miracle. Bharat Ram and Charat Ram kept vigil at their father's bedside till late into the night. The attending nurse finally cajoled them to go to sleep in their room, which was next door. Puran, however, would not be budged. He spread out his thin mattress on the ground and lay there, next to his master.

January in Delhi is cold. 11 January was no different. It was a bitterly cold morning. Room Number 1 needed two heaters to keep it warm. Shri Ram had a restless night. At 5.30 a.m. the attending nurse heard an unevenness in Shri Ram's breathing. Her senses alerted, she went to the bedside and bent over the patient. She checked his pulse, which seemed faint. She then looked at his face. Shri Ram had been in a coma for more than ten hours. His face was pale but now the nurse saw a new pallor creeping in.

She knew she had to get the doctor urgently. But she did not want to leave her patient unattended. Her eyes fell on Puran lying curled up on the thin mattress. She quickly went and tapped him on the shoulder.

'Puran, Puran! Wake up please,' she said urgently.

Puran woke up immediately.

'Kya hua? Lala ji theek toh hain, nah?' was his immediate query.

The nurse shook her head slowly and sorrowfully. Puran understood.

'I have to go get the doctor quickly. Can you watch over the patient? I will not be a minute,' said the nurse as she rushed out of the room.

Puran, wide awake now, stood by the bedside of Shri Ram. He looked at his master, who seemed to be having difficulty breathing. Puran was no doctor, but he knew that the life was ebbing out of Shri Ram. Even though he had been told to watch over the patient, Puran knew that he had to get Shri Ram's sons into the room fast.

He ran to their room next door and woke up Bharat Ram and Charat Ram.

'Jaldi chaliye, jaldi, jaldi. Lala ji ki haalat theek nahin hai,' Puran told the two sons.

Bharat and Charat Ram had slept in their day clothes. They got out of bed quickly. All three rushed to Room Number 1.

As they entered the room they saw the doctor and nurse also run in. The doctor felt for Shri Ram's pulse and, finding none, turned up his eyelids. Curtains had fallen over his eyes. The doctor quietly confirmed that Shri Ram had passed away.

Even though Bharat Ram and Charat Ram had known that their father was in a delicate condition, the news still hit them hard. They looked at and hugged one another, emotions flowing freely between them without either of them needing to say a word. They suddenly felt alone in the world.

As the doctor and nurse waited quietly, the sons got their emotions under control. They knew that they would have to pull out their managerial and organizational skills to get through the next few days. The final rites had to be organized. The sons looked at each other, nodded slightly and then thanked the doctor and nurse for their support. After that they sat in the room and planned for the next few days. Given the stature of Shri Ram, they knew that the final rites and all activities thereafter would need them to be at their managerial best.

There were no mobile phones nor any internet in 1963. But the news of Shri Ram's death spread like wildfire. The newspapers had been printed in the middle of the night but the hawkers selling them yelled out the news of Shri Ram's death as if it were the main headline. All India Radio's morning bulletin broadcast the news to the entire nation. In no time at all, almost everyone, especially in Delhi, had heard about Shri Ram's death.

By the time the ambulance carried the body of Shri Ram back to his Curzon Road bungalow, the lawns were already full of people. The family had taken charge and was ensuring that order was maintained.

The children were all sent to the first floor so that they would be out of the way. Ajay Shriram, Shri Ram's great-grandson and Murli Dhar's grandson, had gone to sleep in his room on the ground floor at night. He was surprised that he was in an unfamiliar room when he woke up. As he rubbed his eyes he saw the other children glued to the window. He too rushed up to it to find out what the commotion was about. He saw that there were over one thousand people in the lawns of the chhoti kothi. And more kept coming.

Shri Ram's body was kept in his spartan room on a bed of flowers. People stood in line to go in and pay their last respects. As the day progressed the line of people became longer. Everyone was sombre and maintained the dignity of the moment.

And then it was time to take the body to Nigambodh Ghat for cremation. The cortege that followed the vehicle carrying the body was the biggest that Delhi had seen in many years. People lined the roads and showered rose petals as the vehicle passed them. These were not merely DCM employees, who were there in all their numbers. Shri Ram, as perhaps the only big Indian industrialist based in Delhi, was respected and revered by ordinary Delhiites. The citizens of Delhi considered Shri Ram to be one of their own, as he had put Delhi in the prime spot on the industrial map of India. They poured out on to the streets wanting to pay their respects to the departed soul.

The cortege reached Nigambodh Ghat. Befitting his status, bundles of sandalwood had been kept ready for the pyre. The two sons performed the final rites and placed the body of their father on the sandalwood pyre.

Amidst the chanting of Vedic chants, the pyre was lit.

As the flames went up, an era ended.

Epilogue

SHRI Ram had, before his death, tried to address the issues of the family and the business by making a will. His elder son, Bharat Ram, was made the head of the business, with the younger son, Charat Ram, as the deputy head. Bansi Dhar, the grandson of Shri Ram and the elder son of Murli Dhar, who had died in the air crash of 1949, was given a substantial role in the business.

The two brothers, Bharat Ram and Charat Ram, were different from each other. Bharat Ram was the public relations and external-facing man while Charat Ram was focused on internal operations. The momentum of working together as a team, as they had done during their father's lifetime, continued for a few years. Both worked closely together and took the DCM Group to even greater success. However, this was not to last for long.

Differences in their working styles started leading to differences of opinion at work. During their father's lifetime, it was the patriarch who had managed these differences and had harnessed each son's ability for the betterment of the business. However, with him gone there was no arbitrator for the two brothers. Bansi Dhar was much younger, and given the culture of the family, could not even dare to intervene when his uncles had arguments. Similarly, intervention by an employee, no matter how senior in the system, was unthinkable.

There was some talk in the family about Bharat Ram and Charat Ram both stepping down from executive positions and letting the next generation take charge. But one would not step down without the other agreeing to do so. The personal differences did affect the working of the business as well. Employees and other stakeholders took advantage of the animosity between the two brothers and formed various factions within the companies. This drove the wedge further between the two brothers, who had to deal with this unwanted factionalism within the teams. This accentuated the problems, and the business dipped further and further and finances became tighter.

But there was more trouble ahead for the already battered DCM Group. In the early 1980s, DCM was the target of a hostile corporate takeover. In those years it was common for Indian families to control their business groups through relatively small equity holdings. So it was that the Shri Ram family together had just under 10 per cent of the shareholding in DCM. The rest of the shares were held by public financial institutions and individual shareholders.

In the 1982–83 budget, the finance minister had made it possible for NRI investors, both individuals and companies, to buy shares of Indian companies subject to certain conditions.

The Indian government had done this with the aim of increasing their foreign exchange reserves. Under the schemes NRIs were permitted to make portfolio investments in shares by buying the shares through the stock exchanges. Further, the purchase of shares in any one company by any one NRI could not exceed 1 per cent of the paid-up equity capital of the company whose shares were being bought.

Swraj Paul, an NRI, was amongst the first to take advantage of the new provision. He circumvented the 1 per cent rule by using thirteen different companies registered in the Isle of Man to buy the shares. Through a web of his companies, Swraj Paul, by May 1983, had already bought 13 per cent of DCM shares. He thus became the largest shareholder of the company.

Swraj Paul had also targeted Escorts, another Indian company, for a takeover in a similar manner. He had bought 7.5 per cent of Escorts while the Nanda family, the owners, had only 5 per cent shareholding. Once it became known that two of India's best-known companies were under a takeover threat, the other family businesses got the jitters.

Many Indian promoters petitioned the government to intervene in the matter. The Shri Ram family themselves approached the Gandhis. Vivek Bharat Ram met with Rajiv Gandhi, who promised to look into the matter. The matter was taken up in the Indian Parliament. Meanwhile, the Indian companies steadfastly refused to register the shares that had been sent by the NRI investor for transfer. And the Reserve Bank of India also refused to clear the transfer of funds to India by Swraj Paul's group.

The matters were discussed heatedly and animatedly in almost all boardrooms. Repeated requests were made to the Indian government by the Indian business owners. Finally, in the middle of 1983 the government established an overall ceiling of 5 per cent of the paid-up capital of the company, which could not be breached by the NRI investor under the NRI investment scheme.

However, the matter of DCM and Escorts still had to be resolved. The matter dragged on. Eventually, in early 1986 the finance secretary, the additional secretary in the Prime Minister's Office and the minister of state for defence mediated between the concerned parties. These gentlemen persuaded Swraj Paul to sell his shares back to the Shri Ram and the Nanda families respectively at a mutually agreed price.

The hostile takeover attempt by Swraj Paul led to further tensions between the two brothers—Bharat Ram and Charat Ram. Each blamed the other for the deteriorating profits of the company leading to a fall in share price, which had emboldened the NRI to make a takeover bid. DCM had been the fourth largest industrial group in the mid-1970s. However, by 1988, the group had slipped further and further down and was a loss-making unit with losses running into Rs 22 crores. Each family member at the helm had his own set of aspirations and each felt that he was constrained by the others.

Finally, the next generation of the family got together and proposed an amicable division of the business. They argued that they all lived in Delhi, they all liked each other and met each other and their families. They did not want the hostile environment of the office to be carried over into the personal relationships between the cousins and their wives/husbands and children.

By 1989–90 it was agreed that DCM would be divided between the three families. DCM Limited went to Bharat Ram's family and Shriram Industrial Enterprises Limited went to Charat Ram's family. Murli Dhar's sons Bansi Dhar and Shri

Dhar wanted a further division within their own companies. Thus, DCM Shriram Consolidated Limited went to Shri Dhar and DCM Shriram Industries Limited went to Bansi Dhar's family.

The family may have been able to divide the businesses amongst themselves without bringing in an outsider; but the financial untangling needed expert advice. The problem was in the shareholding. The shares were in a finance company—Madan Mohan and Shri Ram Pvt Ltd. The Shri Ram family held approximately 55 per cent of the shares and Shankar Lall's family the balance. For the split of the businesses to take place properly, Shankar Lall's shares had to be bought. Further, the Shri Ram family had cross shareholdings in various group companies. These had to be disentangled before the division of businesses could take place. The problem was that no branch of the family had the cash to buy anyone out. It was left to a professional firm to find workable solutions to these complex problems.

Currently there are almost 100 members of the Shri Ram family. The differences in the business have not impacted the personal relations in the family. Even though Bharat Ram and Charat Ram had their differences in the board room, they remained close till the end. They died two months apart—Charat Ram at the age of eighty-nine in May 2007 and Bharat Ram at the age of ninety-three in July 2007.

The families of the three sons of Shri Ram live on and carry on their separate businesses. They meet every Dussehra and Diwali and celebrate the festivals together. For a patriarch there can be no greater joy than the fact that his family carries on the legacy with success in business and harmony in relationships.

Appendix

Shri Ram's Association with Government, Non-governmental and Charitable Institutions

Founder, Commercial Education Trust, 1920

Founder and Chairman, Governing Body, Shri Ram College of Commerce, Delhi University, 1920–1962

Vice President and President, Federation of Indian Chambers of Commerce and Industry, 1929–1931

President, Indian International Chamber of Commerce, 1933

Director of the Central and Local Board, Reserve Bank of India, 1935–1961

Member, Delhi Improvement Trust (Now Delhi Development Authority), 1937–1950

President, Board of Trustees; Chairman, Governing Body, Indraprastha College for Women, Delhi University, 1939–1963

President, All India Organisation of Industrial Employers (AOIE), 1940–1941

Chairman, Governing Body, Ramjas College, Delhi University, 1943–1949

Chairman of the Panel, Post-War Planning on Sugar, Alcohol, Food & Heavy Chemicals, 1944–1945

Member/Architect, Bombay Plan for Post-War Reconstruction (Economic Plan), 1944–1945

Member, Textile Control Board, 1945

Chairman, Northern Regional Committee, All India Council for Technical Education (AICTE), 1945

First Chairman, Kirloskar Oil Engines Limited (KOEL), 1946–1961

Founder, Shriram Institute for Industrial Research, 1947

First Chairman, Industrial Finance Corporation of India, 1948–1954

Member of Board and Governing Body, Council of Scientific and Industrial Research (CSIR), Delhi, 1948–1962

Chairman, Tender Committee, Government of India, 1949

Member of the General Council, and Vice President, Indian Standards Institute, Government of India, 1952–1961

Member, Medical Benefit Council, All India Organisation of Industrial Employers, 1953

Director of the Board, National Industrial Development Corporation Limited (NIDC), 1954

Founder, Lady Shri Ram College for Women, Delhi University, 1956

Member, Research Advisory Committee of Ahmedabad Textile Industries Research Association (ATIRA), 1956–1957

Member, Inventions Promotion Board, Government of India, 1960

Chairman, Madan Mohan Lal Ayurvedic Research Society, Delhi

Chairman, Sir Shri Ram & Sons Charitable Trust Society, Delhi

Chairman, Board of Directors, Rehabilitation Housing Corporation

Chairman, Board of Directors, Kirloskar Pneumatic Co. Ltd

Chairman, Sir Ganga Ram Trust Society and Hospital, Delhi

Chairman, Indian Statistical Institute, Delhi

Chairman, Dr Shroff's Charitable Eye Hospital, Delhi

Chairman, Governing Body, Hindu College, Delhi University

Chairman, Governing Body, Delhi Polytechnic, Delhi

Honorary Treasurer, Indian Council of World Affairs

Member, Mahamana Madan Mohan Malviya Memorial Society, Varanasi

Member, Governing Body, Delhi School of Economics

Member, Governing Body, Commercial H.S. School, Daryaganj, Delhi

Member, Governing Body, Anglo Sanskrit V.J. Higher Secondary School, Delhi

Member, Governing Body, Indraprastha Girls Higher Secondary School, Delhi

Member, Governing Body, Madan Mohan Lal Mahila Shilp Vidyalaya, Delhi

Member, Governing Body, Central Glass Research Institute, Calcutta

Member, Governing Body, National Council of Applied Economic Research, Delhi

Member, Governing Body, Indian Institute of Public Administration

Member, Governing Body, Administrative Staff College, Hyderabad

Member, Governing Body, India International Centre, Delhi

Vice Chairman, Tuberculosis Association of India, Delhi

DCM Group Businesses during Shri Ram's Lifetime

Delhi Cloth and General Mills Company Limited

Daurala Sugar Works

Lyallpur Cotton Mill

Bengal Potteries

Jay Engineering Works

Daurala Confectionery Works

Mawana Sugar Works

DCM Chemical Works

Set up the ferric alum plant

Set up the hydrochloric acid plant

Set up the contact sulphuric acid plant

Set up the superphosphate plant

The power alcohol plant

Captive power plant

Set up the vanaspati plant (Rath and Panghat brands)

Swatantra Bharat Mills

Caustic soda plant

DCM Silk Mills

Hissar Textile Mill No 1

Set up the 20 per cent oleum plant

Set up the active earth plant

DCM Group Businesses after Shri Ram's Death

Caustic soda plant, Kota

Calcium carbide plant, Kota

PVC plant, Kota

Hissar Textile Mills No. 2

Shriram Rayons, Kota

DCM ginning factory, Malout

Stable bleaching power plant

Hissar Synthetics, Hissar

DCM ginning factory, Hissar

SBM Synthetics, New Delhi

Shriram Fertilizers & Chemicals

Set up 65 per cent oleum plant

Agra Engineering Industries

Shri Ram Fibres (SRF)

DCM Data Products

Hindon River Mills

Shriram Piston & Rings Ltd

Set up soap plant

DCM Engineering Products

Grey iron foundry

Set up chlorosulfuric acid plant

DCM Toyota Limited

Shriram Needle Bearings

Cement plant, Kota

Shriram Bioseed Genetics India Ltd

Shriram Alkali & Chemicals

DCM Shriram Ltd, Sugar and Distillery Unit, Ajbapur

Acquired Rupapur sugar unit

Fenesta uPVC window systems

DCM Shriram Ltd, sugar unit

Division of the DCM Group after Shri Ram's death

DCM Shriram Industries Limited went to Shri Dhar (renamed DCM Shriram Consolidated Limited in 1990, which has been DCM Shriram Limited since 2014)

Companies/Plants:

(i) Swatantra Bhagat Mills, Delhi, (ii) DCM Silk Mills, Delhi, (iii) Shriram Cement Works, (iv) Shriram Fertilisers & Chemicals, Kota

DCM Shriram Industries went to Bansi Dhar

Companies/Plants:

(i) Daural Sugar Works, (ii) Hindon River Mills, (iii) Shriram Rayons, Kota

DCM Ltd went to Bharat Ram

Companies/Plants:

(i) DCM Data Product, (ii) DCM Toyota, (iii) DCM Foundry at Ropar in Punjab, (iv) SRF Ltd, (v) DCM Textile Mills, Delhi, (vi) Hissar Spinning Mills

Shriram Industries Enterprises Ltd went to Charat Ram

Companies/Plants:

(i) Mawana Sugar Works, (ii) Shriram Foods & Chemicals, (iii) Jay Engineering Works, (iv) Usha Sales International, (v) Shriram Refrigeration Industries, (vi) Shriram Honda, (vii) India Hard Metals

FOLLOWING A TRADITION OF EXCELLENCE

SIR SHRI RAM'S FAMILY TREE

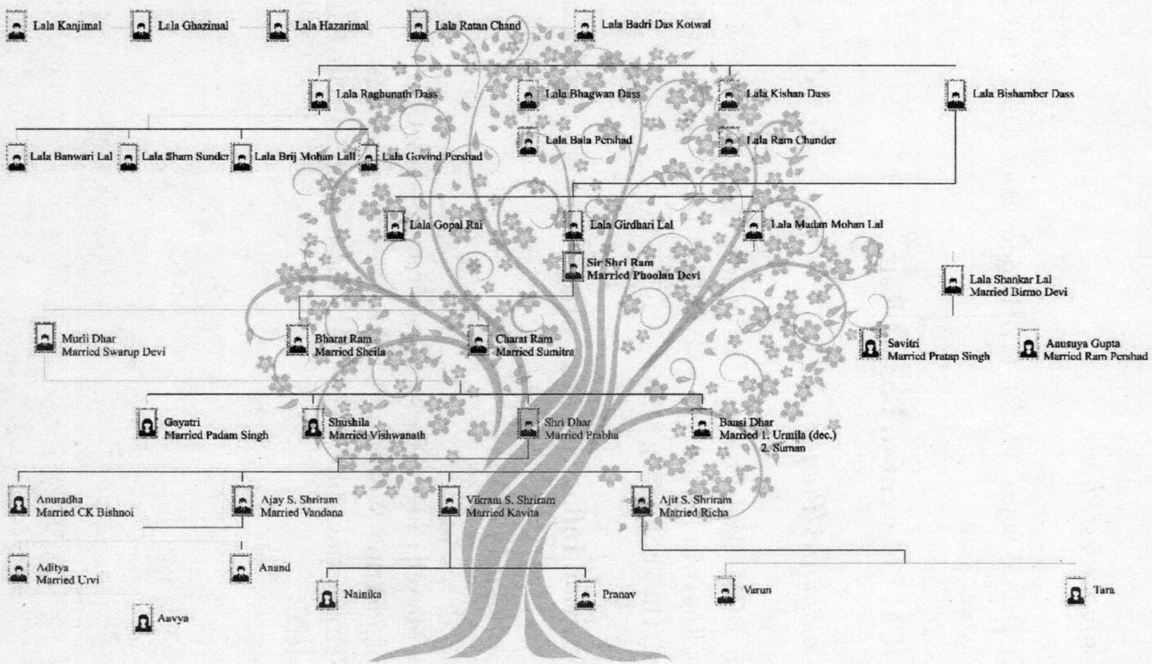

References

Aggarwal, Rajendra Mohan. *Yug Purush Lala Shri Ram*. Kota: Shriram Rayons, 1984.

Aviation Safety Network, https://aviation-safety.net/database/record.php?id=19491212-1

Babu, Venkatesha, 'Ashok Soota: The Mind Behind an Industree', 23 April 2010, https://www.livemint.com/Leisure/1XngF56Svde6WAPfHncwEK/Ashok-Soota--The-mind-behind-an-industree.html

Batabyal, Rakesh, '100 Years of Modern School, Delhi and How the School Combined Innovation with Tradition', 10 January 2021, https://www.nationalheraldindia.com/book-extract/100-years-of-modern-school-delhi-and-how-the-school-combined-innovation-with-tradition

Bhandari, Bhupesh, 'DCM's Split Family Disorder', 20 January 2013, https://www.business-standard.com/article/beyond-business/dcm-s-split-family-disorder-111041400059_1.html

Bhandari, Bhupesh, 'India's First Corporate Agent?', 26 March 2015, https://www.business-standard.com/article/opinion/bhupesh-bhandari-india-s-first-corporate-agent-115032601315_1.html

Bhandari, Bhupesh, 'Remembering Bharat Ram', 9 October 2014, https://www.business-standard.com/article/opinion/bhupesh-bhandari-remembering-bharat-ram-114100901277_1.html

Bhandari, Bhupesh, 'Shri Ram, Ram, Ram...', 21 January 2013, https://www.business-standard.com/article/beyond-business/shri-ram-ram-ram-110041700029_1.html

Bhandari, Bhupesh, 'Those 50 years of DCM', https://www.business-standard.com/article/beyond-business/those-50-years-of-dcm-112041400040_1.html

Bose, Mouli, '76 Years of Japanese Bombing in Kolkata: How World War II Almost Destroyed the City', 14 February 2019, https://www.financialexpress.com/india-news/76-years-of-japanese-bombing-in-kolkata-how-world-war-ii-almost-destroyed-the-city/1419989/

BS reporter, 'DCM Chairman Bharat Ram Dies at 93', 14 June 2013, https://www.business standard.com/article/companies/dcm-chairman-bharat-ram-dies-at-93-107071101012_1.html

BS reporter, 'DCM Loses Stalwart', 5 February 2013, https://www.business-standard.com/article/companies/dcm-loses-stalwart-107051601103_1.html

Byju's, 'NCERT Notes: First Round Table Conference 1930', https://byjus.com/free-ias-prep/first-round-table-conference-1930/

Condair, 'The Importance of Humidity Control in Textile Processing', https://www.condair.co.in/knowledge-hub/the-importance-of-humidity-control-in-textile-processing

Das, Debabrata and Ashish Gupta, 'DCM Shriram: Low on Sugar', 24 July 2018, https://www.fortuneindia.com/enterprise/dcm-shriram-low-on-sugar/102173

DCM Shriram website, https://www.dcmshriram.com/didYouKnow.html

DCM Shriram website, https://www.dcmshriram.com/didYouKnow.html

Desai, Meghnad and Sanjaya Baru. *The Bombay Plan: Blueprint for Economic Resurgence.* India: Rupa, 2018.

Desai, Santosh, 'The Days of Matric Pass', 3 March 2013, https://timesofindia.indiatimes.com/blogs/Citycitybangbang/the-days-of-matric-pass/

Dubashi, Jay, 'Lala Shri Ram (1884-1963): The Merchant of Delhi', https://www.indiatoday.in/magazine/guest-column/story/19840531-lala-shri-ram-1884-1963-the-merchant-of-delhi-803661-1984-05-31

Dubashi, Jay, 'Lala Shri Ram (1884–1963): The Merchant of Delhi', 31 May 1984, https://www.indiatoday.in/magazine/guest-column/story/19840531-lala-shri-ram-1884-1963-the-merchant-of-delhi-803661-1984-05-31

eHeritage Project, 'Shahjahanabad Digital Heritage', https://shahjahanabad.eheritageproject.in/chaurasi-84-ghanta-mandir/

Facebook, DCM Shriram Ltd., https://www.facebook.com/DCMShriramLtd/photos/pcb.1256409414519363/1256408481186123/

Facebook, DCM Shriram Ltd., https://www.facebook.com/DCMShriramLtd/posts/sir-shri-ram-was-elected-representative-of-the-punjab-chamber-of-commerce-to-the/1256409414519363/

Financial Express, 'Bapus Barons', 15 August 2004, https://www.financialexpress.com/archive/bapus-barons/111693/

GK Today, 'Lord Willingdon: Governor General and Viceroy of India (1931–1936)', 11 June 2016, https://www.gktoday.in/topic/lord-willingdon-governor-general-and-viceroy-of-india-1931-1936/

Goswami, Omkar *Goras and Desis: Managing Agencies and the Making of Corporate India.* https://books.google.com/books?id=qBxwDQAAQBAJ&pg=PT84&lpg=PT84&dq=shri+ram+ is+the+story+of+secretaries&source=bl&ots=MUjUVqhiy7&sig=ACfU3U084fyZxTN4OhgykH1SjWksfmYgKQ&hl=en&sa=X&ved=2ahUKEwi0r-TRk4z0AhVzVTABHfQbC3wQ6AF6BAgZEAM#v=onepage&q=shri%20ram%20is%20the%20story%20of%20secretaries&f=false

Grace's Guide, 'Rajputana State Railway', https://www.gracesguide.co.uk/Rajputana_State_Railway

Housing.com, 'Who is a Karta in a Hindu Undivided Family (HUF)?', https://housing.com/news/karta-of-huf/

India Inc: The Shri Ram empire, aired July 2005, https://www.youtube.com/watch?v=oSBBOHCyDmA&ab_channel=NDTV

India Today, '75 Years of World War II Japan Bombing of Kolkata: How the City of Joy Fought Back', 25 January 2018, https://www.indiatoday.in/education-today/gk-current-affairs/story/japan-bombing-calcutta-world-war-2-1108404-2017-12-19

Jagran Josh, 'What Is The Hindu Widows' Remarriage Act, 1856?', 20 July 2020, https://www.jagranjosh.com/general-knowledge/hindu-widows-remarriage-act-1856-1563262916-1

Joshi, Arun. *Lala Shri Ram: A Study in Entrepreneurship and Industrial Management*. India: Orient Longman, 1975.

Kakkar, Himanshu, 'Growing a Legacy', 19 July 2019, https://www.magzter.com/stories/259/357475/5d1f20f3607cb

Khanna, Sundeep, 'Backstory: When Swraj Paul Played the Foreign Hand', 2 July 2021, https://www.cnbctv18.com/views/backstory-when-swaraj-paul-played-the-foreign-hand-9798871.htm

Kothari, Ajay Kumar. *Great Lives.* https://books.google.com/books?id=mryFNM7U8fwC&q=delhi+cloth+and+general+mills&pg=PT14#v=snippet&q=delhi%20cloth%20and%20general%20mills&f=false

Kumar, Nita, 'Labour, Capital, and the Congress: Delhi Cloth Mills, 1928–38', https://scholarship. claremont.edu/cgi/viewcontent.cgi?referer=&httpsredir=1&article=1040&context=cmc_fac_pub

Kumar, Sanjeet, 'Gandhi Irwin Pact', 15 September 2021, https://testbook.com/ias-preparation/gandhi-irwin-pact/

Live History India, 'Delhi Durbar of 1911', 3 July 2017, https://www.livehistoryindia.com/story/cover-story/delhi-durbar-of-1911-2/

Mariwala, Vibhav, 'Remember the Bombay Plan?', 28 October 2021, https://www.deccanherald.com/opinion/main-article/remember-the-bombay-plan-1044827.html

Marsh, Janine, 'Limoges Ancient City with a Remarkable History', https://thegoodlifefrance.com/limoges-ancient-city-with-a-remarkable-history/

Mathai, Palakunnathu G, 'Ailing Rs 624-Crore DCM Broken Up into Three Separate Companies', 15 December 1988, https://www.indiatoday.in/magazine/economy/story/19881215-ailing-rs-624-crore-dcm-broken-up-into-three-separate-companies-797988-1988-12-14

Military History Fandom, 'Victor Hope, 2nd Marquess of Linlithgow', https://military-history.fandom.com/wiki/Victor_Hope,_2nd_Marquess_of_Linlithgow

Mineral Milling, 'Different Types of Clay Used In Making Ceramics', https://mineralmilling.com/different-types-of-clay-used-in-making-ceramics/#:~:text=the%20kaolin%20type.-,Kaolin,clay%20type%20known%20to%20man.

Mitra, Kushan, 'DCM Has Survived Splits and a Hostile Takeover Bid', 28 June 2011, https://www.businesstoday.in/specials/century-old-companies/story/dcm-among-100-year-old-indian-companies-22774-2011-06-27

Mitra, Kushan, 'DCM Has Survived Splits and a Hostile Takeover Bid', 28 June 2011, https://www.businesstoday.in/specials/century-old-companies/story/dcm-among-100-year-old-indian-companies-22774-2011-06-27

Modern School website, https://modernschool.net/our-history/

Mostly Economics, 'Was Mahatma India's First Corporate Agent?', https://mostlyeconomics.wordpress.com/2015/03/27/was-mahatma-indias-first-corporate-agent/

NDTV Profit, 'India Inc: The Shri Ram Empire', aired July 2005, https://www.ndtv.com/video/shows/india-inc/india-inc-the-shri-ram-empire-aired-july-2005-276935

Nutec Bickley, https://www.nutecbickley.com/what-we-do/ceramic-kilns/products-for-ceramics/tunnel-kilns/

Pandey, Pooja, 'Finding Gandhi In The National Education Policy 2020', 2 October 2020, https://www.outlookindia.com/website/story/opinion-finding-gandhi-in-the-national-education-policy-2020/361300

PFAFF website, https://www.pfaff.com/about

Ramki, `Business battles', 6 August 2020, https://www.slideshare.net/ramadd1951/business-battles

Rediff.com, 'Bharat Ram: Relationship Man', https://www.rediff.com/money/2007/jul/12bharat.htm

Sanyal, Amal, 'The Industrialists Behind India's First National Economic Plan', 15 November 2018, https://qz.com/india/1464869/the-story-of-jrd-tata-gd-birlas-bombay-plan-for-india/

Shri Ram College of Commerce website, https://www.srcc.edu/about-us/history

Shri Ram Global website, https://srgpsshalimarbagh.com/lala-shri-ram/

Shriram, Siddharth, 'Sumitra Charat Ram and the Energy of Dance and Music', 15 November 2014, https://www.business-standard.com/article/specials/sumitra-charat-ram-and-the-energy-of-dance-and-music-114111301617_1.html

Shriram, Siddharth, 'The Amazing Story of Lala Charat Ram', 9 June 2007, https://www.rediff.com/money/2007/jun/09bspec.htm

Singh, Khushwant and Arun Joshi. *Lala Shri Ram*. Asia Publishing House, 1968.

Singh, M, 'The Struggle of the Indian Textile Workers', https://www.marxists.org/history/international/comintern/sections/britain/periodicals/labour_monthly/1934/06/x01.htm

Sinha, Shashank Shekhar, 'The Making of New Delhi', 21 December 2017, https://frontline.thehindu.com/arts-and-culture/heritage/the-making-of-new-delhi/article23596392.ece

So Delhi, 'This 200+ Year Old Temple In The Bustling Lanes Of Chandni Chowk Has 84 Bells & An Intriguing Story', 23 May 2021, https://so.city/delhi/article/this-200-year-old-temple-in-the-bustling-lanes-of-chandni-chowk-has-84-bells-an-intriguing-story

Sriram's IAS, 'Facts and Importance of Swadeshi and Boycott Movements', https://www.sriramsias.com/blog/facts-and-importance-of-swadeshi-and-boycott-movement/

Sunder, Sushruth, 'Hostile Takeovers in India: As Mindtree Fights Off L&T, a Look at 3 Major Attempts in Past', 20 March 2019, https://www.financialexpress.com/market/hostile-takeovers-in-india-as-mindtree-fights-off-lt-a-look-at-3-major-attempts-in-past/1522034/

The Editors of Encyclopaedia Britannica, 'Round Table Conference: British-Indian History', https://www.britannica.com/event/Round-Table-Conference

The Editors of Encyclopaedia Britannica, 'Vaishnavism: Hindu Sect', 1 November 2022, https://www.britannica.com/topic/Vaishnavism

The Open University, 'Round Table Conferences, 1930–1932', https://www.open.ac.uk/researchprojects/makingbritain/content/round-table-conferences-1930-1932

The Vegan Indians, 'What Is Bone Char and Does It Make Sugar Non-Vegan?', 1 December 2021, https://www.theveganindians.com/what-is-bone-char-and-does-it-make-sugar-non-vegan/

Tiwari, Anuj, 'Shiv Nadar's Legacy: Meet the Man Who Led HCL to Success', 5 September 2021, https://www.indiatimes.com/trending/human-interest/shiv-nadar-founder-of-hcl-technologies-success-story-548745.html

UK Parliament, '1931 Indian Round Table Conference', https://www.parliament.uk/about/living-heritage/evolutionofparliament/legislativescrutiny/parliament-and-empire/collections1/collections2/1931-round-table-conference/1931-indian-round-table-conference1/

Vivek, TR, 'What Ended the Reign of the Mighty Business Families of Delhi?', 8 August 2008, https://economictimes.indiatimes.com/what-ended-the-reign-of-the-mighty-business-families-of-delhi/articleshow/3339805.cms?from=mdr

Wikipedia, 'Swadeshi Movement', https://en.wikipedia.org/wiki/Swadeshi_movement

Transcript of interview with Vinay Bharat Ram from DCM Shriram Archives

Transcript of interview with Prabha Shriram from DCM Shriram Archives

Unpublished book on Shri Ram by late Bhupesh Bhandari commissioned by Arun Bharat Ram

In-person interviews with Gauri Shriram, Arun Bharat Ram and Ajay Shriram

Index

Afghanistan, 139–40, 203
Agarwal, Bishan, 158
Ahmedabad, 41, 44, 54, 81, 121, 167, 171
alcohol diversification, 223–24
Allahabad, 227, 246
All India Committee for Technical Education, 210
All India Fine Arts and Crafts Society, 243
All India Radio, 242, 273
All-India Textile Workers' Council, 167
All-India Trade Union Congress, 167
aluminium sulphate, 220
American Civil War, 41
anti-mill activities, 128, 215
apprenticeship scheme, 179–80, 204
army contracts, 74–79

Bajaj, Jamnalal, 137
Banaras Hindu University, 145
Barhni, 211–12, 215–16, 218
Barhwali Haveli, 3, 29, 54, 65–66, 99, 102
Basil, Bishandas, 181–84, 186–89, 192, 194, 205
Bavarian town of Bad Kissingen, 188–89
Bazaar Sita Ram, 2–3, 5, 17, 26, 62
Bengal Potteries, 153–65, 177, 181, 202
  finance problem, 159
  profit, 156, 163

Bhagat, Madan Gopal, 155–59, 181, 188
Bhaironji Ka Mandir, 16–17
Birla, G.D., 122, 126, 137, 231
Bishandas, 181–84
black market, 218–19
Bombay, 41, 44, 47–48, 51, 53–54, 81, 97, 121, 143–44, 167, 171, 193
Bombay Plan, 231–32
Bombay Stock Exchange, 51–52
bone sulphate, 131

capital expenditure, 81
capitalists, 125, 232
Central Telegraph Office in Calcutta, 182
Chand, Diwan (Shri Ram's friend), 72–74, 84
Chand, Lala Diwan, 128
Chandni Chowk, 16–17, 25
Chaurasey Ghantey ka Mandir, 2, 16–17
chemicals business, 218–19
Chotalal, Ranchhod Lal, 41
civic amenities, 87
civil disobedience movement, 153
Civil Lines, 87
cloth weaving, 46
Colonel Peart, 156–57
Commercial College, 85, 98
Commercial Education Trust, 85, 262
Commercial School, 1920, 85
Communist movement within India, 84
Congress party, 124
Coronation Durbar, 7
cotton ginning factory, 34–36
Council of Scientific and Industrial Research (CSIR), 209
Curzon Road, 102, 135–36, 141, 239–40, 253–54, 274

Dada & Co. Lever Brothers, 223–24
Dalal, Ardeshir, 231
Dalda vanaspati ghee, 224
Dalmia, R.K., 246
Das, Badri, 1
  British reward, 6
  in danger, 4–5
  death, 6
  in Jullundur Cantonment, 6
  as kotwal in Ferozepur Cantonment, 1–2
  transfer to Delhi, 2
Das, Bishamber, 6–7
  grandson, 9
  sons, 7–8
Das, Gopal, 7
Das, Raghunath, 6
Dass, Benarsi (Gopal Rai's brother-in-law), 8, 40, 44
Dass, Bhagwan, 25
Dass, Krishn, 40, 43
Dass, Ram Kishan, 40–41, 43, 49
  business interests, 43
  nodded in agreement, 44–45
Daurala sugar mill, 131, 134, 136, 138, 155, 177
Davar, Cowasji, 41
DCM Bar Soap, 223

DCM Chemical Works, 219–20
Delhi Cloth and General Mills
  Company Ltd, 40, 175
Delhi Cloth Mills, 28, 49–50
  agreement, 73–74
  capital, 92–93
  civilian market, cloth for, 76
  cloth production at, 56
  diversification, 139
  early successes at, 65–85
  fifty-year milestone, 195–210
  fire, 94
  landmark in Delhi, 55
  production, 234
  profits, 75
  in Punjab, 149
  railways priority, 71
  sales office, 56
  second mill, 104–15
  strike in, 166–76
  workforce, 147
Delhi Iron Syndicate & Company,
  181
Delhi Labour Union, 167, 170
Delhi Municipality, 87–88
Delhi Town Planning Committee,
  135
Delhi University, 209, 262
Delhi Water Works, 220
Desai, Bhulabhai, 173
Desai, C.C., 249–50
Deshmukh, C.D., 150
Devi, Chando (Shri Ram's
  mother), 8–9, 23, 100
Devi, Phoolan (Shri Ram's wife),
  25, 68–69, 261
  death, 226
  epilepsy fits, 146
  marriage, 26–27
  Shobha, meeting with,
    147–48
  son, 28, 35
Devi, Swaroop, 146
Dhar, Murli (Shri Ram's son), 35,
  66, 76, 146, 175, 197, 229, 246,
  248, 253
  death, 277
  Lyallpur mill responsibility,
    150–51, 246
Dhar, Shri (Murli Dhar's elder
  son), 248, 253–54, 265–66
Dharamvira (Jwala Prasad's son),
  145, 218
diversification into sugar, 127–38
Dr Sen's Nursing Home, 268–73

economic depression, 170–71
economic policies, 124–25
educational trust, 84
Emerson, Herbert, 149
Employees Benefit Fund, 202–3
employment, 63
enthusiasm, 34
entrepreneurship, 6
epilepsy, 27
Eureka Pottery Works in Lahore,
  155
European mills, study on, 120

Federation of Indian Chambers
  of Commerce and Industry,
  122–23, 126
fertilizers development, 222
FICCI, 122–23, 126, 209

Gandhi, Mahatma, 98, 122, 125–26, 153–54, 172, 216
Ganju, Jagan Nath (Shri Ram's friend), 31–33
Gauri (Charat Ram's daughter), 253
Gazette, 128
Ghandy, J.J., 249–50
Ghaziabad, 6
ginning, 67
Gita, 21
Goenka, Ramnath, 246
Gopal, Madan, 188–89, 201
Great Depression, 120–21, 127
Gupta, Hans Raj, 181, 188
Gupta, T.R., 187, 205–6
Gwalior Potteries, 156, 160–61

Hanuman Mandir, 17
Haq, Farid ul, 168
Harwood (mills manager), 60
hinduism, 2, 229
Hindu religious practices, 140
Hindu Widows' Remarriage Act, 23
Hope, Victor, 195
Howard, 54
human behaviour, 36
hurricane lanterns production, 264
Hussain, Pirzada Muhammad, 87
Hussain, Zakir, 170–72
hydrogenated vegetable oil, 223–24

Imperial Council of Agricultural Research, 132
in-depth knowledge, 132
Indian Civil Service officer, 89
Indian Institute of Technology, Kanpur, 210
Indian National Airways, 246
Indo Japanese Trade Agreement, 149
Indraprastha College, 261
industrial capital of India, 174–75
Industrial Finance Corporation, 250
institutionalized training scheme, 203

Jain, Mal, 171–72
Jamia Millia Islamia university, 170
Japanese cloth import, 128
Jay Engineering, 187, 192, 217, 230, 234–36, 263
Jay Engineering Works (JEW), 185, 187
Jhajjar, 1

Kalawati (elder cousin), 34
Karim, Fazle, 170
karta, 252
Kashmir trip, 100–101
khaddar production, 122
khadi, 122
Khan, Ahmad Islam, 217
Khan, Allauddin, 241–42
Khanna Babu, 254, 270–71
Kirloskar Industries, 269
Kishen, Jai, 185
Kotwal family, 2
Kucha Mai Das, 9, 12, 26, 54, 57, 86, 101

labour shortage, 200
Lady Shri Ram College, 260–66
Lakshmi Narayan mandir, 16–17
Lal, Brij Mohan, 145
Lal, Girdhari, 7, 12, 22
Lal, Madan Mohan, 7, 57
Lal, Rai Bahadur Brij Mohan, 147
Lal, Shankar (Shri Ram's brother), 28, 30, 65–66, 111–16, 141, 175, 196–97, 199, 227, 229–30, 246–48
Lalbhai, Kasturbhai, 231
Lall, Banwari (Gopal Rai's cousin), 40, 44
Landon, James, 41
Lawson, 60
life insurance, 202
Limoges, 155–56
Lutyens, Edwin, 135
Lyallpur Cotton Mill, 149–52, 177, 246

Madan Mohan Lal Shri Ram & Company, 187–88
Made in India cloth, 79–80
Mahabharat, 21
Majestic Cinema, 43
man-management philosophy, 83
Marchioness, 195, 198–99
Marsh, P.W., 133, 136
Marwari or bania community, 45–46
Mathai, John, 231
Mawana, 216
Memorandum of Association, 130
Messrs Shankar Lall Bharat Ram and Company, 175–76, 187–88
Milner, Doreen Maud, 195
Miranda House, 261
Modern School, 98
Modi, Gujarmal, 223
Mohammed, Ghulam, 247
Mohan, Madan (Shri Ram's father), 7–8, 12, 26–27, 78, 102
  badi kothi, 141
  at DCM, 30, 58
  death, 144
  relationship with Shri Ram, 28, 30
  struggle, 65
Mohan Brothers, 30–31, 33

National Congress, 124
national education, 98
Nehru, B.K., 147
Nehru, Jawaharlal, 249, 263
Nigambodh Ghat, 274
Non-Cooperation movement, 153–54

officer training scheme, 204
Oriental Spinning and Weaving Mills, 41

Pakistani textile industry, 152
paper mills, 220
Pathak, B.D., 187, 227
patriotism, 21, 78
Pershad, Sheo, 95
Petit, Maneckji, 41

Pfaff sewing machines, 183–86, 234
philanthropy and community service, 91
Pitkethly, James, 162
Poddar, Kishen Lal, 185–87
Popular Sugar Company, 211–12
post-war inflation, 81
Prasad, Jwala, 144
profit-sharing scheme, 202
provident fund concept, 77
public endorsement, 199
public service goes hand-in-hand with business, 86–91
Punjab Chamber of Commerce, 87–88
Puran, 270–71

Quit India movement, 216
Qutab Minar, 196

Rai, Gopal, 7–8, 12–13, 25–26, 28–29
  chronic disease, 56–57
  cloth mill in Delhi, 40
  death, 58
  motivation, 54
  reserve fund, 51
  Secretary of Delhi Cloth Mills, 11–12, 35
  setting up DCM, 40–52
Rai Bahadur Boota Singh & Sons of Rawalpindi, 36
Rajpur Road in Civil Lines, 102
Rajputana–Malwa Railway, 54
Rajputana Railways, 54
Ram, Arun Bharat, 241
Ram, Bharat (Shri Ram's son), 76, 99, 140, 175, 197, 213–14
  education, 140–41
  marriage plan, 143
  meeting with Gandhi ji, 172
  Swatantra Bharat Mill setup, 245–46
  wedding, 146–47
Ram, Charat (Shri Ram's son), 76, 99, 140, 175, 197, 217
  in Jay Engineering, 219
  marriage proposal, 144–45
  Swatantra Bharat Mill setup, 245–46
  in textile and engineering divisions, 219
Rama Theatre in Chandni Chowk, 43
Ramayana, 21
Rath and Panghat vanaspati ghee, 225
Reserve Bank of India, 150, 249–50, 269
reward to workers, 83–84
Rohtagi, Binay Krishna, 183, 185–86, 193
Roorkee College of Engineering, 182
Royal Commission of Labour in India, 167
Ryan, Thomas, 162

sales and credit processes, 121
Salt March, 153–54
Satyavati, 168
sewing institutes, 265
sex-determination tests, 8

Shankar, Ravi, 241–42
Shankar, Uday, 241
Shastri, Harihar Nath, 167
Sheila (Bharat Ram's wife), 145–46, 188–89, 240–41, 260–61
Shobha (B.K. Nehru's wife), 147–48
Shri Ram, 9–10
  Anglo Sanskrit High School in Charkhewalan, 17, 24
  army contracts, 74–79
  authority and responsibilities, 69–70
  Ayurveda medicine, 28–29
  back in Delhi, 39
  as Boota Singh's munshi, 36–37
  chhoti kothi, 141–42, 145, 253, 274
  confidence, 70
  dealing with failures, 24–39
  death, 267–75
  in educational institute, 97–98
  emotional attachment with DCM, 94
  for financial and logistical work, 37
  ginning unit success, 68–69
  grandchildren and great-grandchildren, dealing with, 254–58
  growing up in Barhwali Haveli, 11–24
  guidance, 231
  health problems, 103, 267–75
  to Hindu College, 28
  informal guidance, 23–234
  joins DCM, 53–64
  language value, 24
  leadership, 124
  marriage, 26
  matriculation, 24
  overseas trip, 116–26
  passion and the learnings, 63
  patience to listen, 19
  resignation, 269
  second venture, 35
  as Secretary, 70
  shareholding, 78
  stationery business, 33
  stroke, 232
  successes at DCM, 65–85
  sugar diversification, 127–38
  Vaishnava family, 16
  way of living, 102–3
  workers commitment, 83–84
Shriram, Ajay, 258
Shri Ram College of Commerce, 85, 262
Shriram Industrial Research Institute, 270
Shriram Institute of Industrial Research, 209–10
Shroff, D., 231
Sindri Fertilizers, 249–52, 260
Singh, Boota, 36, 70, 72, 155
Singh, Chaudhry Mukhtar, 131–34, 136–37
Singh, Raghubir, 98, 168, 170
Singh, Rai Bahadur Sultan, 98
Singh, Sher (Kalawati's husband), 34, 84
Singhania, Padampat, 140, 188, 232

stationery selling, 31
strikes and lockouts, 200
St Stephen's College, 219, 241
subcommittee, 91
subordinate apprenticeship scheme, 204
Sugar Committee, 132
Sugar Industries Protection Act, 129
sugar mill
- as commodity, 211
- in India, 129
- in Mawana, 138
- new, 211–25

sulphuric acid, 220–22
Sumitra, 144–45, 217, 240–42
superphosphate, 222–23
Swadeshi movement, 59, 79–80, 122–24, 172, 185–86
Swadeshi Prachar Association, 124
Swatantra Bharat Mill, 245

Tata, J.R.D., 231
Tata Group, 249
technical knowledge and skill levels, 208
textile mill at Hissar, 260–61
textiles business, 128–29. *See also* Delhi Cloth Mills
Thakurdas, Purshotamdas, 122, 140, 231
Thapar, Karam Chand, 137, 188
third mill foundation, 121
trade unions, 200, 238

Upanishads, 21
Usha fans, 264
Usha machine, 185–86
Usha sewing machines, 193, 234, 263
Usha silai kendras, 265

vanaprastha, 229
vanaspati ghee, 223–25

wage dispute, 170–71
wage hike for workers, 81
webbing, 74–75
wedding in family and a new mill, 139–52
William, Herbert, 149
workers
- colony, 54
- living and working conditions, 82, 171
- -management relationship, 61, 134
- training, 48

Acknowledgements

As always, I start by acknowledging my family—Juggi Bhasin, my husband, and Karan Bhasin, my son. I have said this earlier and say it again: these two men in my life are my anchors in the choppy seas of life.

I write about family businesses and in that spirit, I must say that I am delighted to be part of the HarperCollins family! It has been a pleasure to work with Sachin Sharma, Executive Editor at HarperCollins Publishers. He has provided valuable inputs in his usual quiet and unassuming manner. But, as I have discovered, behind that calm exterior lies a very active and sharp mind! Thank you, Sachin, for your constant support and guidance.

Shreya Dhawan, with her copyediting skills, sharpened the narrative. Her questions and comments helped me fine-tune the manuscript better. Thank you, Shreya, for your inputs.

The first impression of a book is by its cover. Saurav Das, the designer, has delivered a stunning cover once again. Thank you, Saurav.

The rest of the team at HarperCollins may have worked behind the scenes but their contribution is evident in the presentation of this book. Thank you, Team HarperCollins.

This book is about Lala Shri Ram, and I have had the privilege to spend time with two of his grandchildren—Gauri Keeling and Arun Bharat Ram—and one of his great-grandsons, Ajay Shriram. While interacting with them and listening to them tell stories about Bhaiji (as they all call Lala Shri Ram), it was easy to sense the love, affection and respect they all had for him. It was also evident that the legacy of Shri Ram was being taken forward by them in their own way. Thank you, Gauri, Arun and Ajay, for your time and commitment towards this book.

This book could not have even gotten started if it were not for Kavita Shriram—the great-granddaughter-in-law of Lala Shri Ram. She kick-started the process of getting me in touch with the family and the office of the DCM Shriram Group. Thank you, Kavita, for your invaluable help.

Aman Pannu, part of the DCM Shriram Group, was instrumental in helping me get access to the family as well as the DCM Shriram archives. She was my one-point contact for any and every assistance for any material I needed for my research. Thank you, Aman. I truly appreciate your help.

My acknowledgements cannot be complete without thanking yet another family of mine—the family of my readers. Thank you, dear Readers, for your comments, feedback and suggestions. Do keep them coming as any interaction with you truly encourages me further.

About the Author

Sonu Bhasin is one of the earliest and most senior women professionals in the industry. Bhasin led various businesses in leadership positions during her corporate career, including being part of the TAS (Tata Administrative Service), director at ING Barings Private Banking, president at Axis Bank, group president at Yes Bank, and COO at Tata Capital Limited.

She is an independent director on the board of well-known and reputed domestic and multinational companies. As part of her work now, Bhasin focuses on family businesses, and is the founder of Families and Business (FAB).

She is a family business historian, a business author and the editor-in-chief of Families & Business magazine. She has been named as one of the Global 100 Most Influential Individuals for family enterprises in 2020. Bhasin has a BSc (Hons) degree in mathematics from St. Stephen's College, Delhi University, and an MBA from the Faculty of Management Studies, also Delhi University.

30 Years *of*

HarperCollins *Publishers* India

At HarperCollins, we believe in telling the best stories and finding the widest possible readership for our books in every format possible. We started publishing 30 years ago; a great deal has changed since then, but what has remained constant is the passion with which our authors write their books, the love with which readers receive them, and the sheer joy and excitement that we as publishers feel in being a part of the publishing process.

Over the years, we've had the pleasure of publishing some of the finest writing from the subcontinent and around the world, and some of the biggest bestsellers in India's publishing history. Our books and authors have won a phenomenal range of awards, and we ourselves have been named Publisher of the Year the greatest number of times. But nothing has meant more to us than the fact that millions of people have read the books we published, and somewhere, a book of ours might have made a difference.

As we step into our fourth decade, we go back to that one word – a word which has been a driving force for us all these years.

Read.